Refuge and Renewal

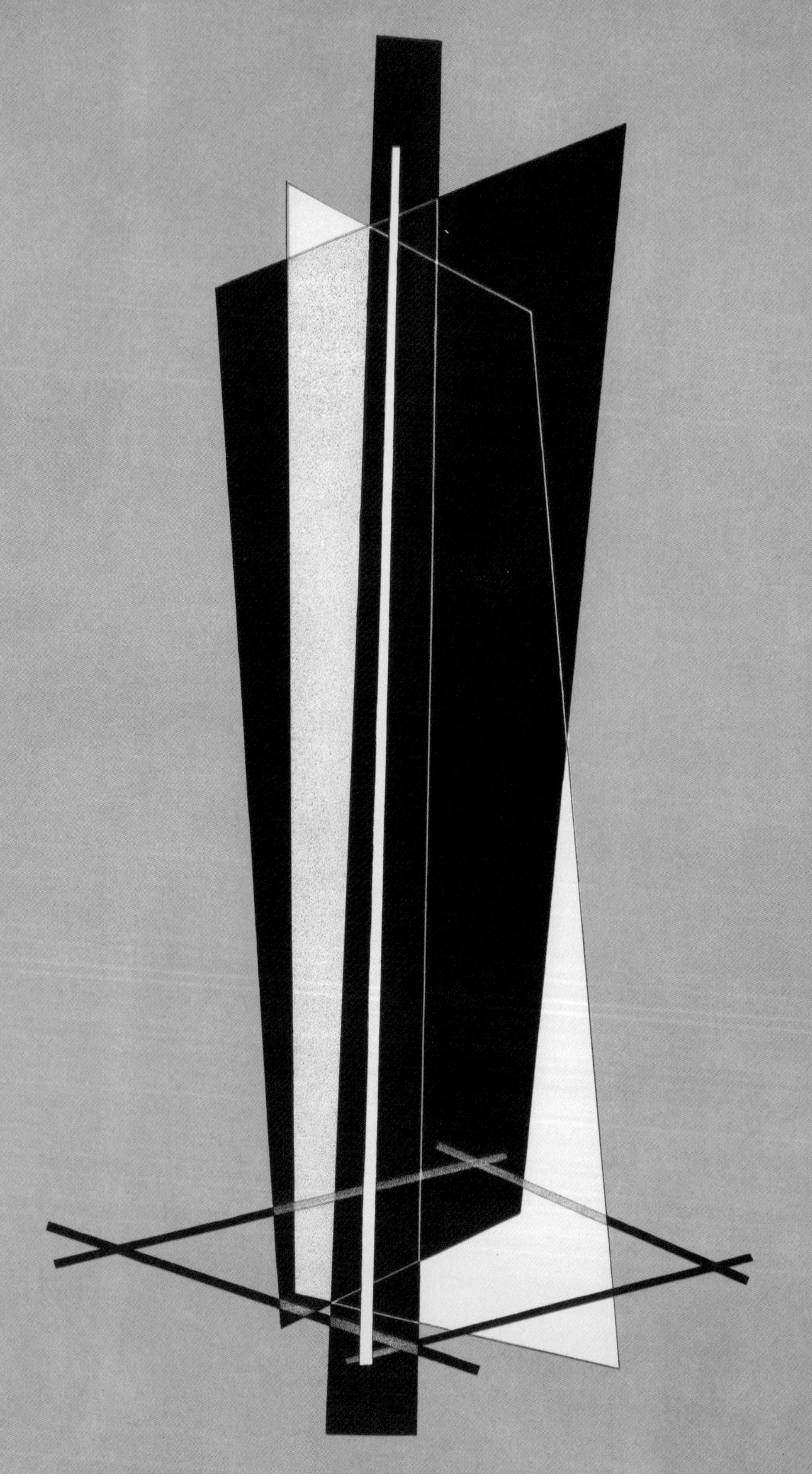

Refuge and Renewal

Migration and British Art

Peter Wakelin

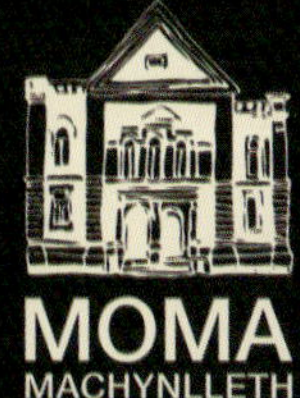

RWA

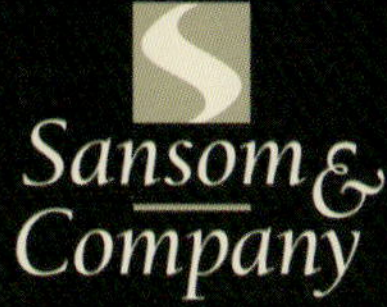

Dedicated to Pip Koppel (Renate Fischl)
born Dresden, Germany, 1930; died Aberystwyth, Wales, 2018

First published in 2019 by Sansom and Company,
a publishing imprint of Redcliffe Press Ltd.,
81G Pembroke Road, Bristol BS8 3EA
www.sansomandcompany.co.uk | info@sansomandcompany.co.uk

In conjunction with the Museum of Modern Art Machynlleth
and the RWA (Royal West of England Academy)

ISBN 978-1-911408-54-3

© Peter Wakelin

British Library Cataloguing-in-Publication Data:
A catalogue record for this book is available from the British Library.

Design and typesetting by E&P Design

Printed and bound by Cambrian Printers, Aberystwyth

Sansom & Company is committed to being an environmentally friendly
publisher. This book is made from Forest Stewardship Council®
certified paper.

Cover:
Camille Pissarro | *La route, effet de neige*
1879 | oil on canvas | 45 x 55 cm
New Walk Museum & Art Gallery, Leicester, UK
reproduced courtesy of Leicester Arts & Museums Service
photo: © Leicester Arts & Museums/Bridgeman Images

Frontispiece:
László Moholy-Nagy | *Untitled* from *Konstruktionen: Kestnermappe 6*
1923 | lithograph | 50 x 26 cm
gift of Suzette M. Hamill (1947.366.2); Chicago (IL), Art Institute of Chicago
photo: © 2019 The Art Institute of Chicago/Art Resource, NY/Scala, Florence

Contents

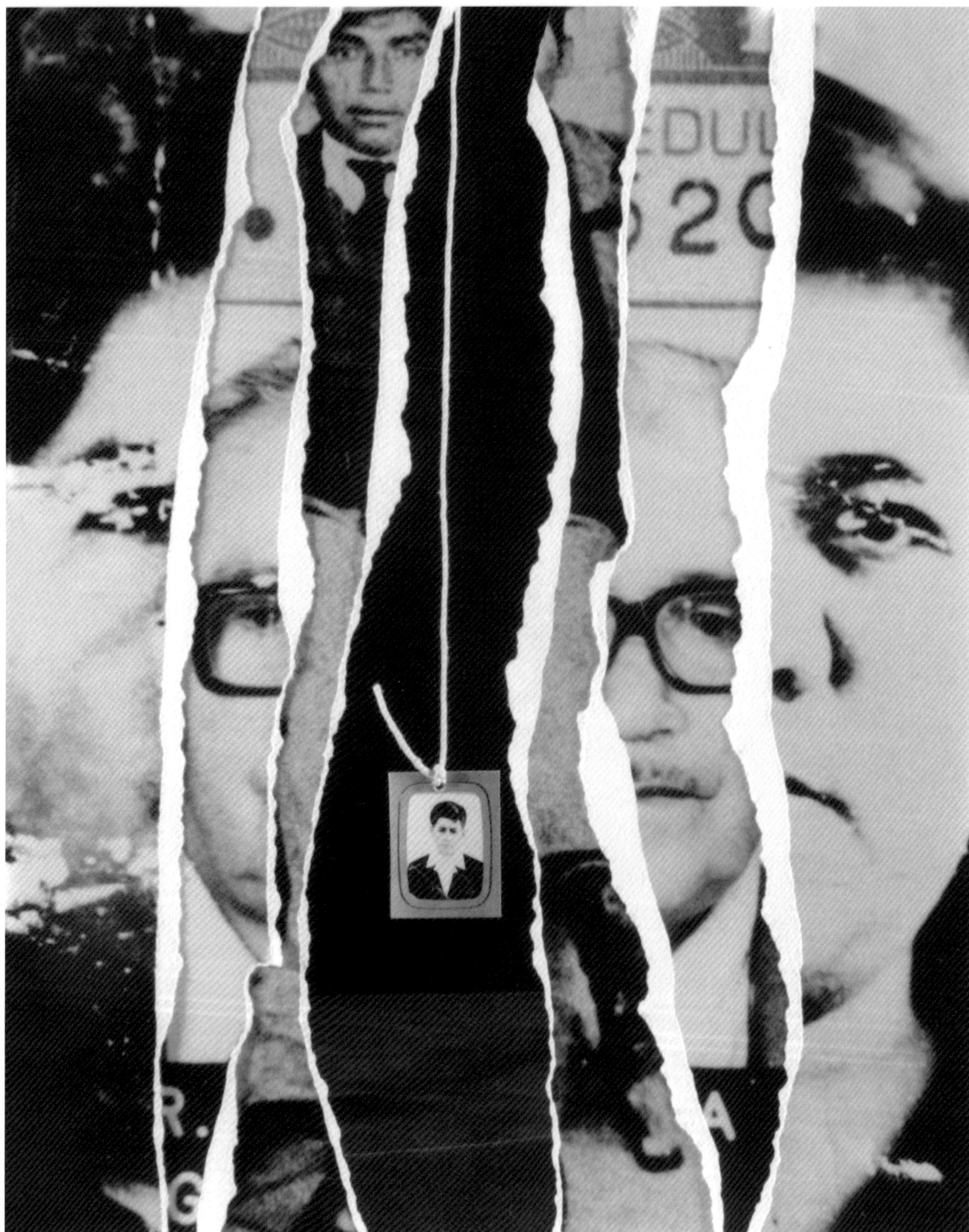

Humberto Gatica (b.1944) | *Destino (Fate)*
2000 | silver gelatin print | 28 x 25 cm
collection of/© the artist

Humberto Gatica left Chile after being detained by the regime of
General Pinochet in 1973. Many of his photographs reflect on Chile's
'disappeared'.

Foreword

THIS BOOK AND THE ACCOMPANYING EXHIBITION seek to communicate, unequivocally, the stories that make up a vital but often hidden strand woven into our shared past, both distant and more recent. The diverse life-stories that make up our communities are compelling, and it is crucial to recognise their value when living through divisive times, in which people may feel vilified or alienated. Historical knowledge, art and creativity all have parts to play in helping us to understand the present and contemplate the future.

This project has been an emotional experience. As well as examining the lives of earlier migrant painters and sculptors, we have worked with contemporary artists who have overcome unimaginable adversity; targeted by oppressive regimes, sometimes imprisoned or tortured, separated from loved ones and forced to leave everything behind and begin their lives again. Yet all of them have somehow maintained a creative practice. Many, like those who came before them, have become influential and helped to shape art in our country. The inspiration and contributions they have brought to Britain are immeasurably significant for those who choose to see them. The exhibition has had personal resonance for me. My own family – divided by two world wars – has just been reunited thanks to an archivist working for the council in the small German town where my grandfather grew up. We will be meeting our relatives again, however momentarily, thereby denying the corrupt purpose that sought to eradicate an entire people and their way of life. Millions were not so lucky.

This project was initiated by the Museum of Modern Art Machynlleth with the support of the Richard and Ann Mayou Fund and curated by Peter Wakelin in collaboration with the RWA (Royal West of England Academy). All of us wish to thank the contemporary artists who have participated and the many public and private lenders and artists' estates who have kindly allowed us to borrow works or reproduce images. We are grateful also for the commitment and support of the publisher Sansom & Company, and of the Insiders/Outsiders Festival, which has done so much already to mark the contribution of émigrés from the Nazi era to British culture.

Nathalie Levi
Head of Programme – Curator of Exhibitions,
RWA (Royal West of England Academy)

Preface

I THINK I WAS 15 WHEN A NEIGHBOUR INVITED ME with my parents to meet someone who was staying with him. The visitor was the Austrian-born typographic designer Georg Adams-Teltscher, who had studied at the Bauhaus in Weimar in the 1920s. I was astonished. The Bauhaus figured in books at home; Paul Klee and Lyonel Feininger were among my favourite artists; my parents, who had trained in architecture before going into the services during the war, often talked about Gropius and Mies van der Rohe. To speak to someone who had studied at the Bauhaus was like reaching out to touch the moon.

I fear I fell on Mr Teltscher with far too many questions but he indulged me and talked openly. I wish I could hear a recording now, but after forty years two images are frozen in my mind's eye. One was described by him: a bus in Trafalgar Square, passengers deep in their newspapers reading about the cricket rather than the Sudeten crisis that threatened to set off a war.[1] The other I saw myself: the rage on his face as he recalled being interned as an enemy alien when he wanted to be fighting Nazism. Both images seem relevant in Britain still, one capturing incomprehension of Europe, the other suspicion of refugees.

I feel honoured to have talked to artists who were refugees across nine decades. Their origins varied but their stories showed a horrible conformity in the repeating pattern of man's inhumanity to man. I doubt I would have survived what they survived – had I lost my family and home, known my work to be destroyed, found neighbours turned against me, experienced imprisonment or seen cruelty reign unopposed. Yet nearly all the refugees in this book overcame such circumstances and went on to quiet triumphs. They forged new lives, contributed to a new society, turned cruelty to kindness.

If the artist refugees are one side of the equation that is the subject of this book, on the other I have been lucky to know British artists whose work was informed and developed by meeting artists from another culture. When I was growing up in South Wales, the influence of Josef Herman was still echoing among those inspired by his perception of the coalfield. Later, I knew many who had been prompted by Heinz Koppel to become artists, or better artists, through the exoticism of his painting, his intellectual rigour and his support for creativity.

In 2015, I gave a lecture on artist refugees to the friends of the National Museum of Wales reflecting on the horrors from which refugees had escaped and the benefits Britain had discovered by giving them a home. While focusing on the 1930s and 1940s, I set them in the context of the recent refugee crisis. Afterwards the chairman let me know the audience had been fascinated 'despite the presentation being so political'. I was taken aback. I thought helping desperate people was a matter of morality, not politics. Would it be a political decision to rescue someone drowning? Was it a political act to save people from torture, bombing or murder?

Of course, I was naïve. It is necessarily a political matter to determine which, and how many, refugees a society will help, or to decide foreign policy towards countries they are fleeing. In a well-ordered world, governments would ameliorate the conditions that drive immigration – they would sanction breaches of human rights, work to quell civil wars and not put their own interests above the stability of their neighbours. They would have better foresight than the passengers drifting into conflagration on Georg Teltscher's pre-war omnibus.

The recent, shocking increase in the stateless is a failure of the world order. Nevertheless, there will always be times and places where cruelty and chaos rule, and there will always be migrants seeking safety. I have learned two main lessons from studying refugee artists for this book. First is that our support or otherwise for refugees is a measure of our national morality. Second is that, when supported and engaged, refugees have frequently contributed dynamically to British life.

THIS BOOK AND THE ASSOCIATED EXHIBITION would not have been possible without the support of the RWA (Royal West of England Academy), the Machynlleth Tabernacle Trust and the Richard and Ann Mayou Fund. I wish to thank particularly my excellent co-curator Nathalie Levi and her colleagues at the RWA, Alison Bevan and Tristan Pollard; Ruth Lambert, Emily Bartlett, Raymond Jones and colleagues at MOMA Machynlleth; and for stimulating the project at its inception, Professor Richard Mayou.

I am very grateful to the lenders to the exhibition: Amgueddfa Cymru-National Museum Wales, the Ben Uri Collection, the British Council Collection, the Glynn Vivian Art Gallery in Swansea, the Government Art Collection, the Gregynog Trust, the National Library of Wales in Aberystwyth, the New Walk Museum and Art Gallery in Leicester, the RWA, Tate, the University of Leeds Art Collection and Estate of György Gordon, the Victoria and Albert Museum, the Martin Bloch Estate, Richard and Montserrat Edwards, Humberto Gatica, Rex Harley, Mona Hatoum/White Cube, Sir Jeremy and Lady Isaacs, Samira Kitman, the Heinz Koppel Estate, Hanaa Malallah, Zory Shahrokhi, Walid Siti, Dee Smart and others who wish to remain anonymous. Many image providers and copyright holders very kindly

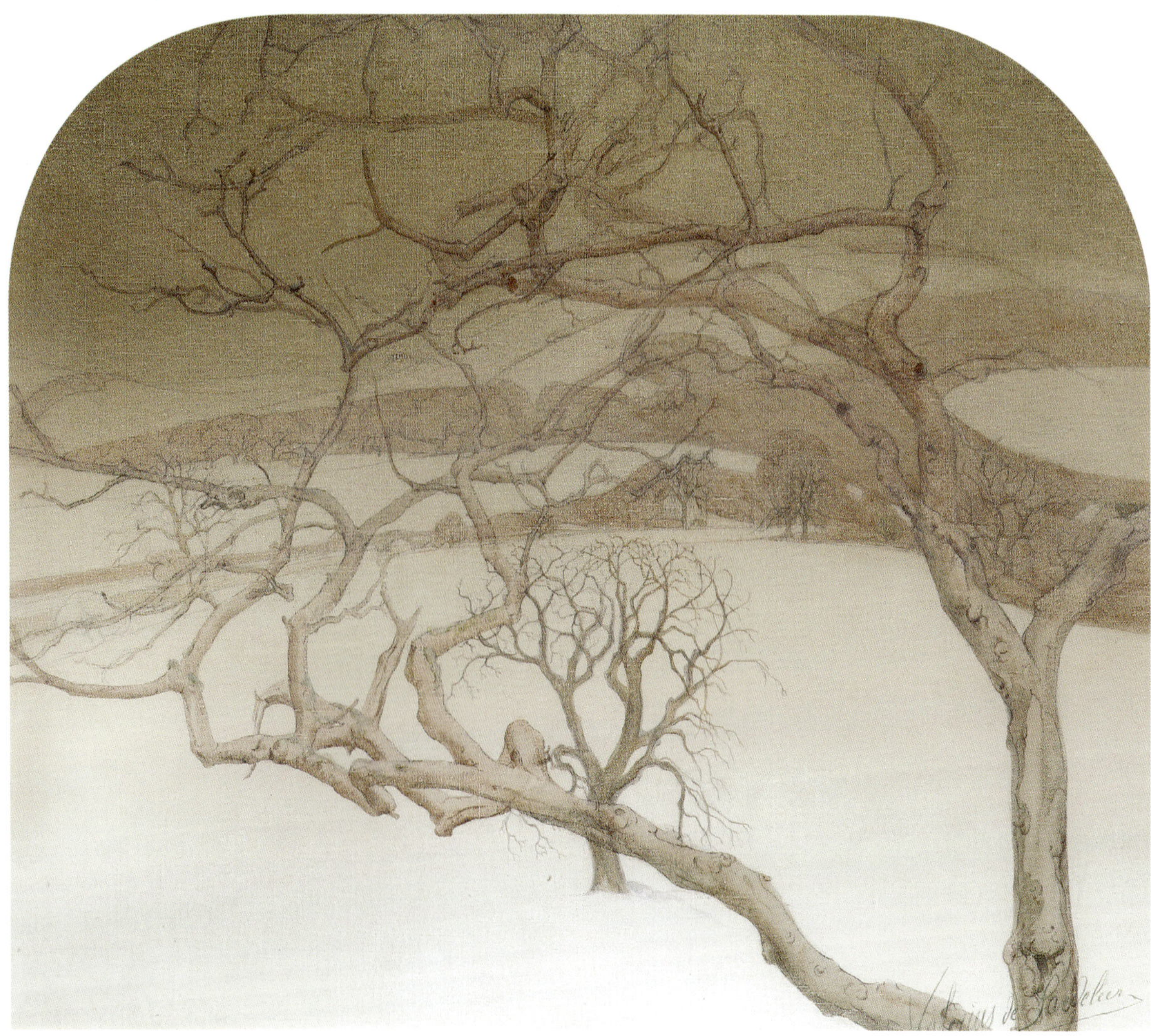

Valerius de Saedeleer (1867–1941) | *Winter Landscape, Aberystwyth*
*c.*1916 | oil on canvas | 47 x 60 cm
The Gregynog Trust

De Saedeleer discovered new landscapes to which he could respond
around his home in mid-Wales throughout the Great War.

allowed us to publish images free of charge; without
that the book simply would not have been possible.
I have made best efforts to trace all copyright
holders and would be pleased to hear from any
whom it was not possible to contact. I have been
very grateful for the commitment at Sansom &
Company of the late John Sansom, Clara Hudson
and Ian Parfitt.

I have been helped as I explored this subject
over many years by: Monica Bohm-Duchen and
Marilyn Greene of the Insiders/Outsiders festival;
the staff of the National Library of Wales in
Aberystwyth, the Centrum Judaicum in Berlin and
the Weiner Library in London; Alun Burge, Carys
Brown, Charles Burton, Paul Cabuts, Richard and
Montserrat Edwards, Oliver Fairclough, Clive
Hicks-Jenkins, Simon Martin, Amir a Nejad, Alan
Powers, Andrew Renton, Caryl and Herbert Roese
and Peter Rossiter. Although I never knew Heinz
Koppel, the friendship of his wife Pip and their
children Hanno, Ruth, Siân, Jess and Gideon has
been of great importance to me for many years.

Peter Wakelin

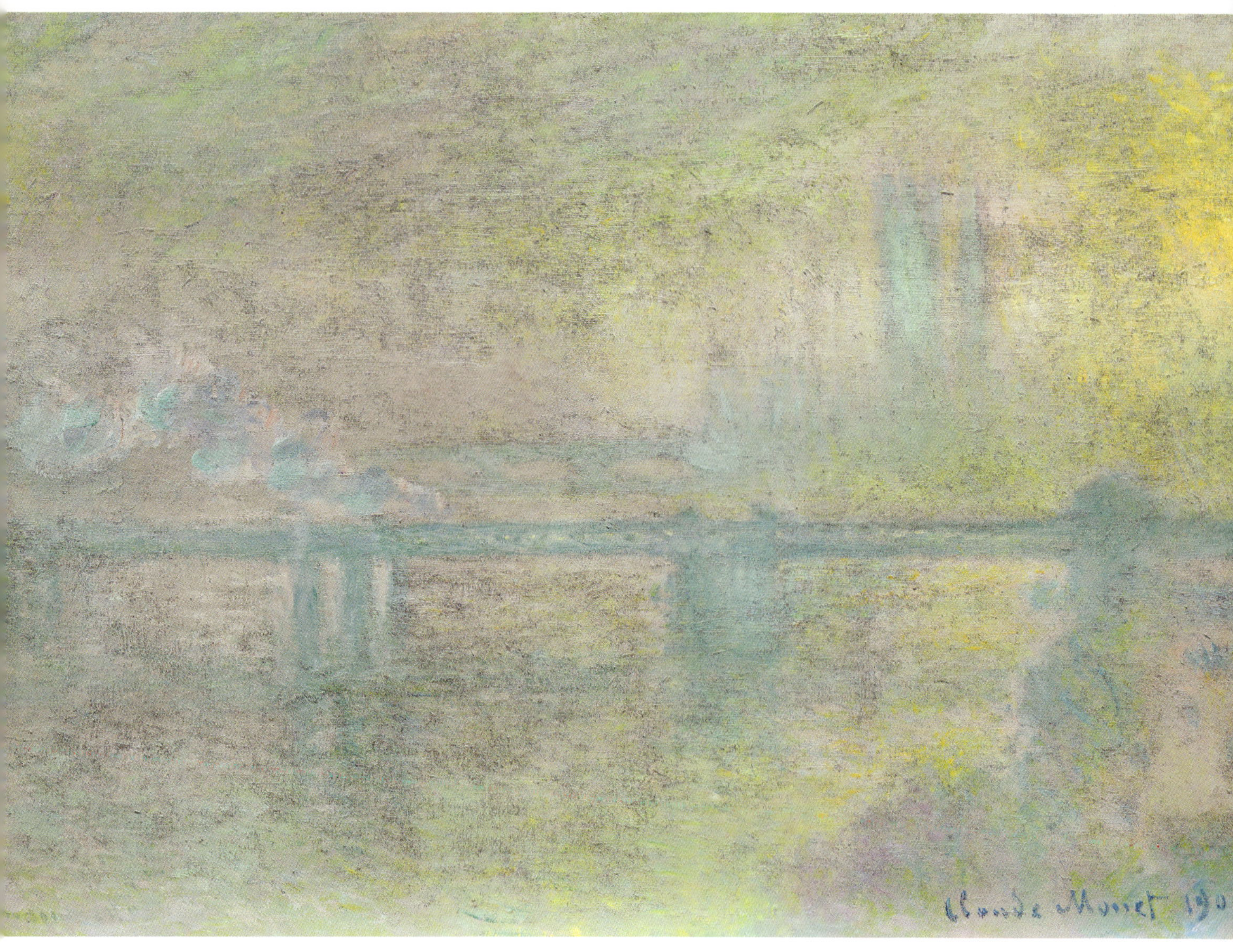

Claude Monet (1840–1926) | *Charing Cross Bridge, London*
1901 | oil on canvas | 65 x 92 cm
Mr and Mrs Martin A. Ryerson Collection, Art Institute of Chicago

Monet was only briefly a refugee in London but he became fascinated by its light and returned to paint. The visibility of his work influenced the next generation.

Refuge and renewal

HOPE AND TRAGEDY ARE INTERTWINED IN THE life stories of refugees who flee oppression, dispossession and destruction. For those who build a future, terrible beginnings may unfold in happier chapters, with kindness, reconstruction and contributions to a new culture.

This book is about artists who have sought refuge in Britain and the impacts that they had – or in some cases might have had – on British artists and British art. Migration has always been a source of cultural fertility, never more so than in the 1930s and 1940s when artists fleeing fascism brought ideas and energy to Britain. Yet the welcome for migrant artists has not always been positive: they have experienced critical hostility, financial struggles and even internment as well as support and respect. Their influence has been determined by circumstances as much as their abilities. British artists left Belgians who took refuge from the First World War largely isolated and missed the opportunity to learn from them. By contrast the 1930s modernists found eager followers. Today, the reception of refugees is as contentious as ever but their contributions to British life have yet to unfold.

John Berger described the twentieth century as 'the century of departure, of migration, of exodus, of disappearance: the century of people helplessly seeing others, who were close to them, disappear over the horizon.'[1] This intensity of exodus has only grown. According to the United Nations High Commission on Refugees, the number of people forcibly displaced worldwide is at an all-time high of over 70 million; conflict or persecution force 37,000 people a day to flee. The great majority remain in their own or neighbouring countries. For the minority who go further, the United Kingdom is a small recipient. It is well down the league of European countries in applications for asylum. Asylum seekers in 2018 represented only one in twenty of new immigrants to Britain.[2]

The numbers may have changed but the movement of refugees and the arrival of ideas with them is the norm not the exception in human history. The Biblical Exodus may represent collective memory of migration episodes in ancient times. In the territory we now call Britain people came and went for millennia, following herds of animals or fleeing conflict, until climate change made it uninhabitable for 100,000 years. People have been here permanently since around 11,000 years ago (say 500 generations), constantly refreshed by movement.[3] Ancient DNA and archaeology show that Neolithic people brought new cultures to a land only thinly occupied by hunter-gatherers, and that they came gradually from the Aegean through central Europe and Iberia.[4] Centuries later, the Angles who gave their name to modern England may have been displaced by the collapse of the Roman Empire.

Artists are no more susceptible to war or persecution on the grounds of race than other refugees but they may be special targets: more visible and more intellectually troublesome than farmers, doctors, miners or mechanics, and more practically dispensable as well. It has been possible to destroy their work and legacy especially easily. Camille Pissarro lost 1,500 works in the war of 1870–1; Emile Nolde had a thousand paintings confiscated by the Nazis. And yet, if they succeed in finding refuge, artists may be better placed than farmers, doctors and others to continue their careers. Visual expression can cross the language barrier and fellow artists are often people eager to discover new ideas.

Hundreds of artists have come to Britain as refugees in the last two centuries and have been among British art's most vital vectors of exchange. Even those who went home when it was safe to do so or moved on elsewhere may have shown their art, taught, or influenced other artists by their presence. On many occasions, refugees have seeded a tradition into British practice – as Jules Dalou did teaching sculpture in the 1870s and 1880s – or given impetus to radical experiment – as did the surge of modernists fleeing fascism in the 1930s.

However, British art has not always been receptive even to the most vivid influences, especially when traditionalism dominated or when those arriving were left isolated, unknown or little understood. Inevitably, not all artist refugees bring ideas of current relevance: the stolid academic painters who escaped the Franco-Prussian War proved creatively a dead end, unlike their Impressionist contemporaries.

This book focuses on refugees who were artists already when they came to Britain. Outstanding contributions have been made by people who became artists after their arrival, but they did not bring mature skills from another tradition. A list of child refugees who became artists might include the Elizabethan miniaturist Isaac Oliver, who fled from Rouen with his family or the painter Alfred Wolmark, who came from Warsaw to escape the pogroms of the 1880s. Child migrants of the Nazi era include the humourist and illustrator Gerard Hoffnung, the 'auto-destruction' artist Gustav Metzger who arrived on the *Kindertransport* aged 13, and two youngsters who became great British painters, Frank Auerbach and Lucian Freud. The Turner-prize nominated photographer Zarina

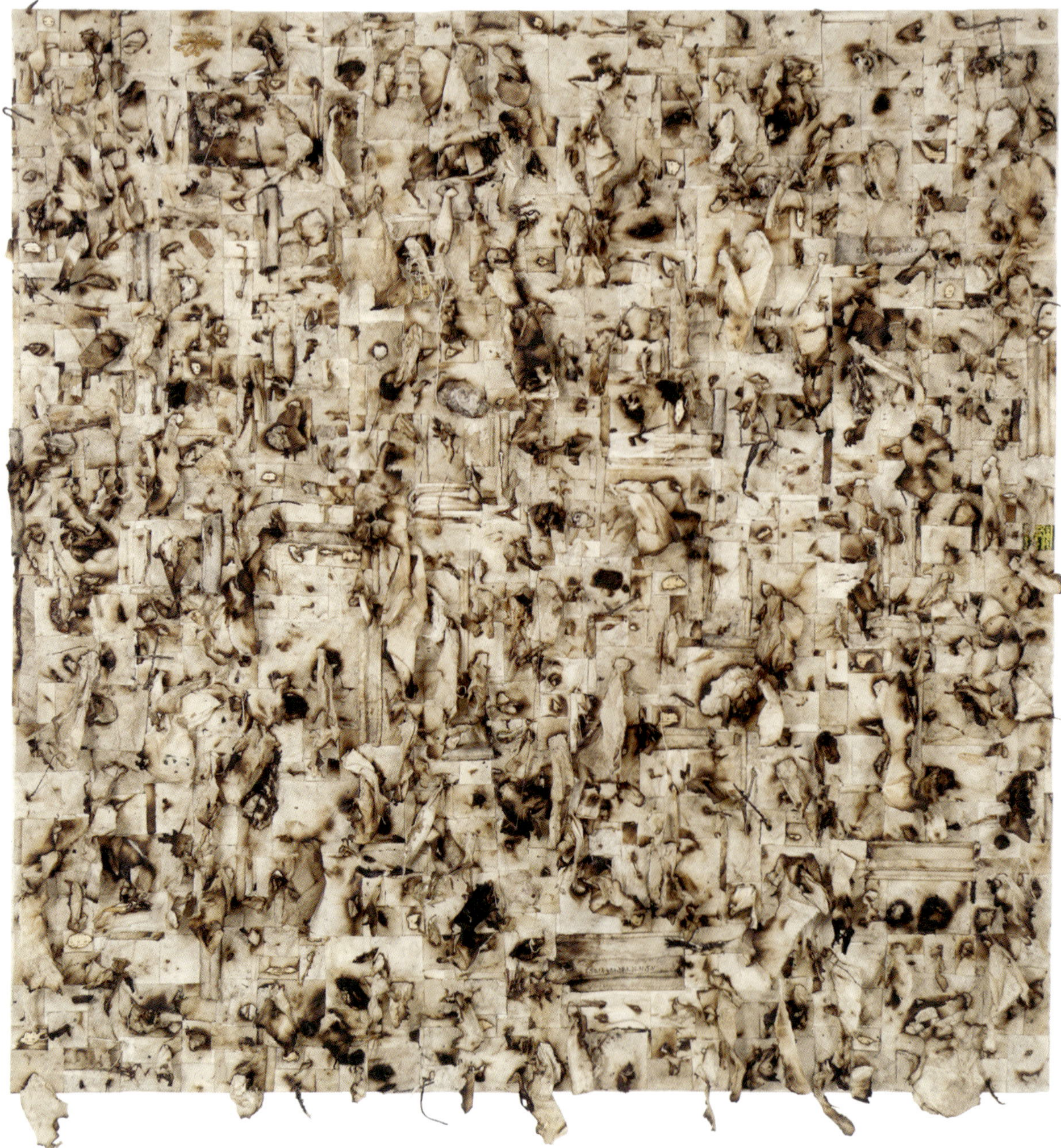

Hanaa Malallah (b.1958) | *Shroud* IV
2012 | mixed media and soft sculpture on canvas | 150 x 150 cm
collection of/© the artist

Malallah studied art in Baghdad but moved to London in 2007.
She says to taste war is completely different from knowing about it
second-hand. This piece was made from pieces of burnt canvas in
which tokens have been folded.

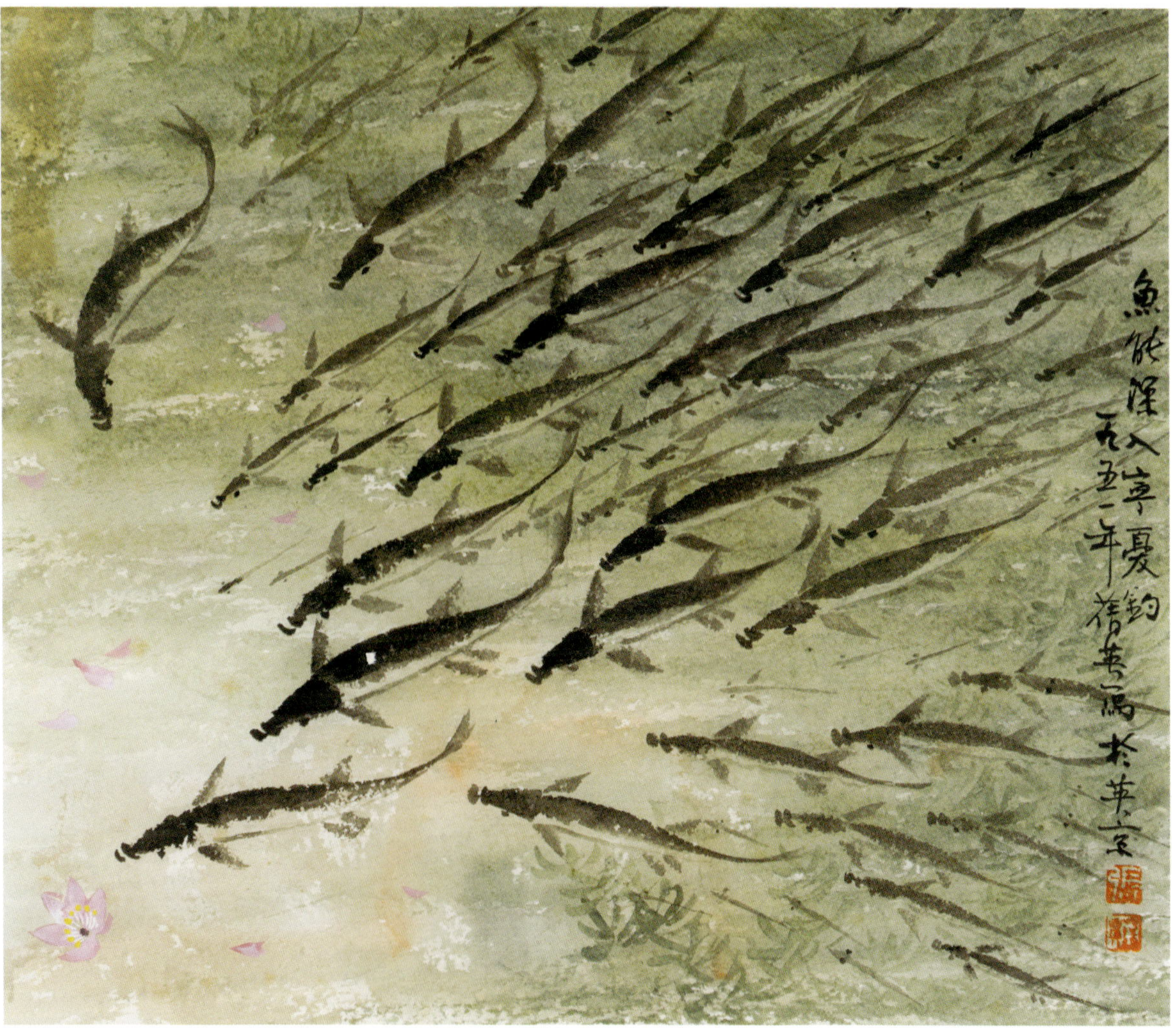

Chien-Ying Chang (1913–2004) | *Fishes in the Pond*
1951 | watercolour | 35 x 52 cm
RWA (Royal West of England Academy) | © Artist's Estate

Chien-Ying and her husband came from China with British Council
grants in 1947 but did not return after hearing about the persecution
of fellow artists.

Bhimji was among the 80,000 Asians expelled from
Uganda by Idi Amin in 1972. Eva Frankfurther
escaped from Nazi Germany and portrayed black
immigrants empathetically until she took her own
life at only 28.[5] Second-generation immigrants
have been important, too, such as children of
some 150,000 Eastern European Jews who came
to Britain from the 1880s to 1914, for example
David Bomberg and Mark Gertler.[6]

Students of migration refer to 'push' and 'pull'.
For those casually seeking a new life, like Britons
who retire to Spain, it is the 'pull' of climate, food
and countryside. Artists have for centuries been
'pulled' to Britain: Philip de Loutherbourg came
seeking work as a scenic painter in the eighteenth
century, Alphonse Legros in the nineteenth
century left France for love, and in the twentieth
century Frank Bowling from Guyana, Kim Lim
from Singapore and Anish Kapoor from India came
to study. For refugees, the 'push' is overwhelming.
Most artist refugees have fled from danger or oppression. Even so, circumstances can be complicated;
individual stories take many forms. Artists may have
been away from home already when circumstances
changed. For example, Feliks Topolski came from
Poland by choice in 1935 but was stranded when
war broke out and became a British citizen 12
years later. The Chinese artists Chien-Ying Chang
and Cheng Wu Fei arrived with a British Council
grant in 1947 but when they heard news of Maoist

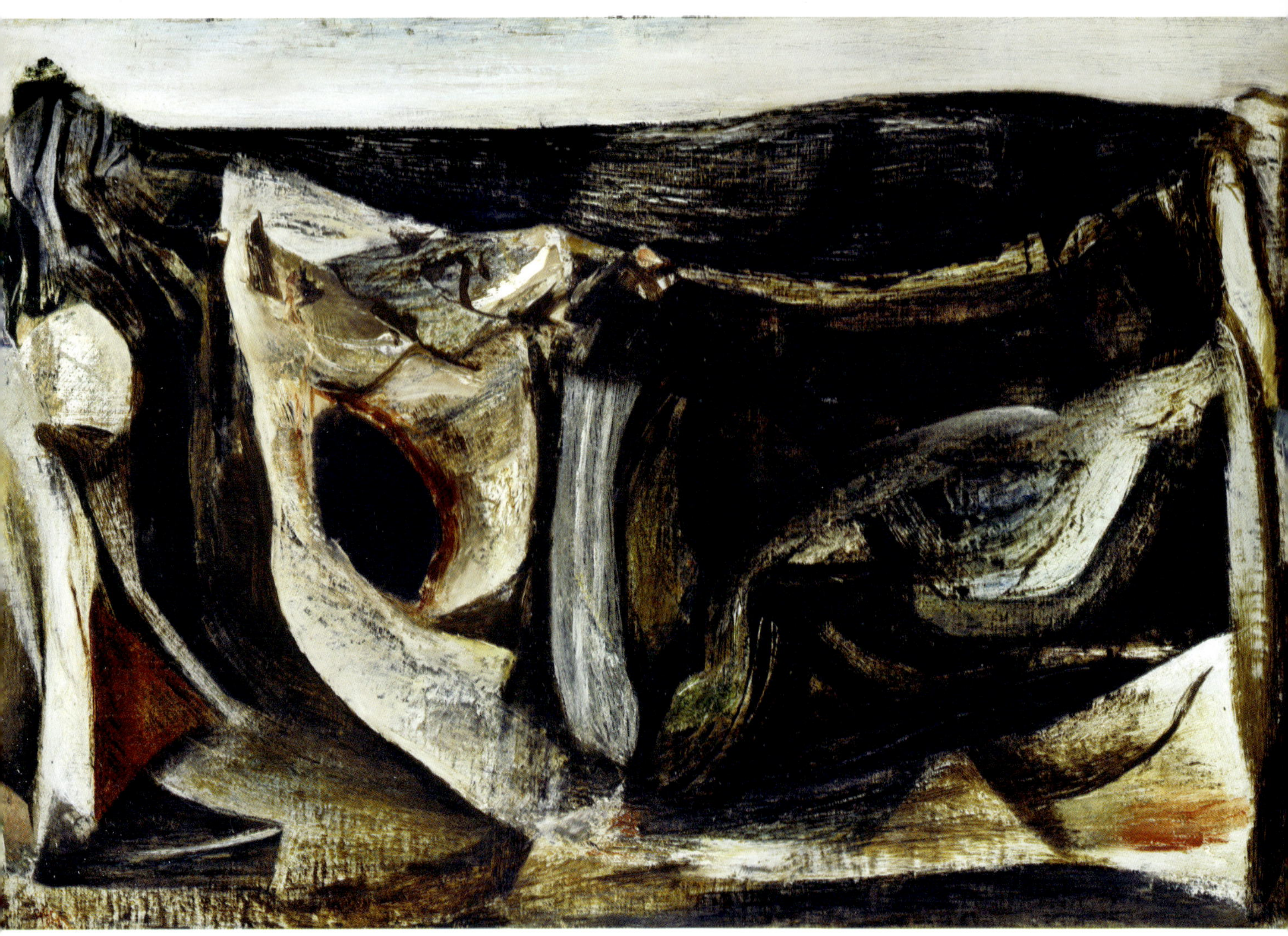

Peter Lanyon (1918–1964) | *Headland*
1948 | oil on canvas | 51 x 77 cm
Tate | © Estate of Peter Lanyon/all rights reserved DACS 2019 | photo: © Tate

Lanyon's semi-abstract landscapes were among the greatest
achievements of the St Ives school, both responding to the nature
of mined headlands and informed by the Constructivist sculpture
of Naum Gabo.

purges they knew it was unsafe to return.[7] Were such artists 'exiles', 'refugees' or 'emigrants' by choice? The philosopher Hanna Arendt who fled Germany for Paris and the USA said: 'We don't like to be called "refugees" We ourselves call each other "newcomers" or "immigrants".' But the playwright Berthold Brecht wrote after reaching the United States:

The name they coined us – emigrants – is fundamentally erroneous, since this was not a voluntary migration for the purpose of finding an alternative place to settle. The emigrants found themselves not a new homeland but a place of refuge in exile until the storm passes – Deportees that's what we are, outcasts.[8]

To 'emigrate' is usually a decision taken voluntarily, though the associated word 'émigré' is used equally for those who had no choice. To be 'exiled' is a condition enforced by the state, frequently through deportation. An 'asylum seeker' is someone hoping that their need for asylum will be recognised and they will be given the status of 'refugee'. That word itself comes from the French *réfugié* – to have taken refuge – brought by the French Protestants fleeing religious persecution in the seventeenth century. Its first use recorded in the *Oxford English Dictionary* is in 1628 but it became commonplace after the arrival of the Huguenots *en masse* in 1685, first to mean French religious refugees specifically and later any person forced to move by war, religious persecution, political troubles or the effects of natural or economic disaster.

Refuge may be temporary, like sheltering from a passing storm, or long-lasting. It may lead to permanent settlement even if conditions improve. If someone has adapted to a new country and built a life, home and family it may be madness to go back. Horrors such as state-sponsored murder of one's loved-ones make returning unimaginable.

For some refugee artists, migration brought gains alongside their losses. James Tissot perhaps stands for many who thrived in their new culture, becoming a wealthy painter in Victorian London. For the Dutch painter Piet Mondrian, who had made his name in Paris, time in London and New York turned his influence global. But for all too many, life was hard and opportunities could never compensate for what they had left behind. In the most important terms, the human ones, no loss was more horrific than that of Jewish artists who learned that their whole families had been murdered in the Holocaust. Others lost their livelihoods and had to live by charity or take work that did not utilise their talents and training. Pamina Liebert-Mahrenholz, highly regarded as a sculptor in Berlin, made her living by restoring broken china; the painter Hilde Goldschmidt sold fur and leather goods.

Even artists of considerable influence and standing have found it hard to be understood in their new country. Expressionism left large parts of the pre-war British audience bemused. Oskar Kokoschka, widely regarded in Austria as the nation's greatest living painter, was perhaps the most distinguished of all the artist refugees who made homes permanently in Britain, yet his arrival roused little interest. He recalled seeking support from the Tate Gallery director, Sir John Rothenstein, who simply offered him tea and sandwiches and asked if he would care to donate a painting.[9] Ludwig Meidner, well-known in Germany, lived in near poverty in Britain for 14 years and took a job as a mortuary caretaker. Expressionists could be caricatured rather than recognised as individuals: 'the British public constructed a concept of "refugee" art', in the words of the art historian Jutta Vinzent, 'defined by the use of rich colour and the free nature of combining feeling, colour and gesture'.[10] Today, artists from Syria or Iraq may meet with similarly undiscriminating views.

Importantly, incomprehension by the public is not necessarily matched by fellow practitioners. In the 1870s, a few younger artists saw the freshness of the Impressionist paintings that appeared in London after the Franco-Prussian War. In the 1930s and 1940s, many in the *avant-garde* embraced the emotion of expressionism as an antidote to French-inspired formalism. Individual artists encountered new ways of seeing and making in places as far apart as Merthyr Tydfil, Hampstead, St Ives, where the young Peter Lanyon got to know the Russian Constructivist Naum Gabo, or Glasgow, where Joan Eardley admired Josef Herman's images of working lives. Many foreign artists taught as they sought to make their livings. Martin Bloch taught Gillian Ayres at Camberwell, and earlier the sculptor William Goscombe John learned naturalistic clay modelling from Jules Dalou at Lambeth.

Refuge is one, albeit vital, feature in a broader picture of migration's importance in art. In the sixteenth and seventeenth centuries, almost all the great names of British painting learned their trade in continental centres: Hans Holbein (German), Hans Eworth (Flemish), Sir Anthony Van Dyke (Flemish, originally Antoon van Dijck), Sir Peter Lely (Dutch) and Sir Godfrey Kneller (German, originally Gottfried Kniller). Kneller exemplifies how ideas were transmitted: born in Lübeck he studied in Amsterdam and Rome before becoming the leading portrait painter in England for almost 40 years and founding London's first proper academy of art in 1711. Such figures came seeking opportunities for patronage but the religious strife of the Reformation was an additional motivation at times. Meanwhile, movement the other way was also critical. It was normal in the eighteenth century for British artists to go to Rome for years on end:

many, like the sculptor John Gibson who went to study with Canova, stayed for the rest of their lives though their market was in Britain. In the early twentieth century, young artists like Christopher Wood and Cedric Morris took time out in Paris before returning home with eyes refreshed. In the 1960s, David Hockney began a double-life in California and Britain.

But for refugees, escape is not for education but survival. For every famous artist refugee who made it to the other side there must have been many who, their time cut short, did not achieve their promise. Charlotte Salomon, a rare example of one known posthumously, perhaps stands for all those lost to us. She was among the last Jewish students to enrol at the Berlin Fine Arts Academy but in 1938 her family decided to send her to take refuge with her grandparents in Nice. When war began her grandmother threw herself out of a window and her disturbed grandfather revealed hidden family tragedies. Charlotte began a sequence of gouache drawings laced with text that traced her family's story under the ironic title *Life? or Theatre?* Among them is her drawing of the mass attacks on Jewish property of *Kristallnacht*. Through a body of 1,000 drawings she showed all but the bitter last chapter. In 1943, she and her partner were denounced as Jews and deported from France to Auschwitz. Five months pregnant, age 26, she was gassed on arrival. Astonishingly, her work was safeguarded and reached the Jewish Historical Museum of Amsterdam. It was reproduced as a literally monumental book in 2015.[11] Her layered text, personal subject matter and autobiographical focus look

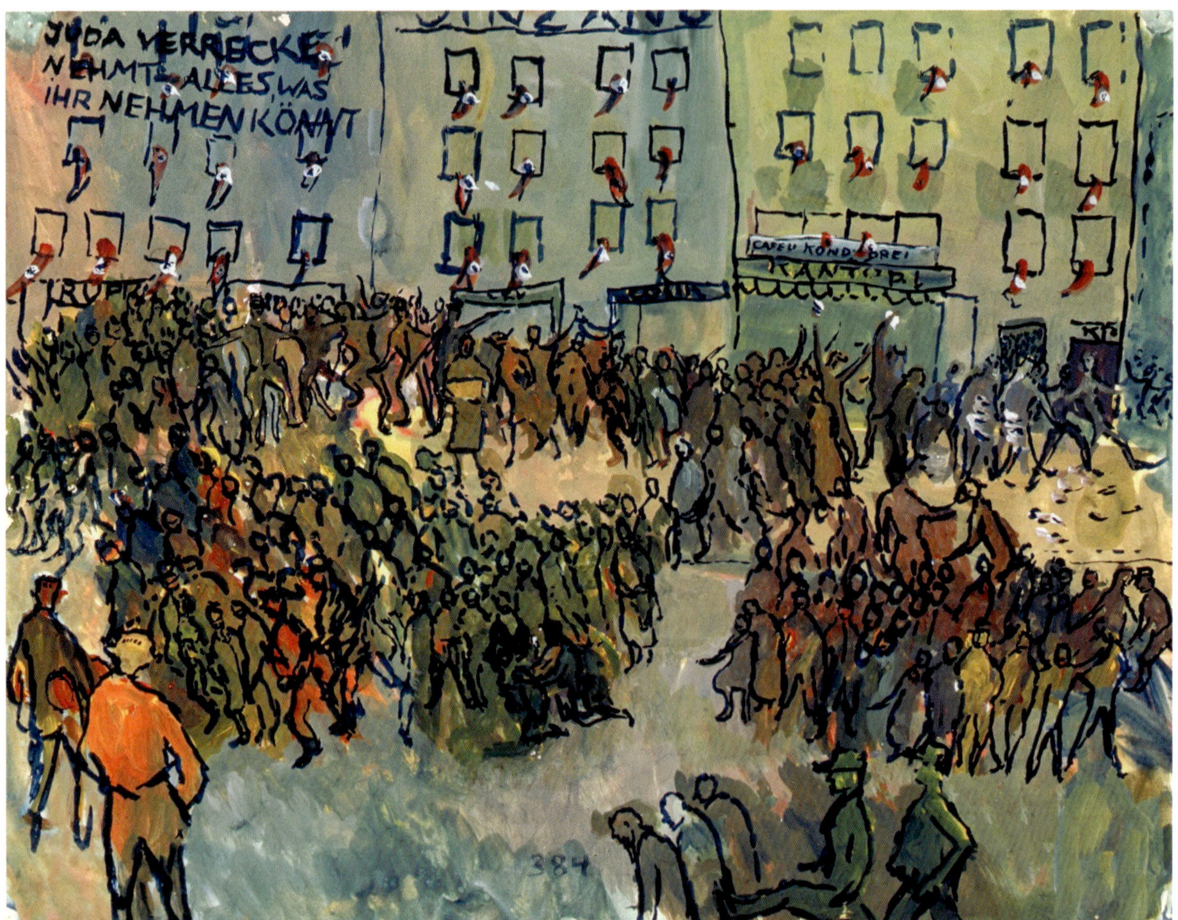

Charlotte Salomon (1917–1943) | *Kristallnacht*
*c.*1940–2 | gouache on paper | 25 x 32 cm
Jewish Historical Museum, Amsterdam | Charlotte Salomon Foundation
photo: Wikimedia Commons

The rubric reads 'Death to the Jews. Grab what you can.' The mob is attacking Jewish-owned shops while Nazi flags hang from the apartments. Flames rise from the square and three figures are detained and kicked by Brownshirts.

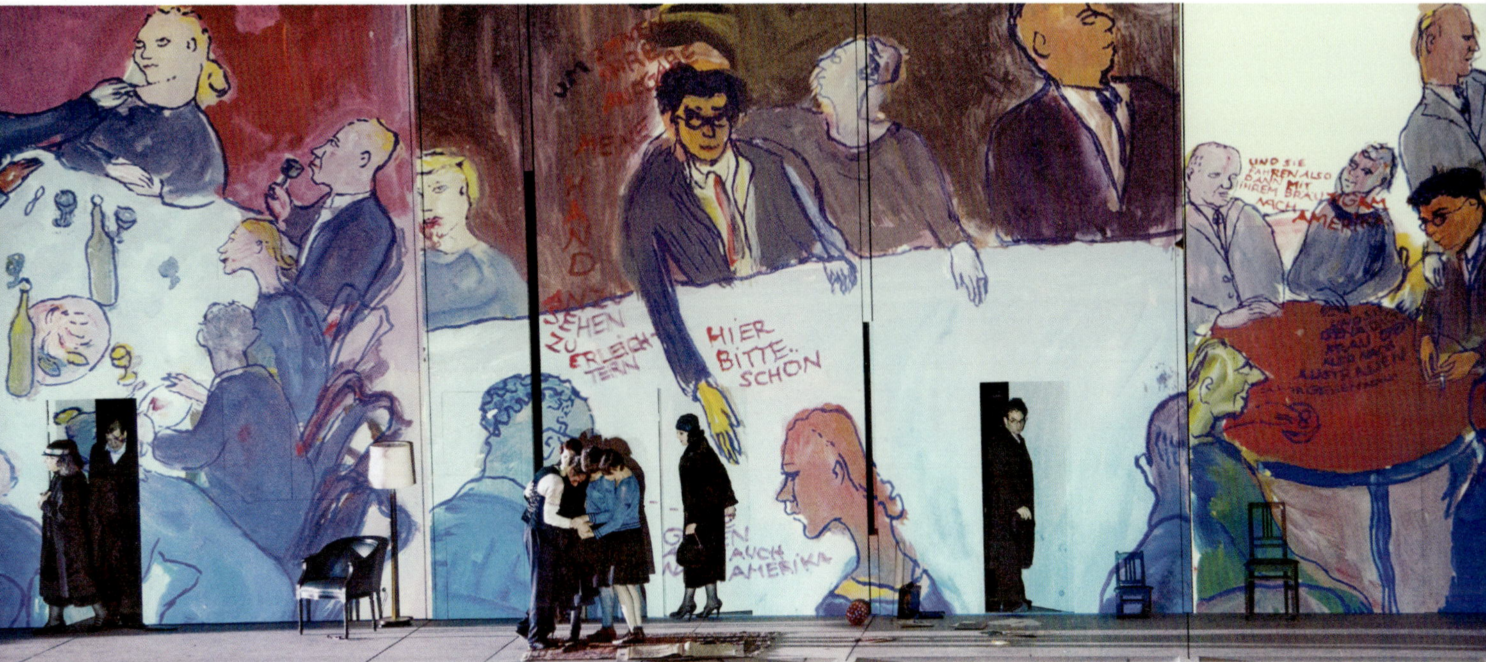

The opera *Charlotte Salomon* by Marc-André Dalbavie and Barbara Honigmann, at the Salzburg Festival, 2014, featuring projections of Charlotte Salomon's watercolours.
photo: Francisco Peralta Torrejón, Wikimedia Commons

as fresh as if they were brand new, prefiguring twenty-first century artists such as Tracey Emin and Marjane Satrapi, author of the graphic novel *Persepolis*. Though Salomon could not influence others in her lifetime, her imagery and story have inspired plays, films, opera and ballet.

The remainder of this book explores successive waves of artist refugees: from religious strife, the Franco-Prussian War, the First World War, the rise of fascism, Soviet oppression and conflicts in the Middle East. How did the conditions of the refugees affect their capacity to create? How did they engage with British artists and audiences, and what has

their influence been on the practice and appreciation of art in Britain?

There is a classic refugee narrative that moves through persecution, flight and asylum to integration and contribution. Woven into this are diverse personal stories. Nevertheless, a pattern holds. Despite repeated tensions, Britain has been for generations a place of safety and as such has gained tremendously. The late comedian and activist Jeremy Hardy wrote in 2002: 'It is a terrible thing that people should ever have to flee their homes because of danger, poverty or discrimination. But for them to be here is our privilege, not theirs.'[12]

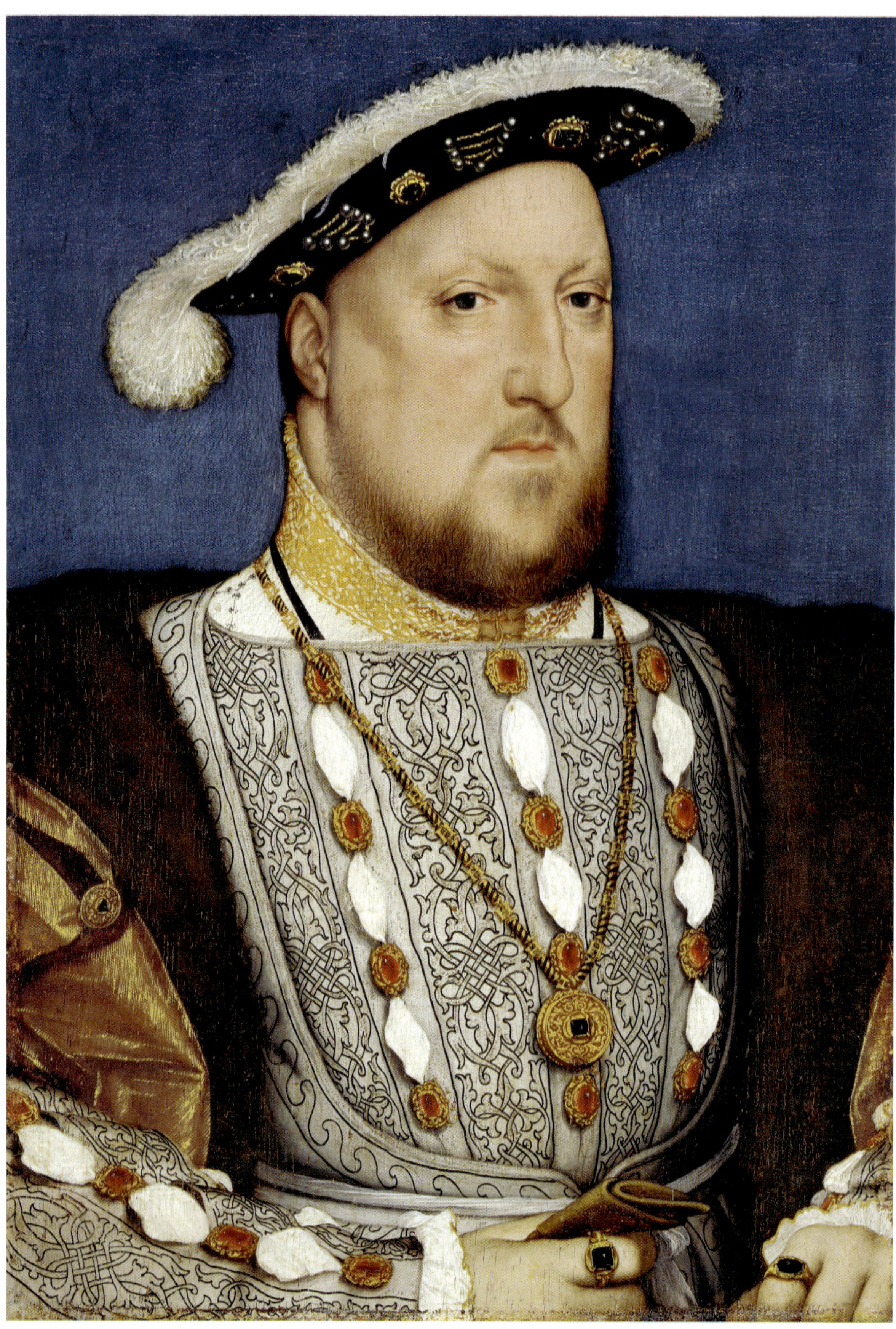

Reformation and religious strife

IN THE TUDOR PERIOD AND FOR SOME TIME afterwards, Britain had fewer distinguished artists who had learned their craft at home than who had come from France, Germany, Italy and above all the Low Countries. Discriminating English clients naturally sought out the best, but many artists came also to escape war or religious persecution during the religious strife following the Reformation. Their arrival transformed art in Britain.

Foremost among them was Hans Holbein the Younger, whose exquisite genius still thrills. His was the greatest single influence on the development of portraiture in seventeenth-century England. Having learned painting from his father, also Hans, he came to Britain speculatively from his home in Basel in 1526 then went home shortly afterwards. However, when religious riots broke out in Basel in 1529 and a strict Protestant regime was established, he saw his work destroyed by Lutherans who condemned it as idolatry. He returned to England in 1532, then still a Catholic country, where he made portraits of German traders and painted his masterful *Ambassadors* of 1533. By 1536 he was painter to King Henry VIII. His paintings and drawings of Henry, Edward Prince of Wales, Thomas Moore, Thomas Cromwell and the Tudor aristocracy are justly famous. He died in London in 1543.[1]

After Henry's separation from Rome in 1537, England became a safer place for Protestants at risk from persecution by the Spanish government of Philip II or from the Eighty Years War that began in 1568. The compelling portrait painter Hans Eworth (originally Euworts) is believed to have been expelled from his home city of Antwerp for the heresy of Protestantism in 1544. He came to Britain shortly afterwards and became perhaps the key figure in British painting in the era after Holbein. It was ironic that as a Protestant he was more closely associated with the Roman Catholic

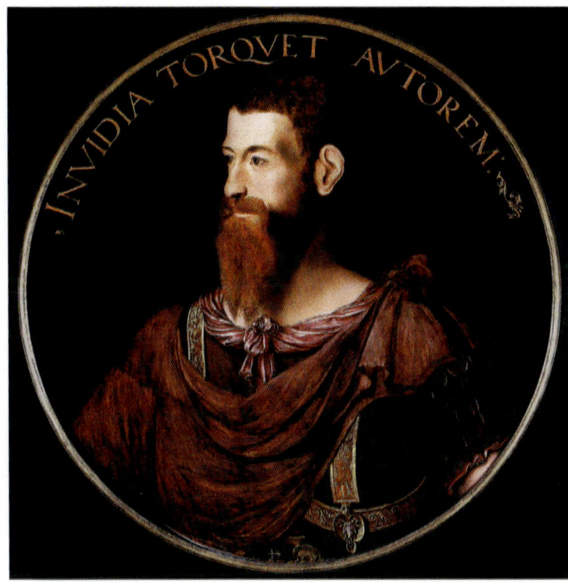

Hans Eworth (*c*.1520–1574) | *Henry Fitzalan, Earl of Arundel*
1550 | oil on panel | 65 cm diameter
Denver Art Museum

Eworth painted this portrait in the year that he was granted 'letters of denization' in Britain.

Mary Tudor than the Elizabethan court that followed.[2]

The Huguenots in France, followers of Calvin, were persecuted until the toleration offered by the Edict of Nantes in 1598 and again after the Edict was revoked in 1685. The earlier persecution reached a crescendo with the St Bartholomew Day Massacre of 1572 when tens of thousands were murdered. Among the earliest French Protestant refugee artists to settle in Britain, around 1595, was the sculptor Maximilian Colt (originally Poultrain). Originally from Arras, he went to Utrecht before moving to London and taking his more English name. He won the most prestigious commission possible, to carve the tomb of Elizabeth I in Westminster Abbey, completed in 1606, and went on to make memorials of unprecedented and influential naturalism.[3]

The greatest influx of Huguenots was after Louis XIV cancelled the civil rights given them by the Edict of Nantes in 1685. They were now subjected to organised abuse, forced to convert and forbidden to leave. Hundreds of thousands sought to weather the storm but around 200,000 fled. Some 35–50,000 came to England; others went to Switzerland, Ireland, Sweden, Holland and the German states. By 1710, about 5 per cent of London's population were Huguenots. They included silk-weavers, paper makers, tapestry makers, silversmiths and painters as well as bankers and merchants and created a boom in skills even as

Hans Holbein the Younger (1497–1543) | *Henry VIII*
1536 | oil on panel | 28 x 20 cm
Thyssen-Bornemisza Museum, Madrid | photo: Google Cultural Institute

Holbein's portrait of Henry is scintillating in its rich detail but also deeply humane. Through dozens of paintings and drawings he set a new standard for portraiture in Britain.

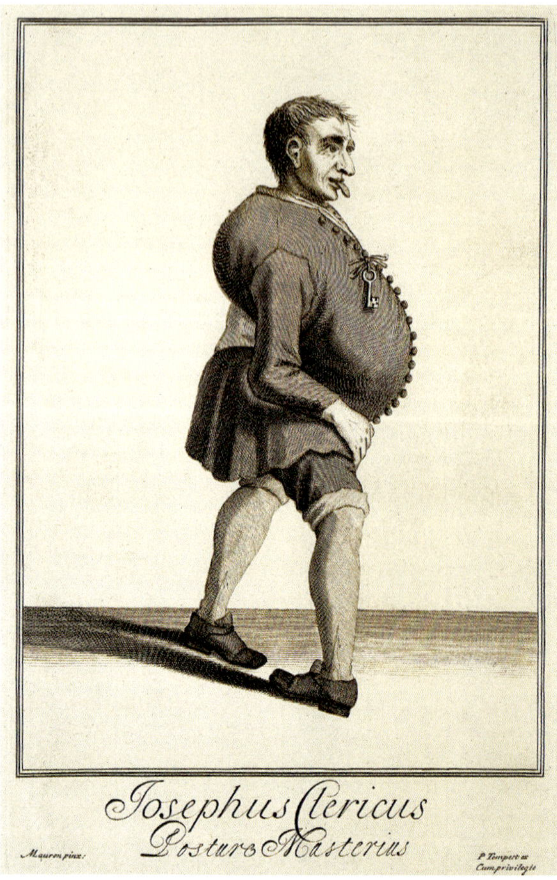

P. Tempest after **Marcellus Laroon** (1653–1702)
Joseph Clark, A Contortionist | 1687 | line engraving
Wellcome Collection

This engraving after Laroon of a street entertainer appeared in his book *The Cryes of London*. Both Daniel Defoe and Samuel Pepys possessed copies.

they denuded France of them. By the mid-eighteenth century probably 600 Huguenot artists and craftsmen had made their lives in Britain. Typically they grouped together, but they branched out creatively in ways that French craft guilds precluded. By bringing both traditional skills and the latest in French taste they began to change the perception of the arts in England, which had never been associated with professional status. The episode proved Britain could benefit from welcoming refugees.[4]

Among the best remembered French Protestants was Marcellus Laroon, born in The Hague in 1648/9. He had trained with his French father and in London in his twenties. He lived in Covent Garden from 1675. His masterpiece was his portrait of Charles II for Christ's Hospital in 1684 but his greatest impact was in recording the community of street vendors and entertainers of his new home in his drawings in 1687 for *The Cryes of the City of London*. The blogger the Gentle Author has written:

> *For the first time, hawkers were portrayed as individuals not merely representative stereotypes, each with a distinctive personality revealed through their movement, their attitudes, their postures, their gestures, their clothing and the special things they sold. Marcellus Laroon's Cries possessed more life than any that had gone before, reflecting the dynamic renaissance of the City at the end of the seventeenth century.*[5]

The Huguenot Jean-Baptiste Monnoyer had studied in Antwerp, the centre of still-life and memento mori, and became a specialist in floral paintings within interior decoration, idioms seldom seen in Britain. He worked at the Louvre and Versailles for Louis XIV, who had some 60 of his paintings. Despite this success, when he was given leave of absence to cross the Channel in 1690 he did not go back.[6] Louis Chéron arrived three years later. He came from a family of painters in Paris and had studied with his father, at the Académie Royale and in Rome. He made a series of paintings for the cathedral of Notre Dame from 1687 to 1690 but continuing persecution determined him to leave. (His sister, the artist Élisabeth Sophie Chéron converted to the Catholic church and stayed.) In England he received commissions at country houses, published engravings and illustrated Milton and the Bible. He taught drawing at Sir Godfrey Kneller's private school and then in 1718 co-founded the St Martin's Lane Academy where he is credited with bringing a female model into a life-drawing class for the first time.[7]

Although ordained as a Protestant priest in Switzerland, Henry Fuseli (born Johann Heinrich Füssli) came from a family of artists. He was advised to leave Zurich aged 20 after co-writing a pamphlet that exposed the corruption of a powerful magistrate. He went first to Berlin and then in 1764 to London, where he was a progenitor of Romanticism. He was notorious as the most original history painter of his generation, regarded by some as Britain's greatest artist and others as one demolishing the great tradition. He became Professor of Painting at the Royal Academy in 1799. His pupils included Constable, Landseer and Benjamin Haydon.[8]

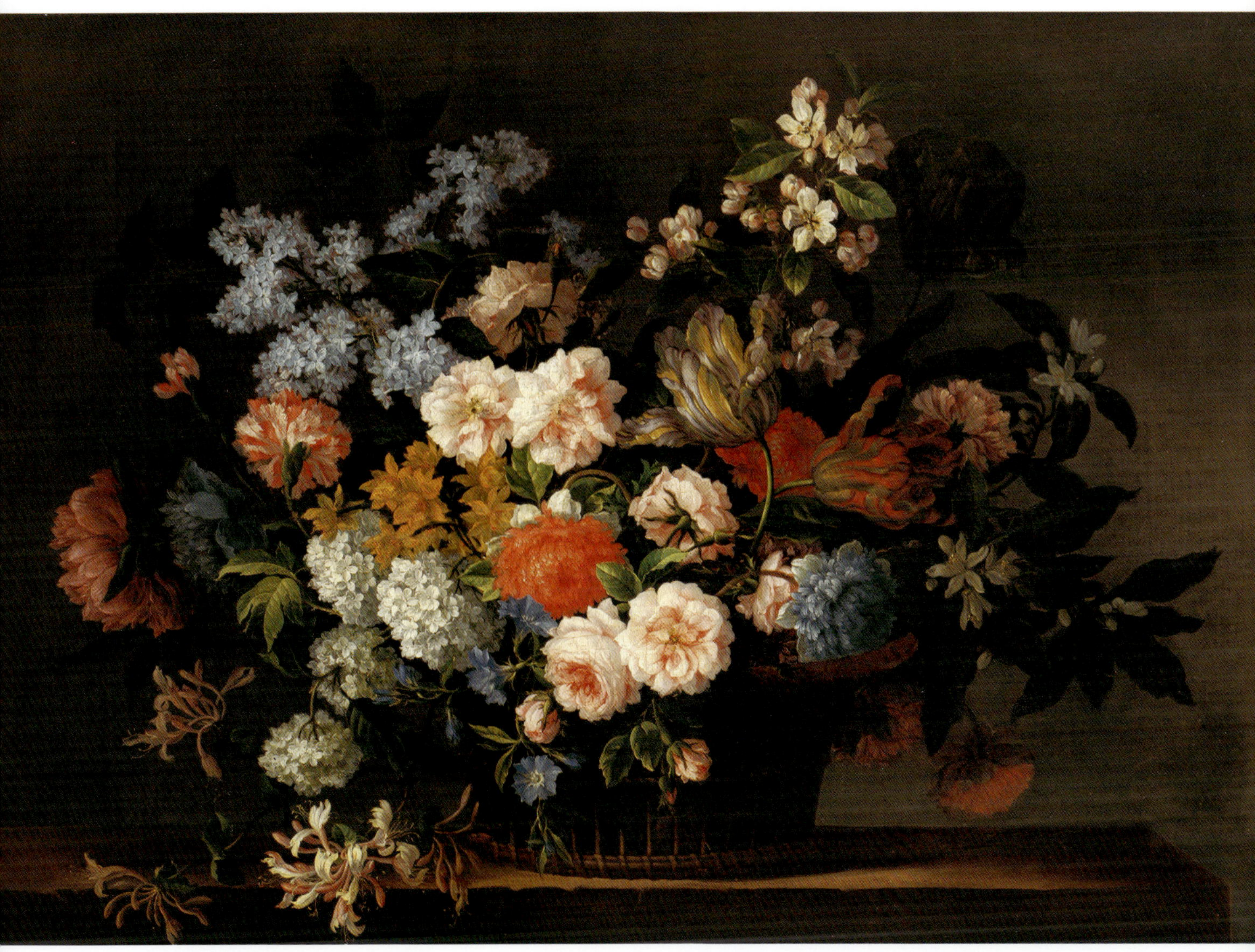

Jean-Baptiste Monnoyer (*c.*1636–1699)
Still-Life with Basket of Flowers | 1690s | oil on canvas | 73 x 103 cm
Art Gallery of South Australia | photo: Google Art Project

The fluid still-lifes of Monnoyer brought a relatively unexploited
idiom to British art.

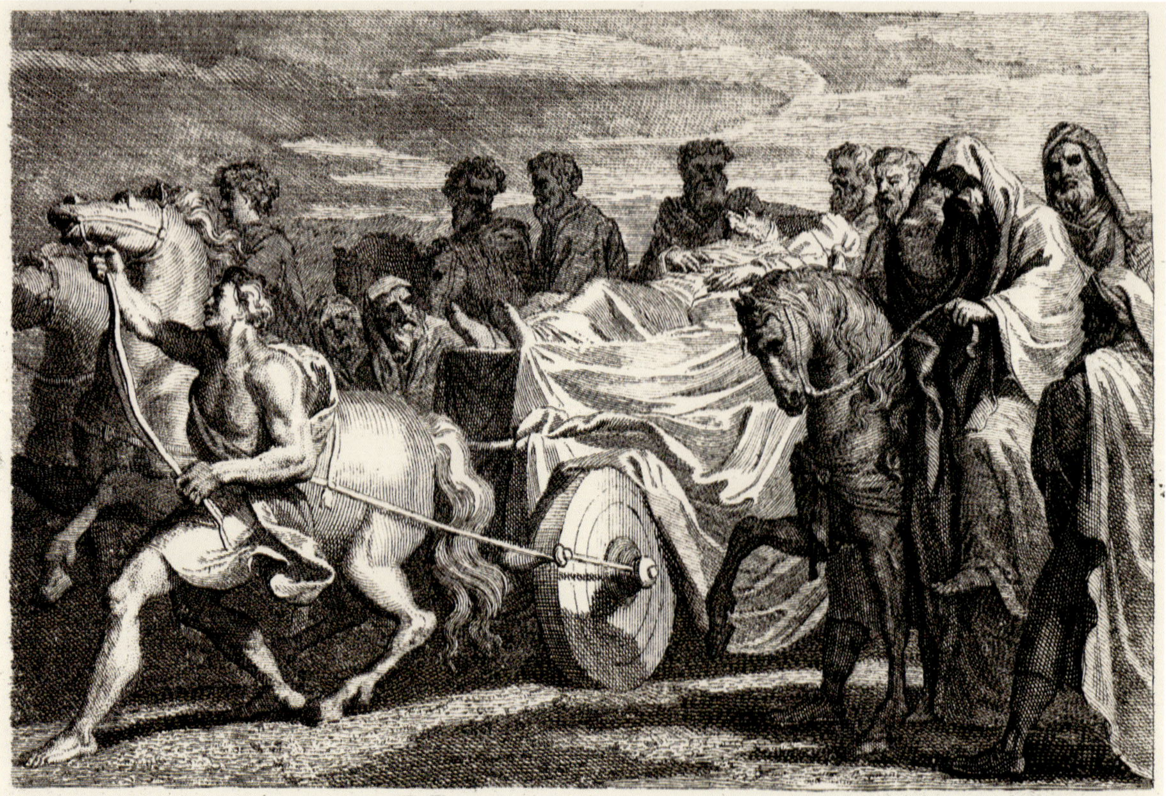

Louis Du Guernier after **Louis Chéron** (1660–1725)
Jacob is taken to the cave in the field of Machpelah by a mournful procession | *c.*1717 | engraving | 11 x 16 cm
Wellcome Library, London

This Bible illustration shows Chéron's ability to deal with complex figure compositions, developed studying Poussin in Rome.

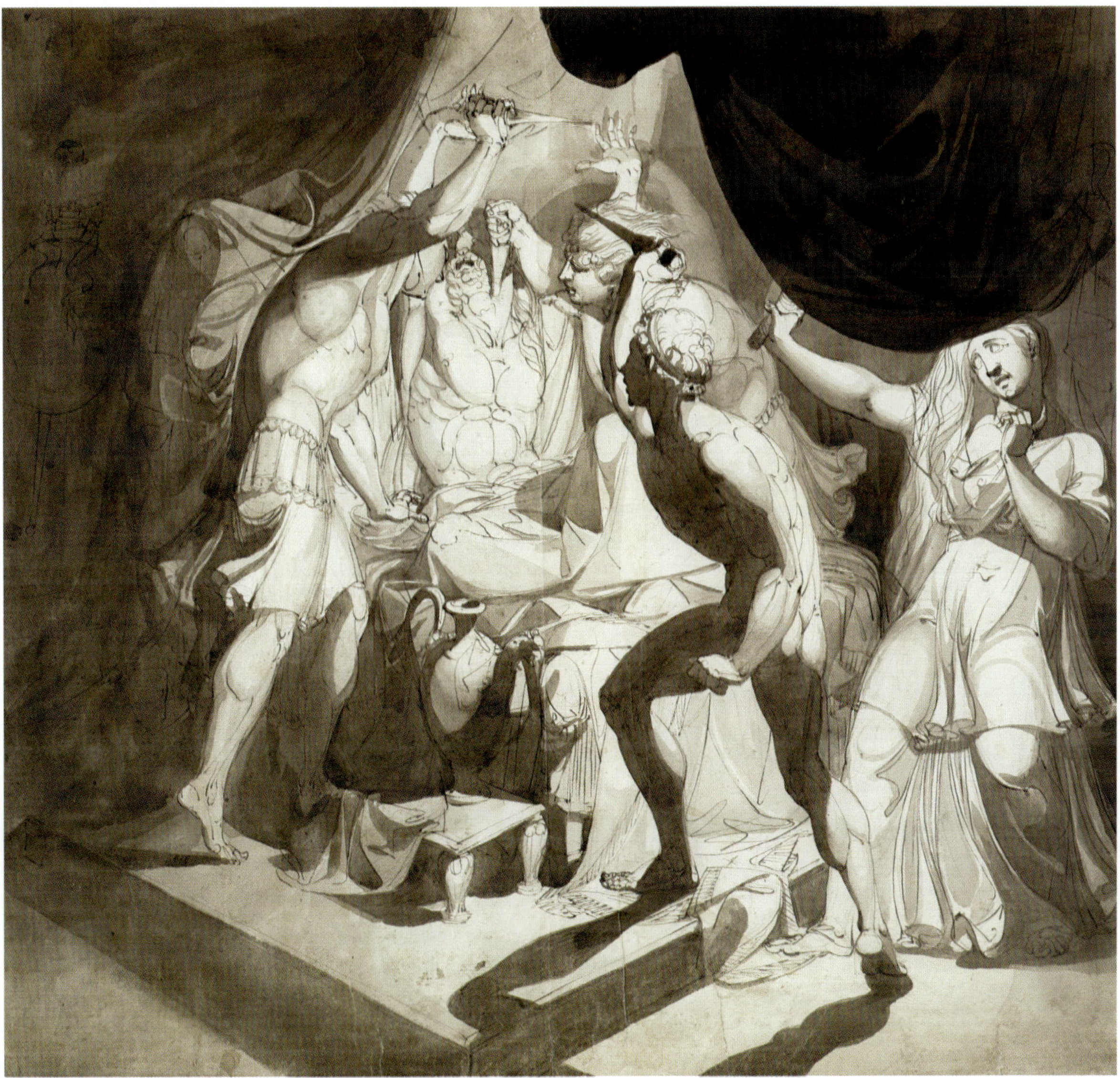

Henry Fuseli (1741–1825)
An Old Man Murdered by Three Younger Men
1770–3 | ink and wash on paper | 42 x 48 cm
The Getty

Fuseli fled his home in Zurich aged 20. He was a progenitor of
Romanticism in England, famous for his fantastical drawings and
paintings of nightmare, murder or bewitchment.

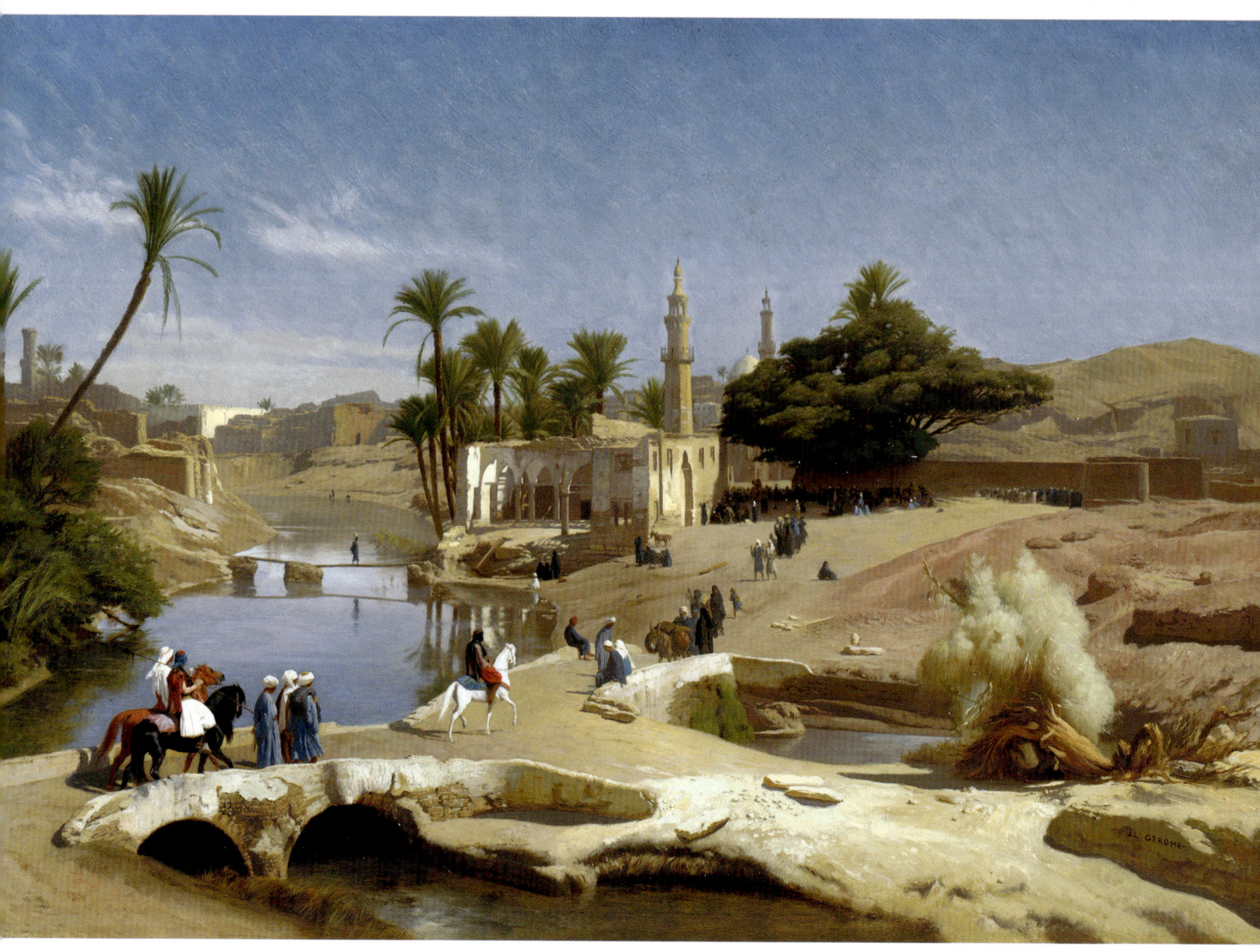

Jean-Léon Gérôme (1824–1904) | *View of Medinet El-Fayoum*
1868–70 | oil on wood | 38 x 56 cm
National Gallery of Art, Washington DC

The academic painter and sculptor Jean-Léon Gérôme was celebrated
for Oriental subjects based on his travels in the Middle East and
North Africa.

When Paris came to London

THERE WAS A MOMENT IN THE 1870S WHEN THE future School of Paris just might have been the School of London. Many artists came across the Channel to escape the Franco-Prussian War or its aftermath. For a year and more London was teeming with French refugees, including many painters. Their experience of refuge was short-lived but not inconsequential.

By 1870 London was the largest city in the world, thriving on the profits of the Empire and Victorian industry, a gateway to wealthy benefactors and customers for art. Some French artists were already succeeding in the metropolis, including the illustrator Gustave Doré who came frequently to prepare his 180 engravings for *London: A Pilgrimage* (1872) and had even opened his own gallery.[1] The painter and etcher Alphonse Legros had come to England in 1863, where he had married, achieved some success commercially and begun teaching at the South Kensington School of Art.

The war and its aftermath were disastrous. Victor Hugo christened it the '*année terrible*'. Rattled by German ambitions for unification, France declared war on Prussia in July 1870. The French invaded but the German coalition's troops flooded back, capturing Emperor Napoleon III. A new French government, the Third Republic, continued the war for five more months during which Paris was under siege. After the capital fell in January 1871, the revolutionary Commune took control, ruling from mid-March to the end of May, when it was put down in a bloody civil war that resulted in trials, executions and reprisals against its supporters and left 10,000 dead. The painter Gustave Courbet was among those imprisoned. He subsequently went into exile in Switzerland.

Since 1826 Britain had exercised almost no restrictions on immigration, attracting both the workforce it needed and radical thinkers exiled from their own counties such as Karl Marx. The artistic radicals of 1870–1 were two painters who would eventually be household names though as yet they were relatively unknown, the emerging Impressionists Claude Monet, aged 30, and Camille Pissarro, 40. Also in London was their more senior friend Charles François Daubigny,

born in 1817. Ironically, the one Impressionist of British nationality, Alfred Sisley, stayed in France, where his house was ruined and all his paintings were destroyed.[2] Also escaping the war, and to become an important influence on British taste, was the dealer Paul Durand-Ruel, who rushed all his stock to London in September 1870 and opened a gallery in New Bond Street.

Many French artists of an academic tradition rushed to England too. Foremost among them was Jean-Léon Gérôme, best known for glowing historical and Oriental subjects. Gérôme's hostility to innovative contemporaries, including Monet and Dalou, made his work unfashionable in later years.[3] Others who stayed for the duration of the war were Ferdinand Heilbuth, Alexandre Prevost, Guillaume Régamey, Jules Le Rechenoire, who specialised in animals, and Jacques Clément Wagrez, though none had much relationship with art in Britain.

The period in London was significant for the French artists because circumstances threw them together – many met regularly at a café in South Kensington. However, it was stimulating in other ways too. They saw British collections and found inspiration in the work of Turner, Constable and others, and they had new environments in which to paint.

Making connections was challenging but critical. When François Bonvin arrived in October 1870 the first thing he did was call on Legros, who told him of others already there.[4] Daubigny already knew people in London from visits in the 1860s. Like refugees before and after him, he was anxious to support his fellow émigrés and help people back home, joining a committee for 'An Exhibition for the Benefit of the Distressed Peasantry of France'. He introduced Monet and Pissarro to Durand-Ruel, who would be a crucial supporter for both.[5] Monet later said that it was thanks to Durand-Ruel that he and his friends survived a 'miserable time' and did not die of hunger.[6] Through him he was to sell more than 23 paintings in London in 1872.[7] It was Durand-Ruel who put Monet and Pissarro in touch in their temporary lodgings, writing to Pissarro in January 1871: 'Your friend Monet asked me for your address. He did not know you were in England.' Bonvin, who had moved from academic still-life and portraits towards more Realist inter-ests, was a regular contact but it was especially significant to be close to Daubigny, who was associated with the Barbizon School in the 1840s and settled in Auvers-sur-Oise. His practice of paint-ing unembellished, atmospheric views of nature in-fluenced Impressionism: he handled paint broadly and worked *en plein air*, often from his floating studio in the Oise. Monet and Pissarro had already admired and emulated Daubigny's paintings and he had supported their submissions to the annual Salon, but in London they were thrown together.

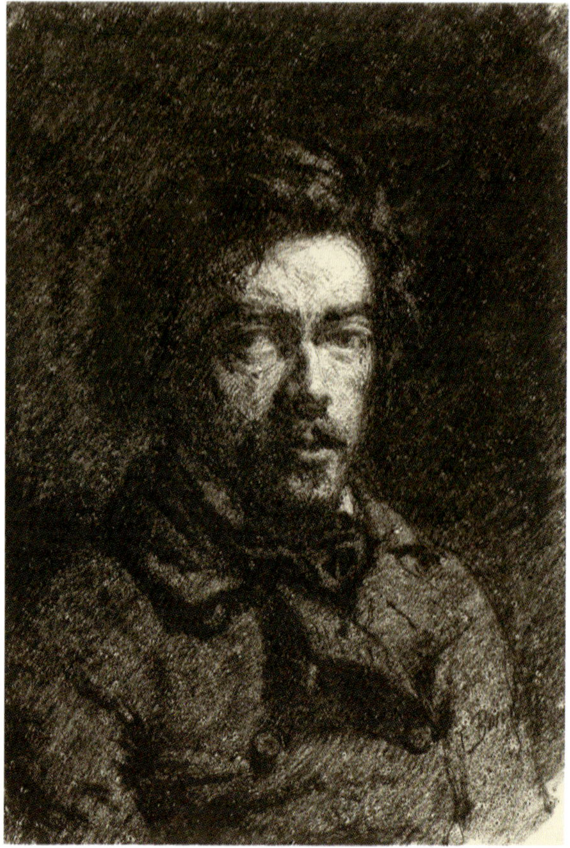

François Bonvin (1817–87) | *Self-Portrait*
1846–7 | chalk on paper | 33 x 24 cm
J. Paul Getty Museum

Bonvin had moved from academicism towards the depiction of
everyday life under the influence of Courbet and became a close
associate of Daubigny, Monet and Pissarro in London.

Monet had been on an extended honeymoon
when war broke out. He headed to London quickly,
concerned about being called up into the French
army. Camille Pissarro was Danish by birth but
his home at Louveciennes was near the German
heavy artillery and he took his family to Brittany
and then, when the Third Republic was declared,
joined the rush of refugees to escape through Le
Havre in September 1870.[8] They came to stay with
his half-sister at Norwood in South London. His
wife detested England and despaired of her ability
to speak the language. At home their rented house
was taken over by Prussian troops. His landlady
described its condition in a letter to London:

*There were two carloads of dung in it. In
the small room beside the living room horses
were kept; the kitchen and pantry were used
as a sheepfold [...] The former occupant also
put fire to your house [...] we have some of
your pictures well taken care of. However*

*there are a few which those gentlemen for
fear of dirtying their feet, put on the ground
in the garden; they used them as carpets.*[9]

Pissarro estimated only 40 of the 1,500 pictures he
had left behind survived the occupation. All record
of his work before the age of 40 had been largely
destroyed. However he and Monet were doing
new work in London. He recalled 30 years later:

*Monet and myself were very enthusiastic
over the London landscapes. Monet worked
in the parks, whilst I, living at Lower Norwood,
at that time a charming suburb, studied the
effects of fog, snow and springtime. We
worked from nature.*[10]

London confirmed Monet in painting open-air landscapes, which he had begun to do in 1866 but now
became part of his permanent practice. The Thames
seems to have initiated his interest in the atmospheric
effects of fog; also perhaps his interest in subjects
such as bridges, railways and steamships. He often
wrote later of how he adored looking at London:
'a mass, an ensemble [...] above all the fog'.[11]
Christopher Lloyd sees in the canvases painted
by both Monet and Pissarro while in London and
shortly afterwards, 'a lighter, more spontaneous
touch and a brighter palette, the colours applied
in smaller patches so that the surfaces appear to
be crisper and more active.'[12]

However Monet was dissatisfied with London
as a place to live and left in May 1871. While it

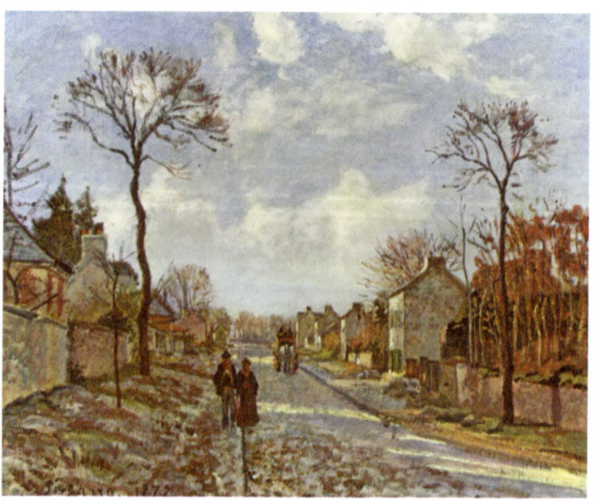

Camille Pissarro (1830–1903)
La route de Versailles, Louveciennes
1872 | oil on canvas | 60 x 73 cm
Musée d'Orsay | photo: Yorck Project

Pissarro painted this view of his village soon after he returned
home from London to find nearly all his previous work had
been destroyed.

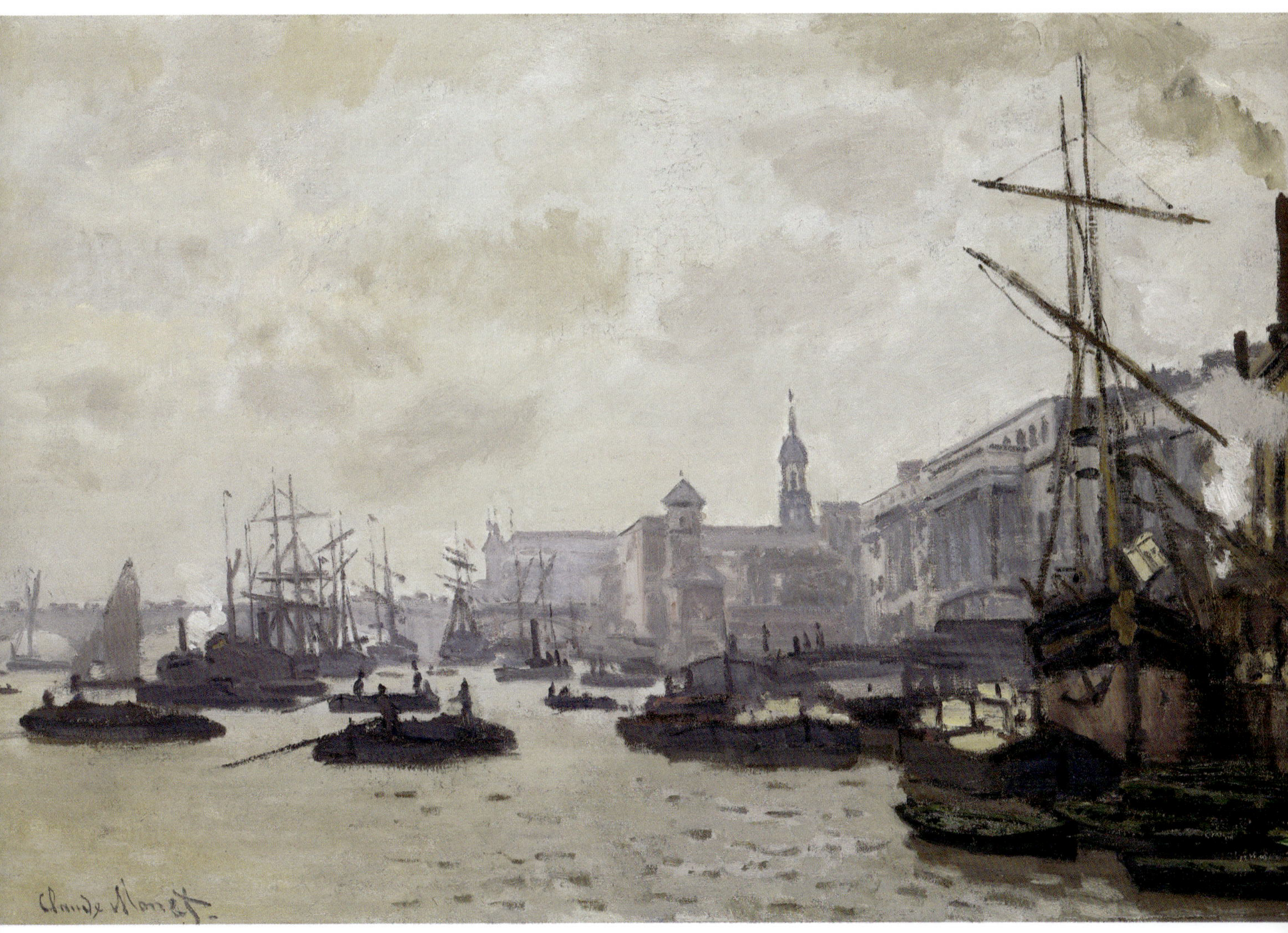

Claude Monet (1840–1926) | *The Thames at London*
1871 | oil on canvas | 48 x 74 cm
Amgueddfa Cymru-National Museum Wales

The Thames offered new effects and subjects to which Monet returned
repeatedly and may have influenced his development.

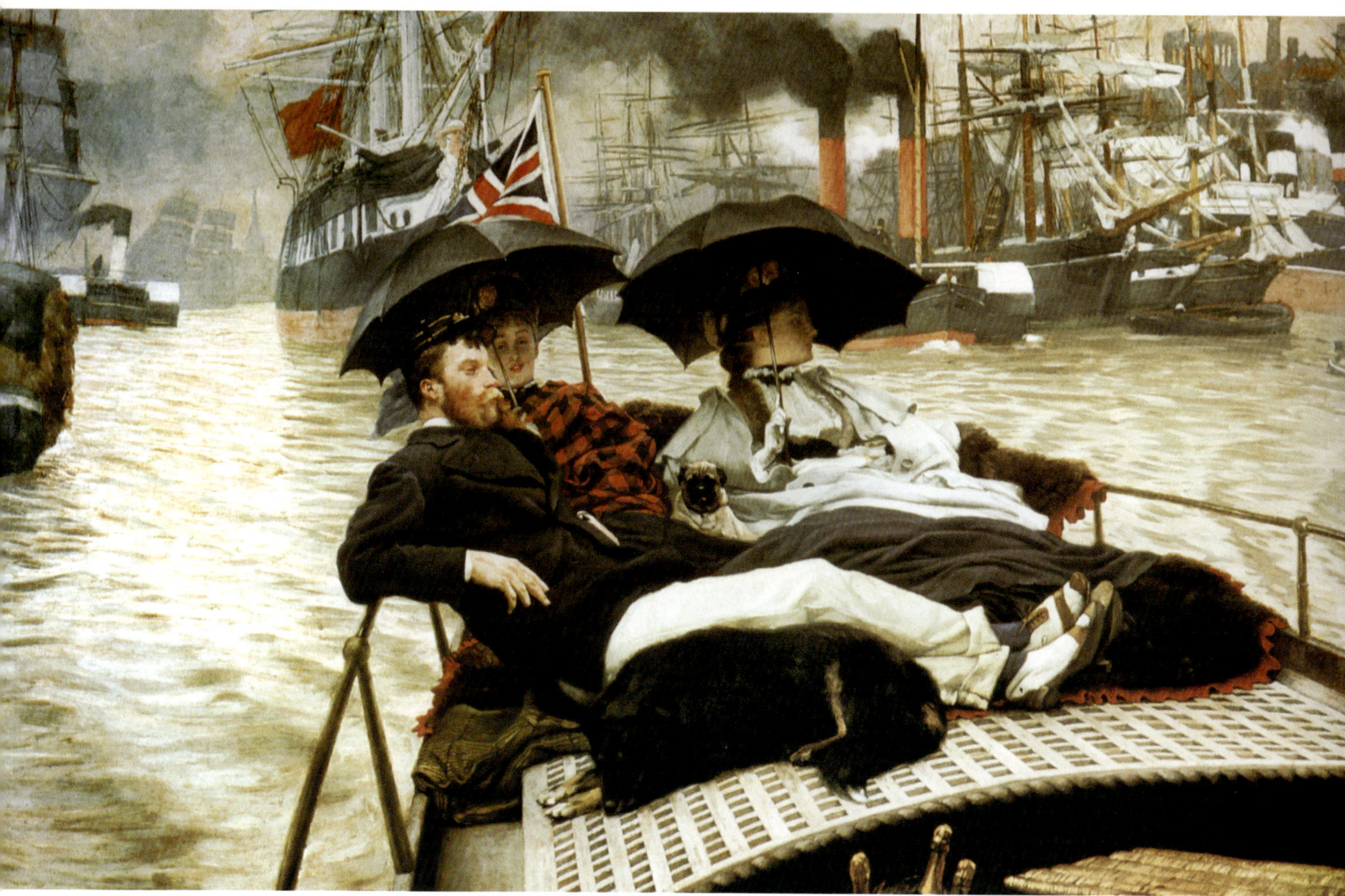

James Tissot (1836–1902)
On the Thames (or How Happy I Could Be with Either)
1876 | oil on canvas | 75 x 188 cm
The Hepworth, Wakefield

Tissot's painting of a louche young man and two female companions
in a launch on the river with champagne bottles and a picnic was
considered risqué at the Royal Academy in 1876.

was unsafe to go home he spent several months at Zaandam in Holland. He perhaps took something of his experience with him, pursuing the effects of light on water in fresh, gestural paint, though now on the Achterzaan rather than the Thames. He came back later in life to paint London again, not as an impoverished refugee but as a respected artist in the best hotels. Pissarro, too, returned three more times by 1897, making almost a hundred paintings.[13]

The importance for them of seeing British art has been debated. They met few British artists but discovered affinities with their own attempts to record effects of light and colour. Whistler's technique may have influenced Monet after 1871 and they saw a mass of Turners and Constables at the South Kensington Museum, the National Gallery and the Royal Academy, including *The Hay Wain* and *Rain, Steam and Speed*. Pissarro always recommended that younger artists, including his own sons, should study Turner and with Monet, Sisley, Renoir, Morisot and others he wrote a public letter in 1885 praising him as 'un grand maître de l'école anglaise'.[14] He recalled this period visiting galleries with Monet:

> *The watercolours and painting of Turner and Constable, the canvasses of old Crome, have certainly had an influence on us. We admired Gainsborough, Lawrence, Reynolds, etc, but we were struck chiefly by the landscape painters, who shared more in our aim with regard to 'plein air', light and fugitive effects.*[15]

What, if any, was the effect in Britain of this French invasion? The reception of the nascent Impressionists and their colleagues was problematic in a climate of confident late-flowering Romanticism and lionised Pre-Raphaelites. Dante Gabriel Rossetti saw in the work of the French School 'nothing but decay and decomposition.'[16] Pissarro wrote from London to the critic Théodore Duret, who was planning to come: 'Here there is no art, everything is a question of business […] My painting doesn't catch on, not at all.' Duret came anyway and wrote to Manet:

> *The English, with regard to French artists, like only Gérôme, Rosa Bonheur, etc. Corot and the other great painters don't exist as yet for them. Things here are the way they were 25 years ago in Paris.*[17]

Similarly, the young Italian painter Giuseppe de Nittis, who was associated with the Impressionists in Paris, was unsuccessful and unhappy: he hated the climate and the food, couldn't speak the language and struggled with his clients.[18]

Neither Monet nor Pissarro met with great

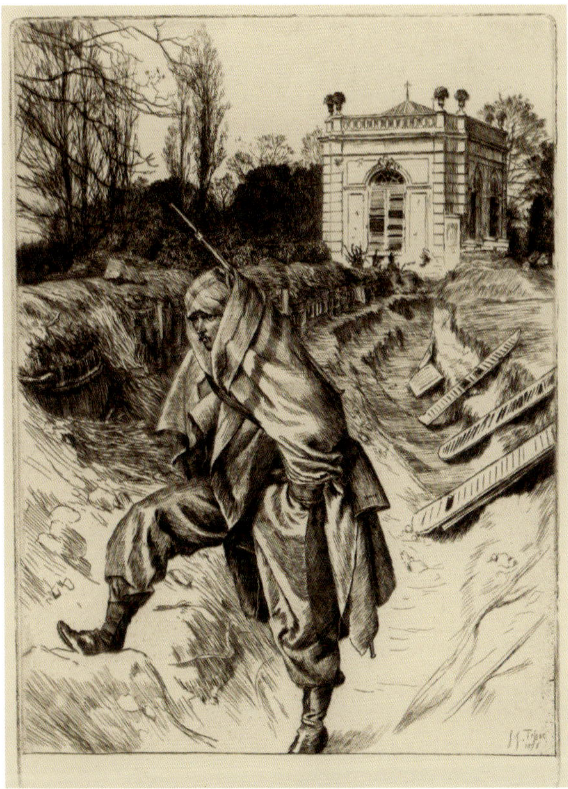

James Tissot (1836–1902) | plate from *Souvenir du siège de Paris* 1878 | etching and drypoint | 28 x 20 cm
Elisha Whittelsey Collection, Metropolitan Museum

While in London Tissot looked back on his experiences in the siege of Paris, making prints that showed snipers such as he had been himself.

success in London at this time. Both were rejected by the Royal Academy's annual exhibition of 1871. However, pictures by them were accepted for the International Exhibition at South Kensington Museum, as were paintings by Corot, Courbet, Daubigny, Fantin-Latour and Jongkind.[19] A gradual acclimatisation brought appreciation and favourable reviews for both the Barbizon school and the developing Impressionists. Durand-Ruel was spreading awareness of their ideas. He held numerous exhibitions from 1870 onwards and maintained a presence in London after his return to France. The Impressionists would have a significant impact after their exhibition in Paris in 1874 but in the meantime young British painters who frequented Durand-Ruel's gallery included Fred Brown, Alfred Webster and George Clausen, who was deeply influenced towards French art. Nevertheless, even as late as 1905 Durand-Ruel's huge exhibition of some 300 Impressionist pictures, of Monet and Pissarro alongside Cassatt, Degas, Manet, Morisot, Renoir and Sisley, attracted hostile reviews and few sales.[20]

A different clutch of artists arrived shortly after

the war. The German painter Otto Scholderer had rushed home to Frankfurt from Paris during the war. Unable to go back to France despite the end of hostilities, he moved instead to England early in 1871. He stayed for nearly 20 years, achieving some success before falling out of favour. Two French artists who fled Paris after the fall of the Commune were Jules Dalou and James Tissot. Both stayed much longer than their colleagues had done and achieved great success.

Jacques Joseph Tissot had been at the siege Paris as a sniper in the National Guard. He seems then to have supported the Commune, which was probably his immediate reason for fleeing. However, he clearly hoped to make a success of life in London. He was already an anglophile (he began calling himself 'James' early in his career), he saw British art as less hidebound by academic conventions and he hoped to be patronised by rich industrialists. His friends in London included Whistler and the proprietor of *Vanity Fair*.[21] Having arrived penniless, he became far more successful in Britain than any of his French contemporaries (Berthe Morisot, visiting him in 1875, said he was 'living like a prince'). His English pictures were his best. Nevertheless, he did not attract followers; Atkinson Grimshaw, the painter of nocturnal townscapes, seems to have been his sole English disciple.[22]

Tissot was much influenced by Baudelaire's essay of 1863, *Le Peintre de la vie moderne*, which urged the mundane details of life as fit subjects. Many of his paintings caught the manners and customs of contemporary lovers – society balls, days out together, teas on the terrace. Some attracted criticism, even mild xenophobia. Commentators wondered if he was making fun of the British in a way only the British should be allowed to do. He moved back to Paris after his lover, Kathleen Newton, died of tuberculosis in 1882, and devoted himself to religious themes.

Jules Dalou was a political refugee, an enthusiastic Communard whom the regime had appointed as a curator at the Louvre. With the fall of the Commune he was forced to flee. Tried in absentia, he was sentenced to life imprisonment. His acceptance in England was remarkable in the circumstances, for example he was appointed a professor at the South Kensington School of Art and commissioned by Queen Victoria to make a memorial for the Royal Chapel at Windsor. His work showed a fluid naturalism (he and Rodin had been friends since they were teenagers) and had an important influence on the diverse New Sculpture movement in Britain, specifically the strand that sought naturalism in contrast to Neoclassicism. Dalou recommended to a young French sculptor, Édouard Lantéri, that he should come to England in 1872. Alex Miller wrote in *Tradition in Sculpture* (1949):

> *Both as a teacher and as a working sculptor, he exercised a great influence on the group of English sculptors and his inspiration was continued in his pupils well into the twentieth century.*

Dalou returned to Paris following the amnesty of 1879 and was appointed to important public commissions.[23] One of his British students, Alfred Drury, followed him to Paris as his assistant from 1881 to 1885 before returning to London, where he created the statue of Sir Joshua Reynolds in

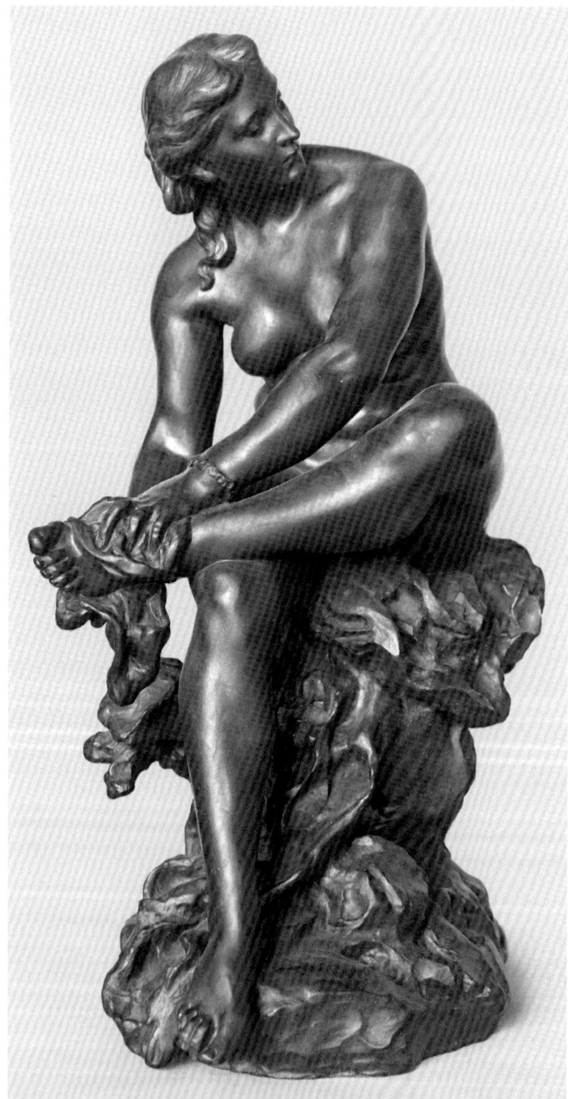

Jules Dalou (1838–1902) | *Woman Bathing*
*c.*1870–80 | bronze | 43 x 26 x 20 cm
Metropolitan Museum, New York

Dalou and Rodin had grown up together and they were at one in their commitment to naturalistic modelling.

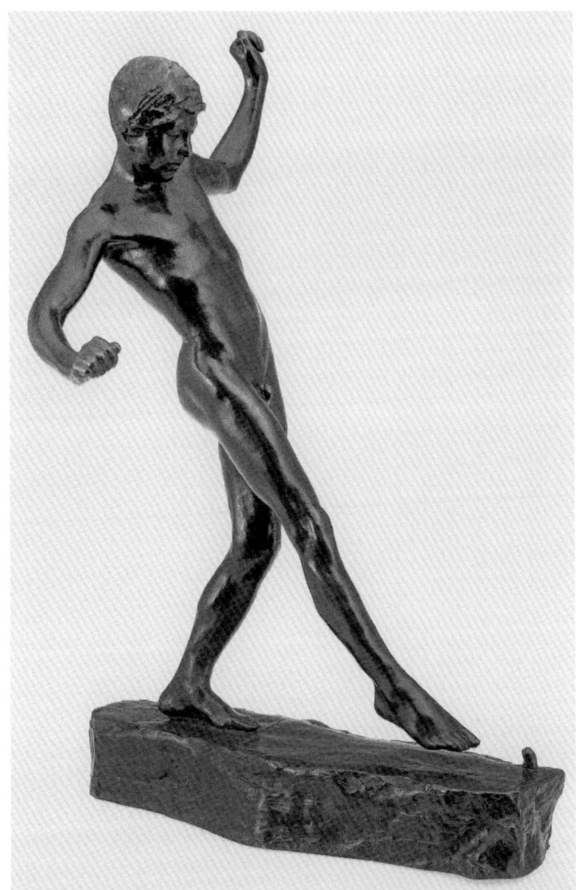

Sir William Goscombe John (1860–1952) | *Boy at Play*
*c.*1896 | bronze | 45 cm high
Amgueddfa Cymru-National Museum Wales | © Artist's Estate

Goscombe John's figurine shows the naturalistic influence of his time spent studying clay modelling with Jules Dalou.

the forecourt of the Royal Academy.[24] Perhaps the most influential sculptor moulded by Dalou was William Goscombe John, who was to become a leading member of the younger generation of 'New Sculpture' after studying with Dalou at Lambeth. He learned naturalistic clay modelling from him before going on to study with Leighton and Thorneycroft at the Royal Academy Schools.[25]

In the end, none of the refugee artists of the Franco-Prussian War and the Commune stayed permanently. Nevertheless, they took something of Britain back with them to France in their knowledge of different traditions. In Impressionism, the formative movement of modern art, small echoes rang of Turner, Constable and the London fog. On the British side of the Channel, an openness to French art was engendered that changed taste and supported British followers of Impressionism and the New Sculpture movement to develop their work and find receptive audiences in the years to come.

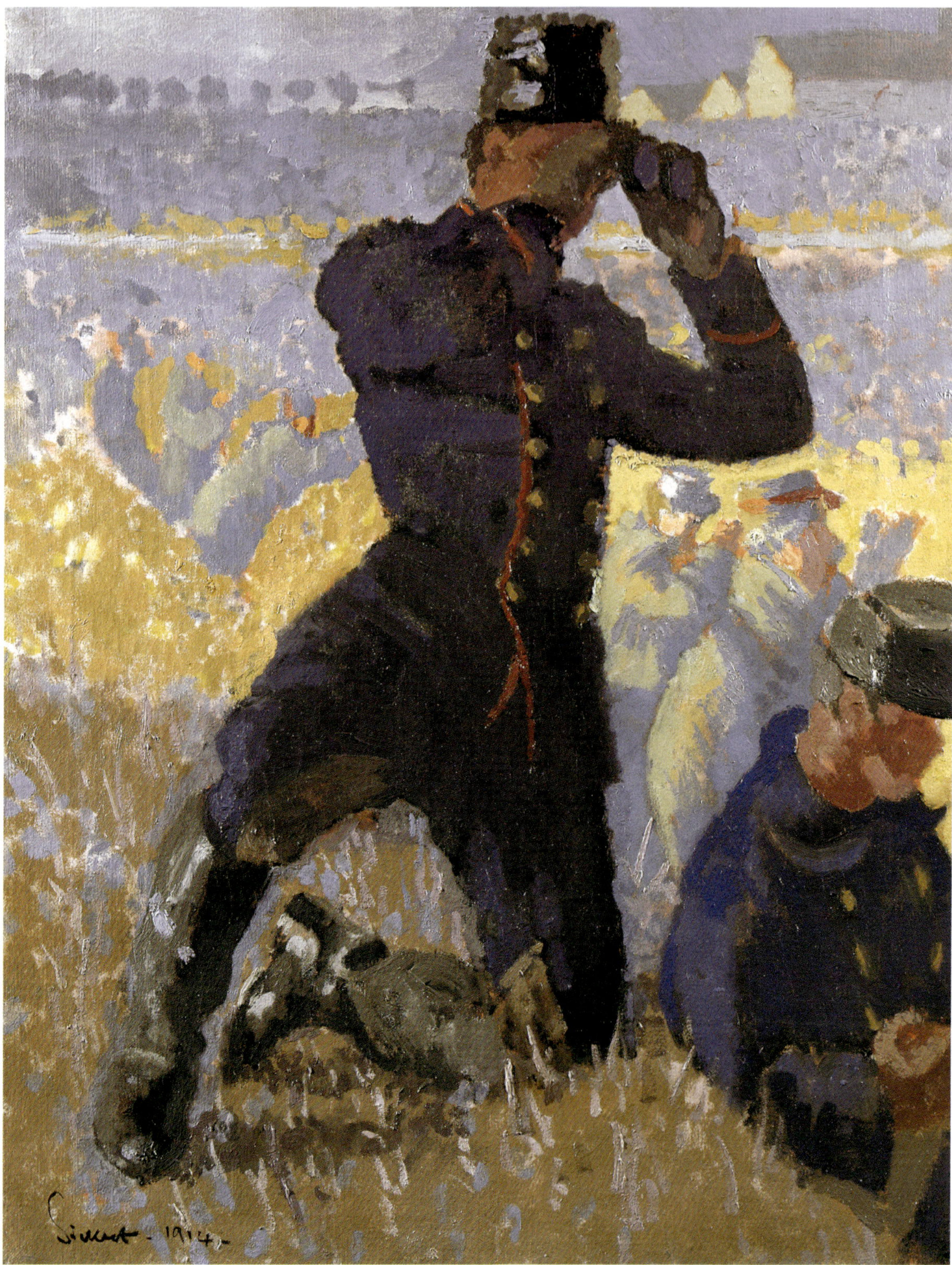

Walter Richard Sickert (1860–1942) | *The Integrity of Belgium*
1914 | oil on canvas | 92 x 71 cm
Government Art Collection | photo: © Crown copyright: UK Government Art Collection

This image of Belgian soldiers at the front line was shown at the
Royal Academy in 1915 and sold by Sickert in aid of refugees.

The war to end wars

IT WAS 'THE WAR TO END WARS' THEN 'THE GREAT War' until it became 'the First World War'. By any of these names it was a period of unprecedented conflict and turbulence. Up to 15 million people were displaced. Artists were among them and a significant number came to Britain.

Mass migrations of civilians arose from the German occupations in Belgium, France, Poland and Lithuania and from Russia's invasion of East Prussia; in the Habsburg Empire, Jewish, Ruthenian and Polish civilians fled or were deported. Movement continued long after the end of hostilities. While Belgium, France and Italy survived as states with borders intact, other territories shifted, leaving refugees with uncertain status even if they could go home. The disintegration of the Russian Empire caused strife across the edges of the Baltic states, Poland, the Ukraine and the Caucasus and extended to central and eastern Asia. A Red Cross official said: 'almost everybody was either going somewhere else or expected to do so soon, and meanwhile, was living in a makeshift fashion.'[1]

Against this challenge, there was no organised recognition of refugee status and rights: that had to await the creation of the United Nations in 1945. Britain had reversed its historically liberal policy of open immigration with the passage of the Aliens Act in 1905 and the Alien Restrictions Act of 1914, largely in response to the 2 million Jews who had abandoned the Russian Empire since the 1880s, of whom 150,000 made lives in Britain.[2]

The greatest concern for Britain in 1914 was the displaced of Belgium, its nearest neighbour and the seat of conflict. Between August and October around 1.5 million Belgian civilians fled their homes. Over a million of them (nearly a sixth of the population) crossed out of the country and around 600,000 remained in the Netherlands, France and Britain.[3] Belgium was subject to violent fighting and the first ever aerial bombing. Atrocities were reported, including summary executions, hostage taking and the razing of towns and villages, and while some accounts were subsequently discredited a great many took place. Within four days of the invasion, 850 civilians had been killed and 1,300 buildings set on fire. Through 1914, 5,500 civilians were deliberately killed by the German army in Belgium. Panic was widespread. Antwerp had seemed a safe place of refuge but it too would fall in October. The Belgian government had agreed with the British an escape route to Tilbury and 10,000 took this in September. Following the fall of Ostend at least 26,000 refugees arrived in Folkestone in mere days. In all 250,000 Belgians landed – the largest refugee movement in British history.[4] Many went home or joined the armed forces to leave around 160,000 still in Britain at the end of 1916. Around 65,000 of these lived in and around London.

The conflict was seen by the public as a new kind of war that targeted civilians. Images of the exodus became part of wartime propaganda and help for refugees was mobilised by charities and fundraisers. Helping was judged both patriotic and moral and by the end of 1914, 2,000 relief committees were lending aid. The War Refugee Committee was the largest. It placed tens of thousands with families or in hostels; as the historian Neil Evans put it: 'no society hostess was complete without at least one Belgian family to display'.[5] The reception was almost rapturous. A local paper reported:

> *A contingent of Belgian refugees reached Aberystwyth on Saturday evening by the express train from Euston and received a hearty welcome by the inhabitants. The Station precincts were crowded and the visitors were cheered on making their appearance [...] It is stated that the adults are distinguished professional teachers, musicians, and painters of a high station in life. [...] In the evening a large crowd of students and townspeople assembled in front of the hotel and the visitors joined in singing the national anthems.*[6]

Among the Belgians who came to Britain were about 60 artists. Some were of considerable reputation and some brought radical ideas. However, while they well supported, they were largely isolated from other artists. The opportunity was missed to bring new impetus to British art. Unlike refugees from other conflicts, it was realistic for them to go home to pick up the pieces of their lives – on average they were in Britain for only four or five years. *The Studio* carried articles on 'Belgian Artists in England' in December 1914, February 1915 and April 1915 and the magazine *Colour* issued a portfolio of works by Belgian artists in 1916, but this did not translate into substantive connections. Few even now are represented in British collections. Such lack of impact was disappointing given the impetus for change from Roger Fry's Post-Impressionist exhibitions of 1910 and 1912, sometimes considered the dawn of modernism in Britain.

Several of the Belgian refugee artists were associated with the artist's colony of Laethem-Saint-Martin (or Sint-Martens-Latem) near Ghent.

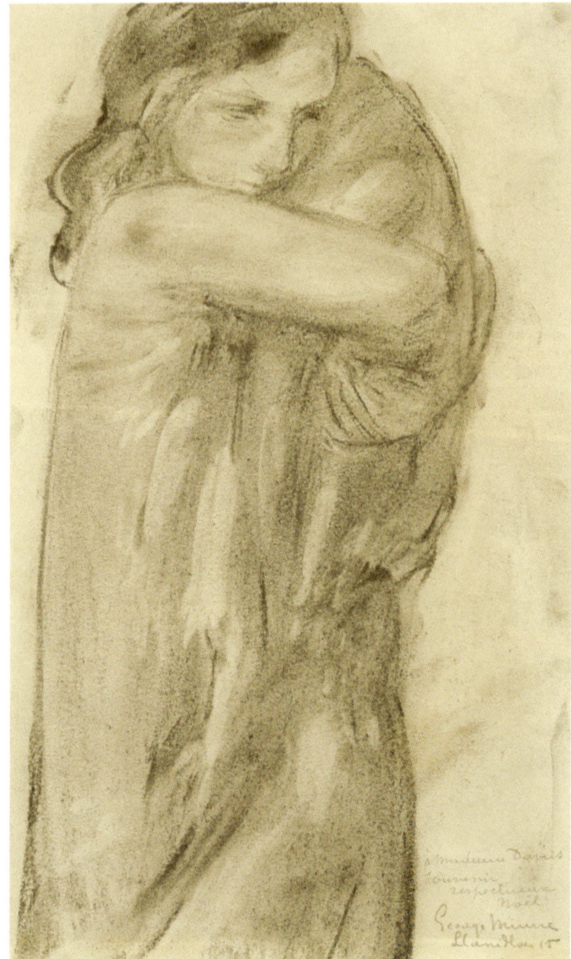

George Minne (1866–1941) | *Mother and Child*
1915 | charcoal on paper | 27 x 17 cm
The Gregynog Trust

Minne gave this emotive drawing of a protective mother with her child to one of the Davies sisters, benefactors of the Belgian artists, in 1915.

This had attracted radical artists since 1898 who saw Impressionism as superficial and were associated variously with Symbolism, a mystical realism and Belgian Expressionism. Those who came to Britain included George Minne, Valerius de Saedeleer, Gustave Van de Woestyne and Constant Permeke.[7]

Permeke is perhaps best known in Britain now, but his influence came later and indirectly, through artists who knew his work in post-war Belgium, including the Polish émigré Josef Herman and Peter de Francia. Permeke had studied at Bruges and Ghent before moving to Laethem-Saint-Martin in 1909. He joined the army at the outbreak of the war and was severely wounded almost immediately. He was sent to Folkestone where he was reunited with his wife and where his son was born. They moved on to a succession of villages in Wiltshire and Devon, where he painted bold, almost primitive landscapes until their return to Ostend 1919. Later Permeke became a figurehead of Belgian Expressionism and was judged 'degenerate' by the Nazis.[8]

Among the most generous patrons of the Belgian artists were the Davies siblings of Llandinam in Montgomeryshire. In September 1914 they sent representatives to Belgium to make arrangements and in October they went to the Alexandra Palace resettlement centre to seek the Laethem-Saint-Martin circle among others, bringing them to Wales for cultural renewal as well as philanthropic need. They eventually assembled 91 artists or musicians and their families. Even at this early point, concerns were expressed that connections would be missed. An article in *The Welsh Outlook* of November 1914 concluded:

> *The study of painting and sculpture is in a deplorably backward condition in Wales. Shall we take full and immediate advantage of the unexpected presence in our midst of this brilliant group; take counsel with them; give them facilities to exercise their genius; give our young art students a chance to see their work? What will the three colleges do? and the Art Academies? and the Art Schools? The opportunity is unique but we may be too parochial to seize it.*[9]

George Minne was the most internationally recognised of the Laethem-Saint-Martin group at the time – a sculptor aged 48 when war broke out. His work had been exhibited in Venice and Vienna, where it attracted the interest of Gustav Klimt and Egon Schiele. He came with his wife and six children to Llanidloes but his time in Wales represents a common pattern among refugee artists of all periods – one of disruption to creativity. The grief of fleeing his country was debilitating. He found himself unable to sculpt, completing only drawings evocative of peace, of which he took 400 home after the war. He said shortly before departing in 1919: 'We are completely isolated here. Our only distractions are occasional walks in the surrounding countryside, which has great beauty. But we feel ourselves to be terribly alone.'[10]

The Symbolist painter Valerius de Saedeleer left Belgium in 1914 with his wife, five daughters and 90-year-old father and was found a substantial house near Aberystwyth, Ty'n-lôn, where he became a recognisable figure locally in wide-brimmed hat and cape. He said that the landscape was beautiful and the people were kind, and he developed a relationship with his new home that seemed to go deeper and last longer than most of his colleagues. His paintings of the coast and hills around Aberystwyth simplified and regularised the land-

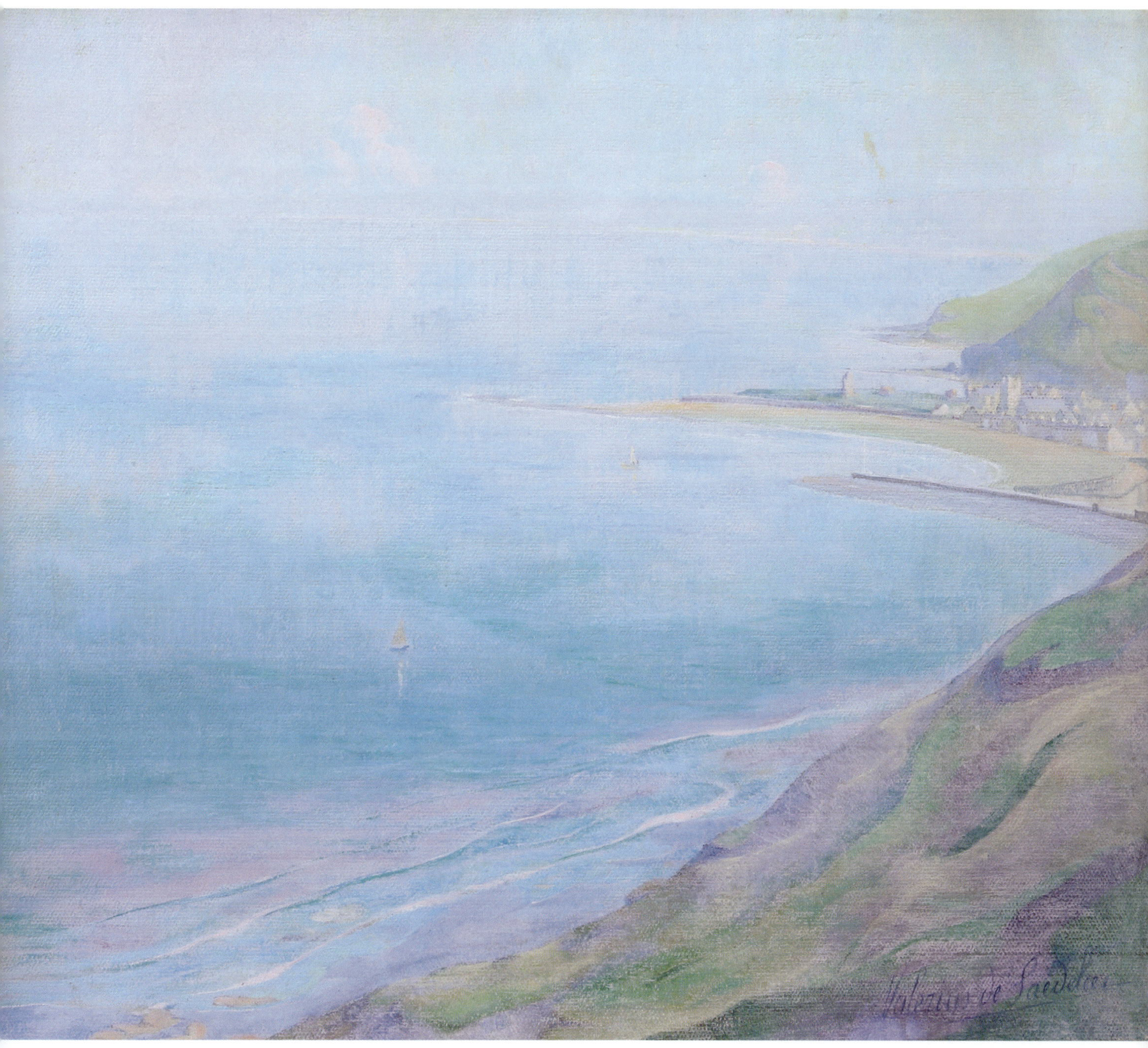

Valerius de Saedeleer (1867–1941) | *Untitled*
*c.*1916 | oil on canvas | 37 x 43 cm
collection of Rex Harley

De Saedeleer's delight in his new home is apparent in his view of
Aberystwyth from the south, nestling in pearlescent light next to
a calm Cardigan Bay.

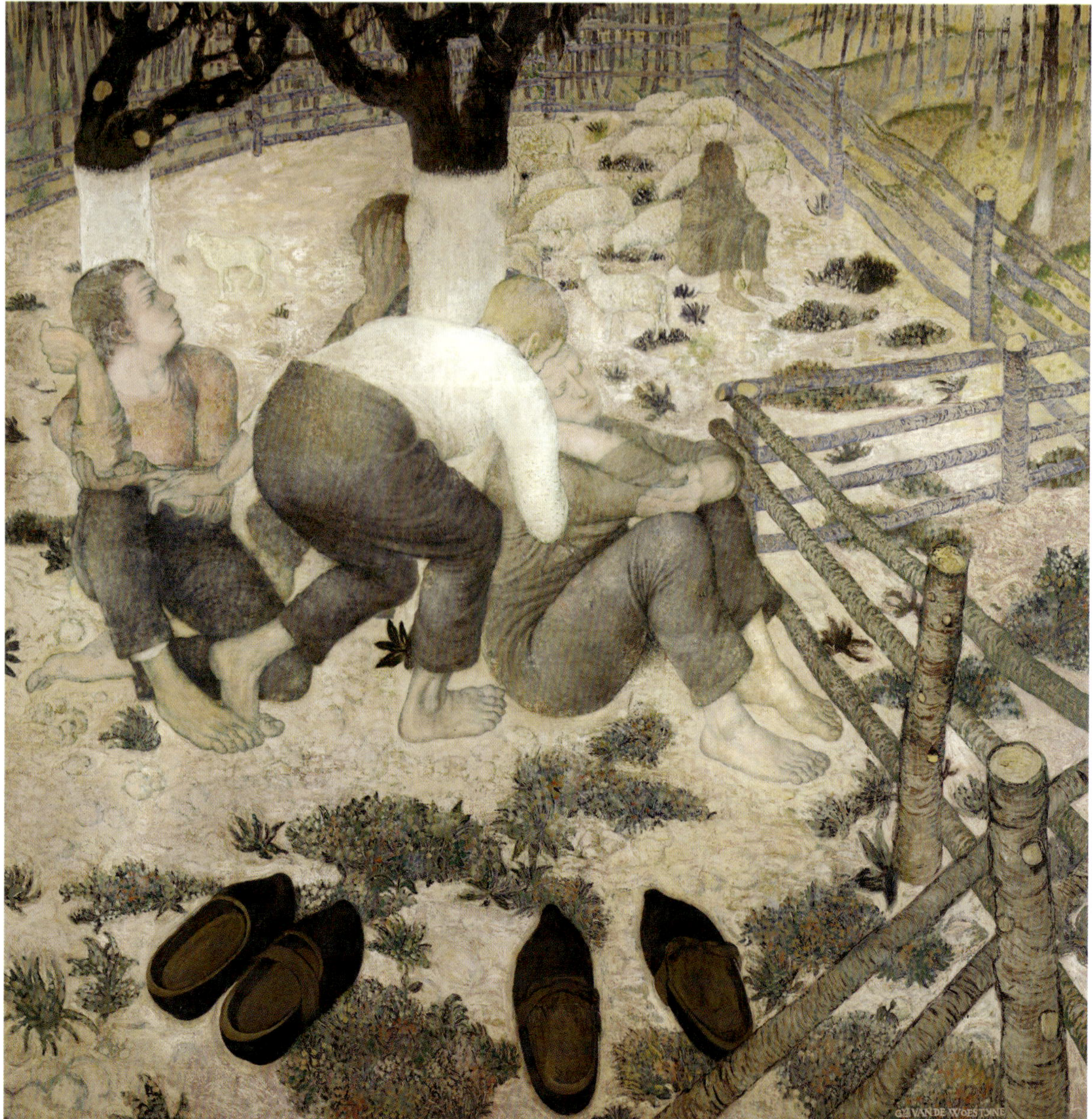

Gustave Van de Woestyne (1881–1947) | *The Sleepers*
1918 | oil on canvas | 202 x 202 cm
Royal Museum of Fine Arts, Antwerp

This sophisticated painting was done in London before Van de Woestyne left Britain but went unseen by British audiences.

scape into plains of colour and he found some commercial success with an exhibition in Aberystwyth in 1916 (he also bartered paintings with his doctor, dentist and tailor). A review in the local paper warned that he 'has the eyes of a primitive'. Two of his daughters began weaving and tapestry making and de Saedeleer may have contemplated staying to run the new Arts and Crafts Department in the university. He did not return to Belgium until 1921. Once settled, he named his new house 'Tynlon' after his home in Wales.[11]

The painter Edgard Gevaert joined the army and was wounded in Belgium. From a hospital in Wrexham he wrote to his mother: 'Here it is as though we had tumbled into heaven, into the promised land'. He sought help from the famous artist Frank Brangwyn, who sent painting materials to the hospital. Still suffering from wounds and shellshock he was released to stay with the de Saedeleers at Aberystwyth. He started painting again, recording their garden from an upstairs window and completing a commission for a local chemist. In 1916 he married George Minne's daughter Marie and moved across the mountains to Llanidloes. After the war he went to live in Sint-Martens-Latem where he designed a studio and home for his wife and their eleven children. He became a peace campaigner for the rest of his life and in 1940 had to flee the Nazi invasion to south-west France.

Gwendoline and Margaret Davies purchased from several refugees to support them, acquiring works by de Saedeleer, Minne, Pierre Paulus and the Impressionist Emile Fabry.[12] Another Symbolist from Laethem-Saint-Martin they brought to Wales was Gustave Van de Woestyne, along with his wife and three children (a fourth born there was named after David Davies). However, he moved on to London where he was better able to make a living from portraits and commissions. His expressive, allegorical figure paintings might have been of great interest to younger British artists such as Stanley Spencer or Mark Gertler but few people other than his benefactors saw his work.

Frank Brangwyn was one of the few British artists who had a close association with the refugees, no doubt prompted by his Flemish-Welsh heritage. In addition to giving materials to Gevaert he sent woodcutting tools to Minne and produced art works of his own to raise funds and interest.[13] He gave lodging in his London home to Pierre Paulus, a social realist who had designed the Walloon flag in 1913 and later became Baron de Châtelet. However, he seems mostly to have assisted at a distance. Another supporter was Walter Richard Sickert, who had been a refugee as a child himself after the Prussian annexation of Schleswig in 1866 and identified with the poverty of those trying to establish themselves in a new country.

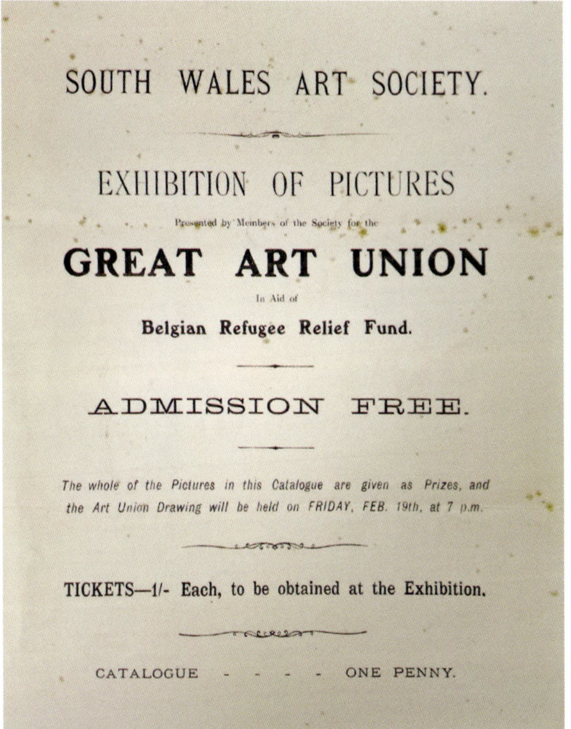

In February 1915 the South Wales Art Society put on an exhibition of works donated for 'the Great Art Union in Aid of the Belgian Refugee Fund'. 128 items were given for a prize draw, most by amateur artists. Catalogues were sold for a penny.

He too made propaganda pictures for the Belgian Relief Fund, borrowing Belgian uniforms from hospitals in London and finding soldiers to pose for him.[14] *The Integrity of Belgium* was a tribute to the courage of the Belgians in the defence of Liège. It was described as a realistic battle image: 'in the foreground is a soldier leading the attack; to the left are faintly discerned the ranks of resolute Belgians'.[15] Sickert never visited the front, and painted it in his studio.

The senior Impressionist painter Emile Claus felt deeply unsettled in exile. Though he was given a home in London with the Duchess of Somerset he felt the need to get away from the city. He went to Cardiff hoping to find the company of his Wales-based colleagues without understanding that they were many miles away. Within a few months he headed back to London and the fellowship of Pierre Paulus and Albert Baertsoen. He created a studio in a tower overlooking the Thames and worked unceasingly, following Monet's precedent, and broke into a mistier, more subdued colour-scheme than his pre-war work. Other Belgian artists in London included Hippolyte Daeye, who made a living from portraits, Jan de Clerck, Jules de Bruycker, Marcel Jefferys and Edgard Tytgat, who confined himself to printmaking. Also in London was Jean Delville,

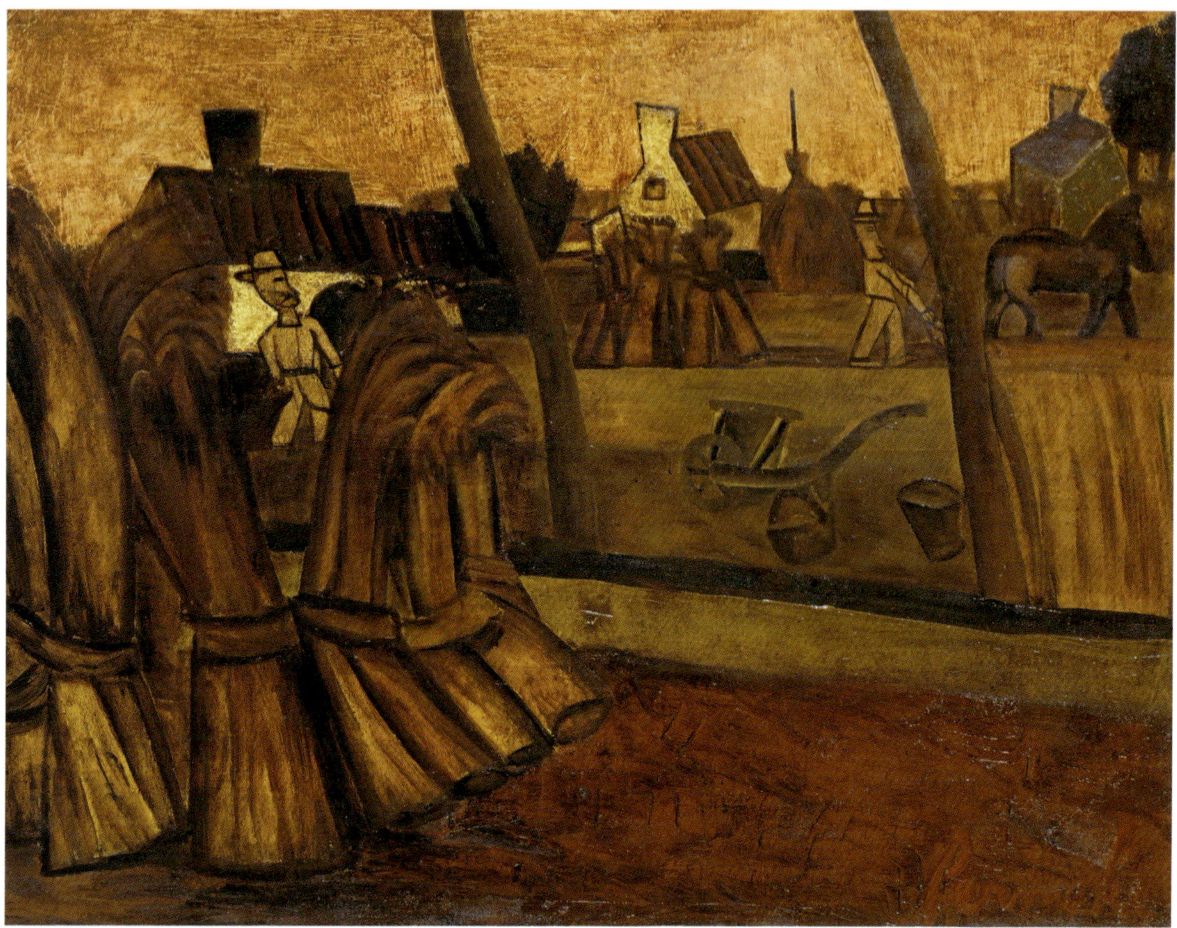

Constant Permeke (1886–1952) | *Harvest (De Oogst)*
1924–5 | oil on canvas | 128 x 165 cm
Tate | © DACS 2019 | photo: © Tate

After his experiences in the war Permeke painted working people and
the labour of farmers and fishermen with a monumentality that became
influential.

Frank Brangwyn (1867–1956) | *Antwerp, the Last Boat*
1915 | lithograph | 102 x 63 cm
Musea Brugge | www.lukasweb.be | © Artist's Estate/Bridgeman Images

Commissioned by the Red Cross, this image of refugees huddling
onto ships after the fall of Antwerp was a propaganda poster as
well as a marketable lithograph to raise funds for refugees.

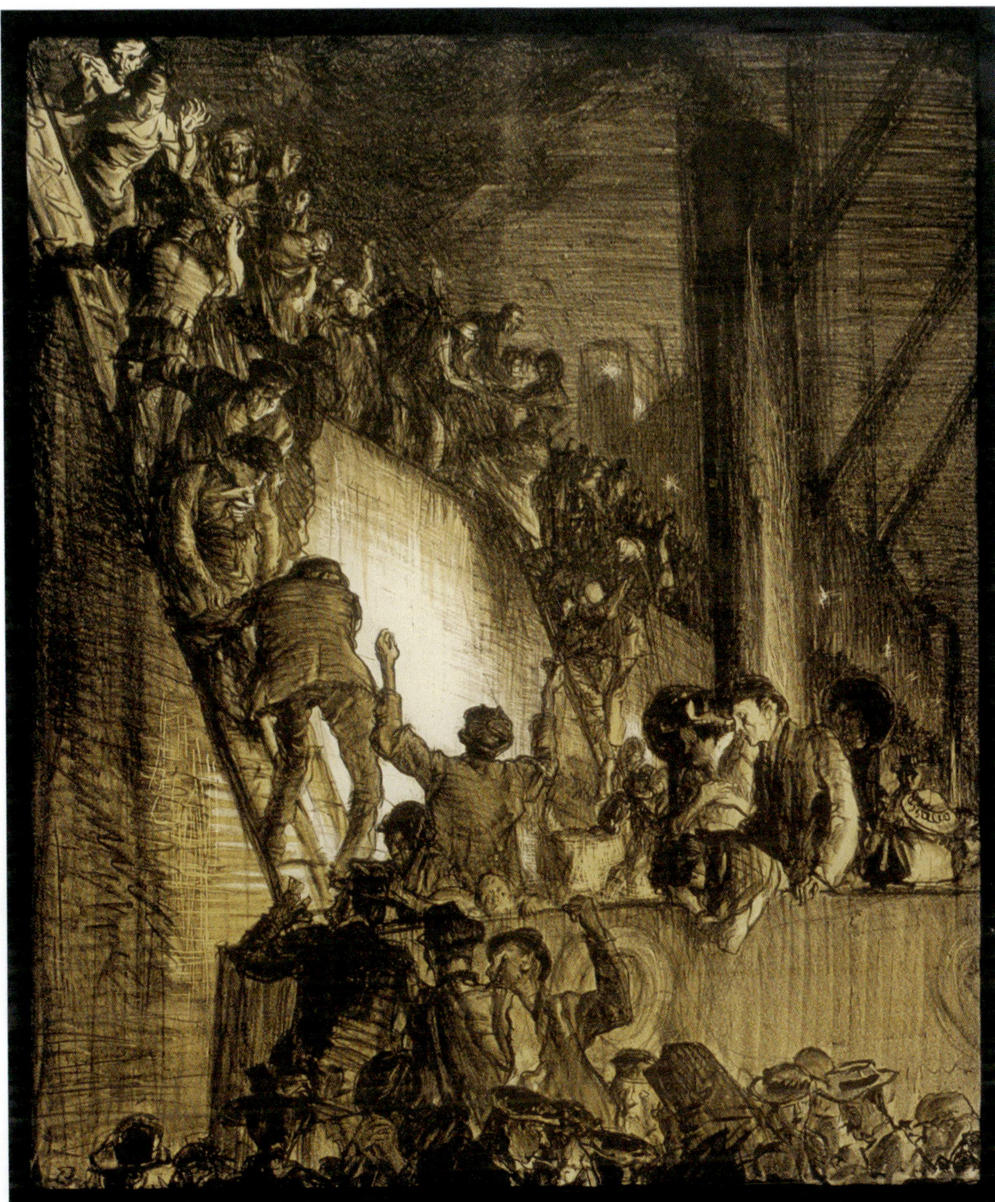
ANTWERP. THE LAST BOAT
SPECIALLY DESIGNED FOR THE
BELGIAN RED CROSS FUND BY
FRANK BRANGWYN A.R.A.
A LIMITED EDITION OF PROOFS OF THE ABOVE DESIGN
ON SALE ON BEHALF OF THE FUNDS OF THE BELGIAN RED CROSS
can be obtained at
THE AVENUE PRESS (L. UPCOTT GILL & SON L?) 57 DRURY LANE W.C

who had taught at Glasgow School of Art for seven years from 1900 and so had connections that he used to organise a philanthropic society and a fundraising publication *Belgian Art in Exile*. Only one artist had continuing work in Britain, though it was so dispersed as to be overlooked: the sculptor Joseph Reubens. Having been given a new home at the tiny village of Llanwenog in Carmarthenshire, he carved a complete scheme of rood-screen, pews and pulpit to refurnish the medieval church. The project brought him at least 20 commissions long after his return to Belgium.[16]

The other strand of refugees during the Great War and its aftermath was Russian. Unlike the Belgians, they did not go home. Many Jewish artists had already spent time out of Russia, mostly in Paris, before the Revolution owing to the hostile environment at home and opportunities abroad.

More came west after the Revolution of 1917, not necessarily for opposition to Communism but for fear of Bolshevik reprisals and daily hardship. Among those who came to Britain in wartime were Lena Pillico and her husband Leopold Pilichowski. Leopold was a successful painter of genre scenes of Jewish life at Łódź in Russian Poland. They travelled back and forth to Paris and then settled in London in 1914, where Leopold began to make a contribution to British art as President of the Ben Uri Art Society. A landscape painter, Lena was a member of the 7&5 Society in the 1920s alongside such well-known artists as Ben Nicholson, Cedric Morris and Eric Ravilious, yet her own reputation did not grow as theirs did. The Russian Impressionist Nadia Benois came to Britain when she discovered she was pregnant in 1920 (her son was the future actor, writer and director Peter Ustinov). Benois had

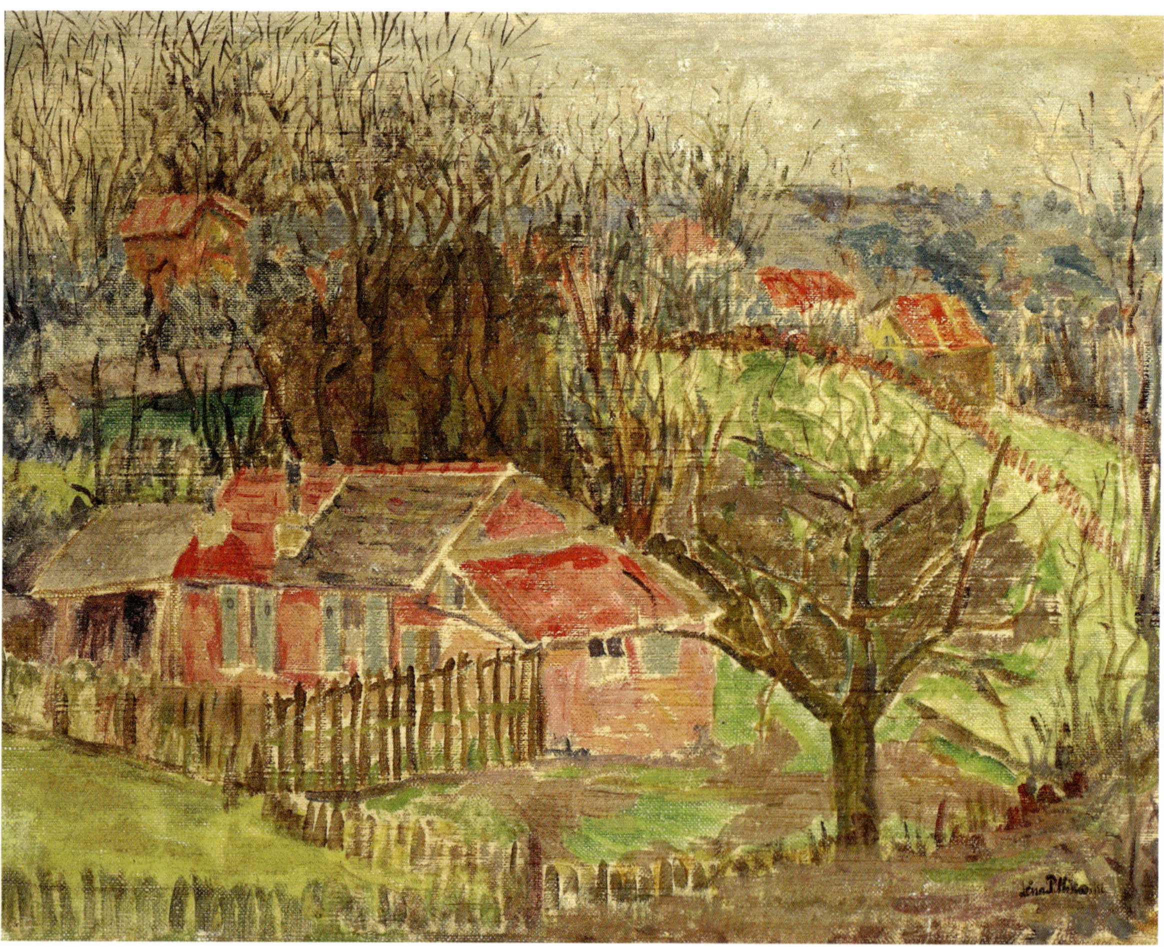

Lena Pillico (1884–1947) | *Cottages in the Country*
1932 | oil on canvas | 50 x 65 cm
Ben Uri Collection

This could almost be a Russian landscape but it has shared qualities with the faux-naïve idiom of the other 7&5 artists in the 1920s such as Christopher Wood, Cedric Morris and Winifred Nicholson.

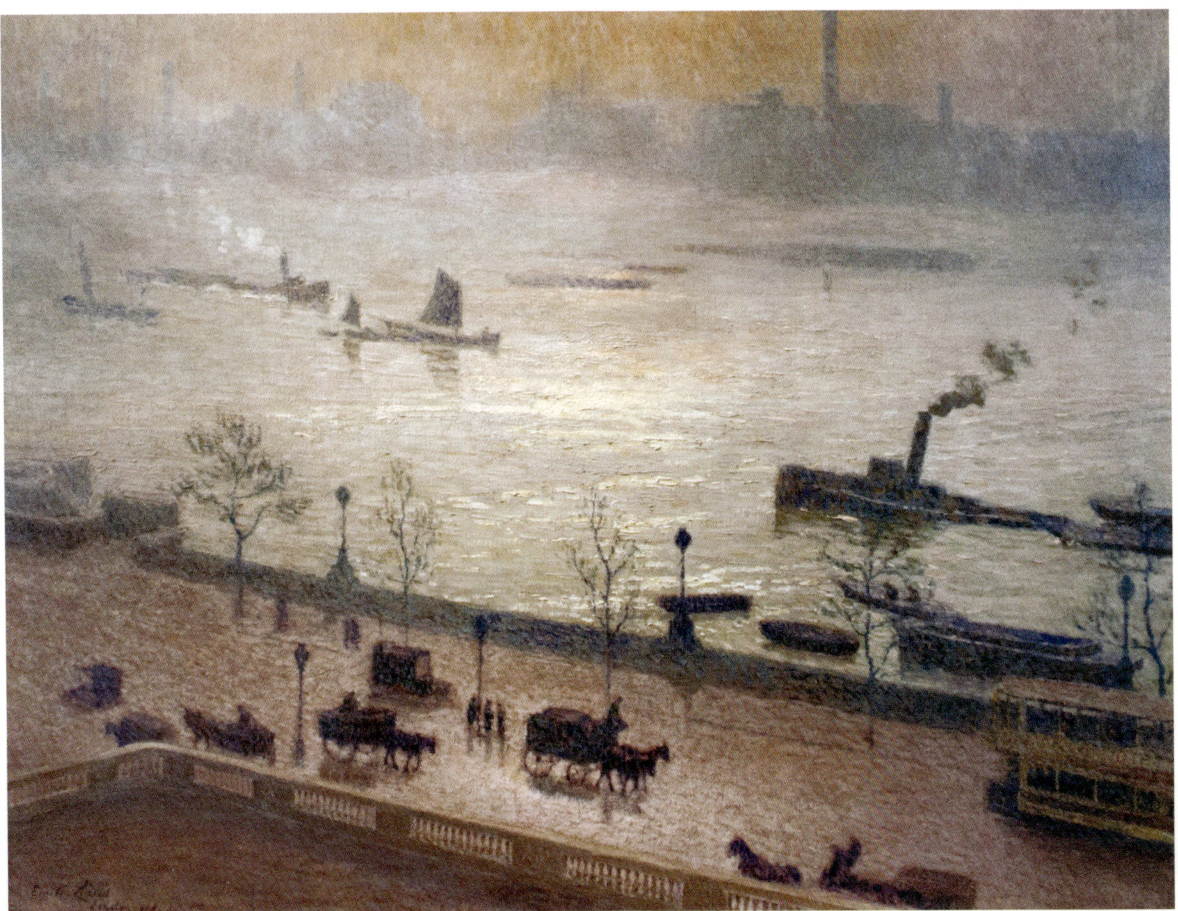

Emile Claus (1849–1924) | *Morning Reflection on the Thames in London* | 1918 | oil on canvas | 72 x 92 cm
Museum of Fine Arts, Ghent

Aged 69 when he arrived in London, Claus was deeply disconcerted by being separated from his countrymen but he devoted himself to Monet's example by painting the Thames in all its moods.

studied at St Petersburg Academy and designed for Diaghilev; in London she designed for the Royal Ballet and Marie Rambert, who herself had come to Britain at the outbreak of the war in 1914.

For all the failures to engage with artists during the war, one artist had a clear impact on British art. Lucien Pissarro, the son of Camille, was embedded more deeply in London than other refugees. He had come during the Franco-Prussian War aged seven and returned to learn English for a year when he was 20. He married in London in 1892. However, it was the Great War that decided him to take British citizenship. His younger brother Ludovic-Rodo also became more integrated than most, having fled to join him at the outbreak of the war. He stayed until 1922, making prints of London scenes.[17]

Lucien's artistic heritage was rich. His main influence was the Impressionism of his father, but he learned from Monet, Cézanne, Gauguin and Van Gogh.[18] He cross-fertilised this with the Pre-Raphaelites, William Morris, Arts and Crafts, and the new Aesthetic Movement. Though his father disapproved of the Symbolist elements in his work these informed the ethos of the Eragny Press, which he created with his wife Esther.[19] In 1911, he had been among the founders of the Camden Town Group with Sickert, Harold Gilman, Augustus John, Wyndham Lewis and Spencer Gore as a response to Fry's first exhibition.[20] Gore called Lucien a 'fountain of true principles'. Sickert, who was becoming one of the greatest painters of his generation, wrote of 'the exceptional position at once of an original talent, and of the pupil of his father, the authoritative depository of a mass of inherited knowledge and experience.' Acknowledging that he had started to 'observe colour in the shadows' and increase his use of violets and greens, Sickert

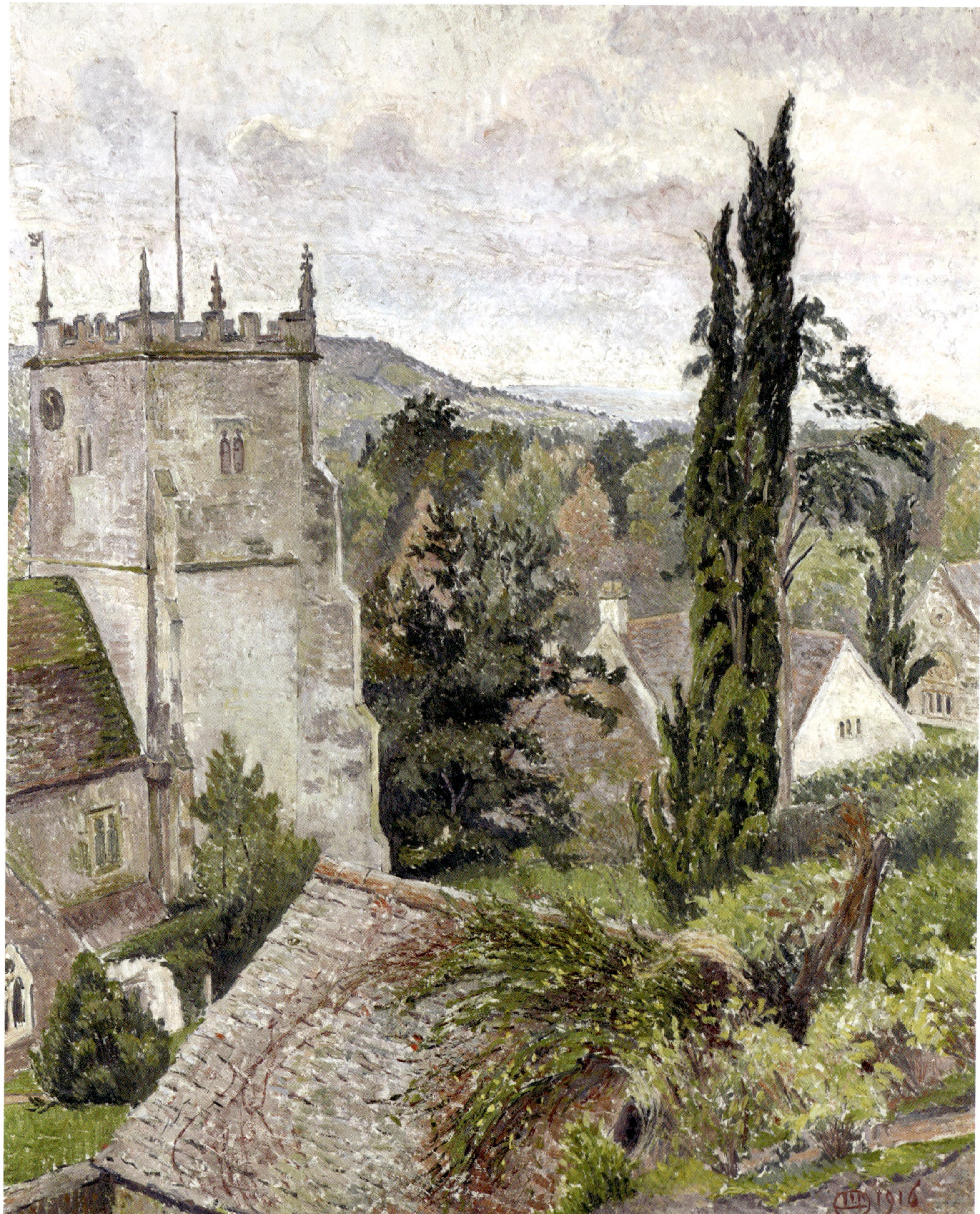

Lucien Pissarro (1863–1944) | *The Church, East Knoyle*
1916 | oil on canvas | 73 x 59 cm
Government Art Collection | photo: © Crown copyright: UK Government Art Collection

Painted at the mid-point of the Great War when Pissarro became a British citizen, this seems a celebration of Englishness and distance from conflict as well as a demonstration of Neo-Impressionist principles.

nevertheless denied that he recast his painting based on Neo-Impressionism (he did not abandon black as Pissarro advocated). Although the Camden Town Group was short-lived, through Sickert, his contemporaries and followers, Lucien Pissarro would be a powerful influence on British painting for many years.[21]

Few of the artist refugees could contribute to the war effort. Most were too old to join up or else, like Permeke and Gaevert, had been wounded and discharged. Once British troops were engaged in the war and privations were increasing, support began to wane. At Christmas 1914 many refugees were returned to London by host families and local committees who had run out of money or empathy.[22] In spring 2016 it was noticed that Belgian men were not conscripted like the British and the slogan became widespread, 'Fight or go!' Stories spread about Belgians profiteering, stealing jobs or sleeping with soldiers' wives. The accusations echo xenophobia towards refugees since: stealing jobs, crowding together, demonstrative in public, dirty, immoral, lazy.[23] In July 1916, Belgians began to be called up by the government in exile. By 1918, 30,000 Belgians were employed in British ammunition factories.

Repatriation was policy for both governments. The British, concerned about a predicted economic crisis, announced a few days after the Armistice:

From the British point of view it is desirable that the whole of the working-class refugees, and all the others who are not able to support themselves, should be repatriated as early as possible. Unless this is done, labour difficulties are likely to arise.[24]

From December 1918 to May 1919 the British authorities paid for the return of over 65,000 people, while many more returned with their own resources. Going back was not easy. Belgians who had lasted out the war in hunger and oppression regarded the returners almost as deserters. The area most devastated had become a desert 60 km long by 10–20 km wide where houses had been wiped from the map. Barrack huts were used until the mid-1920s. Nevertheless, fewer than 5,000 Belgians settled permanently in Britain.[25] Like nearly all the refugee artists of the Great War, their presence was substantial but they were soon forgotten.

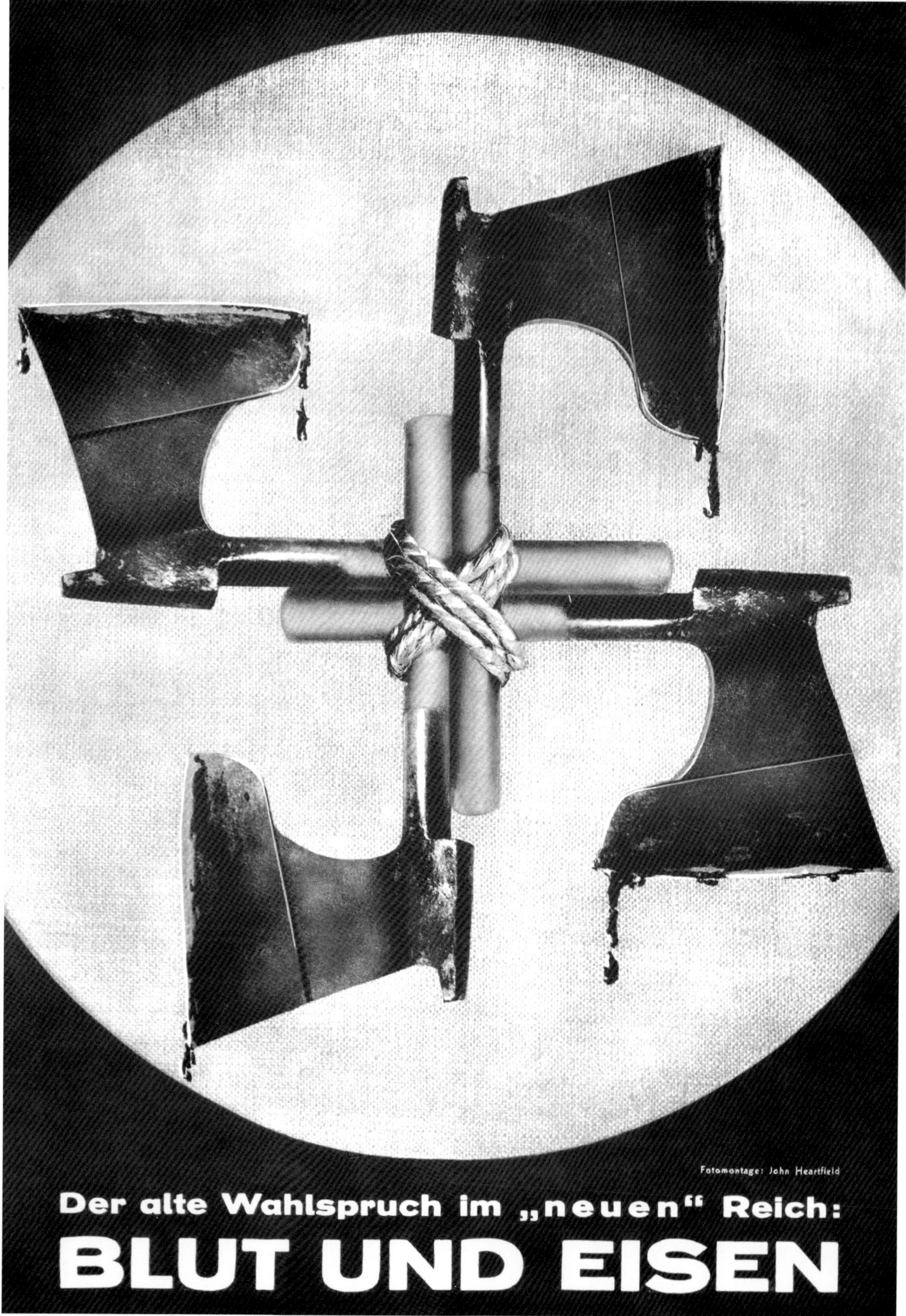

Der alte Wahlspruch im „neuen" Reich:

BLUT UND EISEN

The thirties
oppression and escape

THE 1930S WAS A DECADE OF ESCALATING oppression. It began with anti-semitic gangs and political victimisation, it grew into state-led exclusion and violence; it ended in concentration camps, war and the Holocaust. The epicentre was Nazi Germany but totalitarianism or racism spread wide: Stalinist Russia, Franco's Spain, Italy, Hungary, Poland and Austria. People in all walks of life sought to escape. Britain, though it flirted with fascist elements, was to be a vital refuge, especially as countries thought to be safe havens did not remain so. It settled 50,000 people from central Europe between 1933 and 1939 (a fifth of them children accepted in the *Kindertransport* just before the war broke out). Over 300 artists were among them.[1] Their impact on British art and culture would be remarkable.

The National Socialists took power in Germany on 30 January 1933; their regime would last 12 years. As their territory extended, so too did their policies against 'non-Aryans' and opponents – to Austria, Czechoslovakia and then through invasion to much of continental Europe. Artists could be their victims on several grounds. Far the greatest number were people of Jewish heritage or religion. Also targeted for their race were Africans, Romani, Poles, Slavs and Ukrainians. Further attacks were political (against communists and social democrats) or religious, for example against Jehovah's Witnesses and Roman Catholic clergy. People were imprisoned or murdered for homosexuality. Hundreds of thousands with disabilities were sterilized or killed. From 1935 the Nuremberg Laws decreed only those of 'German or kindred blood' could be German citizens and made it a crime for Jews to marry or have sexual relations with them. Savage, co-ordinated attacks on Jewish people and property

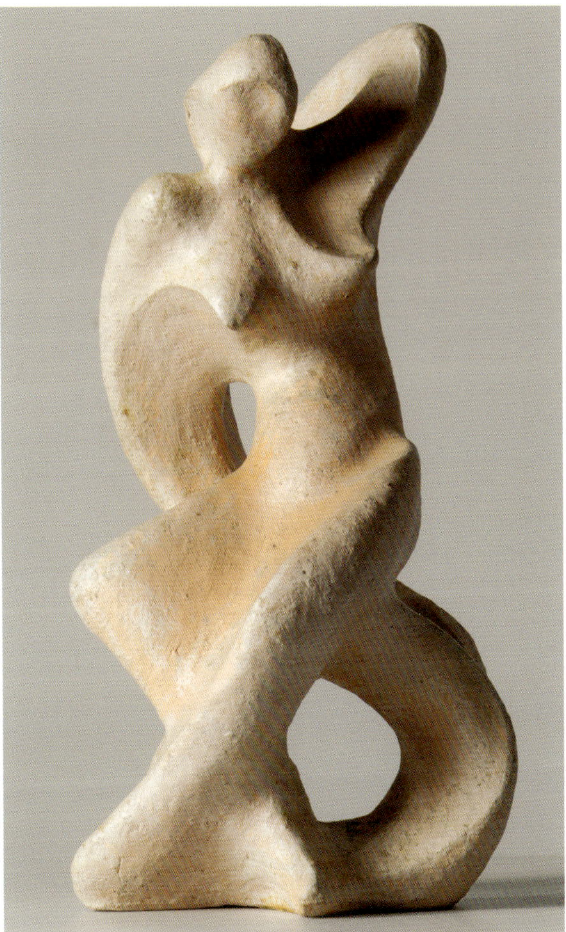

Ernst Blensdorf (1896–1976) | *Bathing Woman*
1933 | terracotta | 32 x 14 x 14 cm
RWA (Royal West of England Academy) | © Artist's Estate

Blensdorf's outspoken opinions on world peace made him one of first artists branded degenerate, in 1933. He left for Norway and then Scotland.

exploded on *Kristallnacht*, 9–10 November 1938. Marion Berghahn has written: 'The beating, torture, humiliations and shootings they suffered or witnessed made it abundantly clear to them that this was only a prelude to what was in store for all Jews.'[2]

Art, for the Nazis, was a critical force. It was personal for Hitler, who had failed to win a place at the Vienna Academy of Fine Arts. As nationalists and militarists the Nazis deemed avant-garde art outside German tradition, internationalist, while art movements in German-speaking countries – the Blaue Reiter, expressionism and the *Neue Sachlichkeit* or 'new objectivity' – were 'degenerate' in departing from conventional standards. In September 1933, Goebbels established the *Reichskulturkammer* (the Reich chamber of culture) and its fine art subsidiary, the *Reichskammer der Bildenden*

John Heartfield (1891–1968) | *Blut und Eisen*
1934 | printed poster | 40 x 29 cm
Victoria and Albert Museum, London; given by Erica Millman
© The Heartfield Community of Heirs/DACS 2019 | photo: V&A

Heartfield used photomontage to attack fascism. Bismarck's nationalist phrase 'Blood and Iron' is placed with a swastika composed of executioner's axes and the words 'The old slogan and the new Reich'.

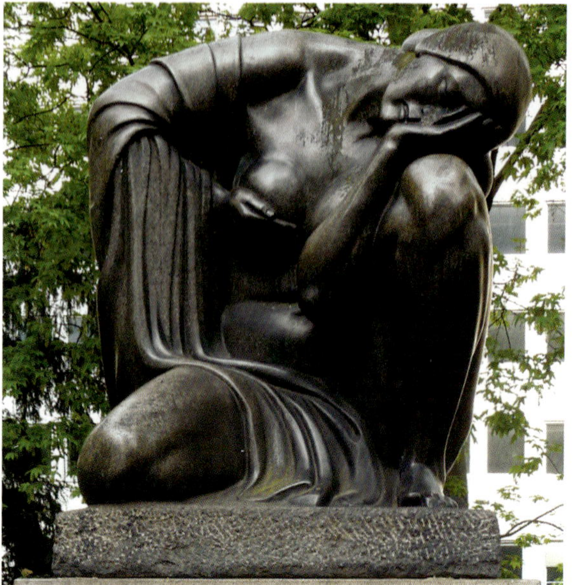

Benno Elkan (1877–1960) | *Den Opfern*
1920 | marble war memorial in Frankfurt-am-Main
(cropped from) photo: Frank Behnsen, Wikipedia

As a symbol of universal mourning with the inscription 'The Victims', this memorial to the Great War was felt to represent a broken Germany. It was removed in 1933 and Elkan fled to London. It was restored in 1946.

Künste. These excluded 'non-Aryans' and modernist 'undesirables' and non-members would be dismissed from museums, art colleges and academies. Goebbels' department watched individuals so closely as to make intellectual freedom impossible.

Artists might fall simultaneously into several categories as enemies of the state: for example Ludwig Meidner was communist, expressionist and Jewish. Such discrimination was almost incomprehensible to many. Martin Bloch had never considered himself a Jew before Hitler; he complained when his work was removed from exhibitions and found himself threatened and expelled from the *Reichskammer*. In 1937, the Nazis pressed down on *entarte kunst* or 'degenerate art' with the mass confiscation of art works by German modernists and foreigners such as Picasso and Matisse. The public focus was an exhibition of confiscated works that attracted 2 million visitors in Munich even before its tour; five times more than the partner exhibition of 'approved' art. It has probably never been exceeded in attendance by any art exhibition. Many works were burned ceremoniously by the Berlin fire brigade; others were sold off in Switzerland.

Expressionist painters were in the first rank of confiscations from state collections, in which they had figured powerfully: Emil Nolde's 1,052 works were the largest number removed even though he was a member of the Nazi party, followed by Erich Hechel's 729 and Ernst Ludwig Kirchner's 639. Goebbels ordered the confiscation of all works of modernist art in institutions – often the artists' most important and defining works – so that over 21,000 were seized in total. Many artists were compelled to hand over their own collections to the Reich Chamber for Visual Arts; Nolde lost 48 paintings in 1940 that were never to be seen again and in 1941 was forbidden to paint.[3]

One of the most striking figures among the regime's artist enemies was John Heartfield, a politically engaged communist on the Gestapo's most-wanted list. He had anglicised his name from Helmut Herzfeld as a statement of opposition to the Great War and now he attacked the Nazis in searing photomontages (he said in 1966: 'the pencil was too weak to convincingly hammer it home to people what one had to say at the time.'). He escaped to Prague in 1933 and continued his campaign from there. Another highly visible enemy was Kurt Schwitters, who had written after the last war: 'The past has collapsed […] we must build anew from its fragments', which he did in collages that included three-dimensional objects, taking the word *merz* or 'rubbish' to describe them.' Nazi Party members began barracking him at lectures long before they came to power.

Meanwhile, oppression was intensifying in other countries. In Austria the Dolfuss regime rounded up 800 communist sympathisers in 1933. The Bauhaus-trained photographer Edith Suschitzky (later Edith Tudor Hart) was stopped with communist documents and had all her photographic negatives confiscated. She and her brother Wolfgang escaped to England. Their father, the owner of a social democratic bookshop, killed himself. The great expressionist Oskar Kokoschka left Austria for Prague and took out Czech citizenship not so much in direct conflict with the regime as in search of a sympathetic culture for his painting. The organisation to promote artists in exile was named after him and he was branded 'un-German'. By 1938, when the Nazis moved into Sudetenland, 417 of his works had been confiscated. He painted his *Self-Portrait of a Degenerate Artist* and flew to London. Public sculptures were affected too: after Siegfried Charoux turned down a commission for a memorial to dead policemen in Vienna he was boycotted and his memorial to the writer Gotthold Ephraim Lessing, which he considered his most important work, was destroyed (a copy was re-erected 30 years later).[4]

In Poland life had long been harsh for a Jewish, left-sympathising, modernist art student like Josef Herman. He recalled: 'My motherland, since I could remember, had been governed by a military dictatorship. Anti-Semitism was part of state policies.' In the late 1920s, aged 16, he was imprisoned for ten

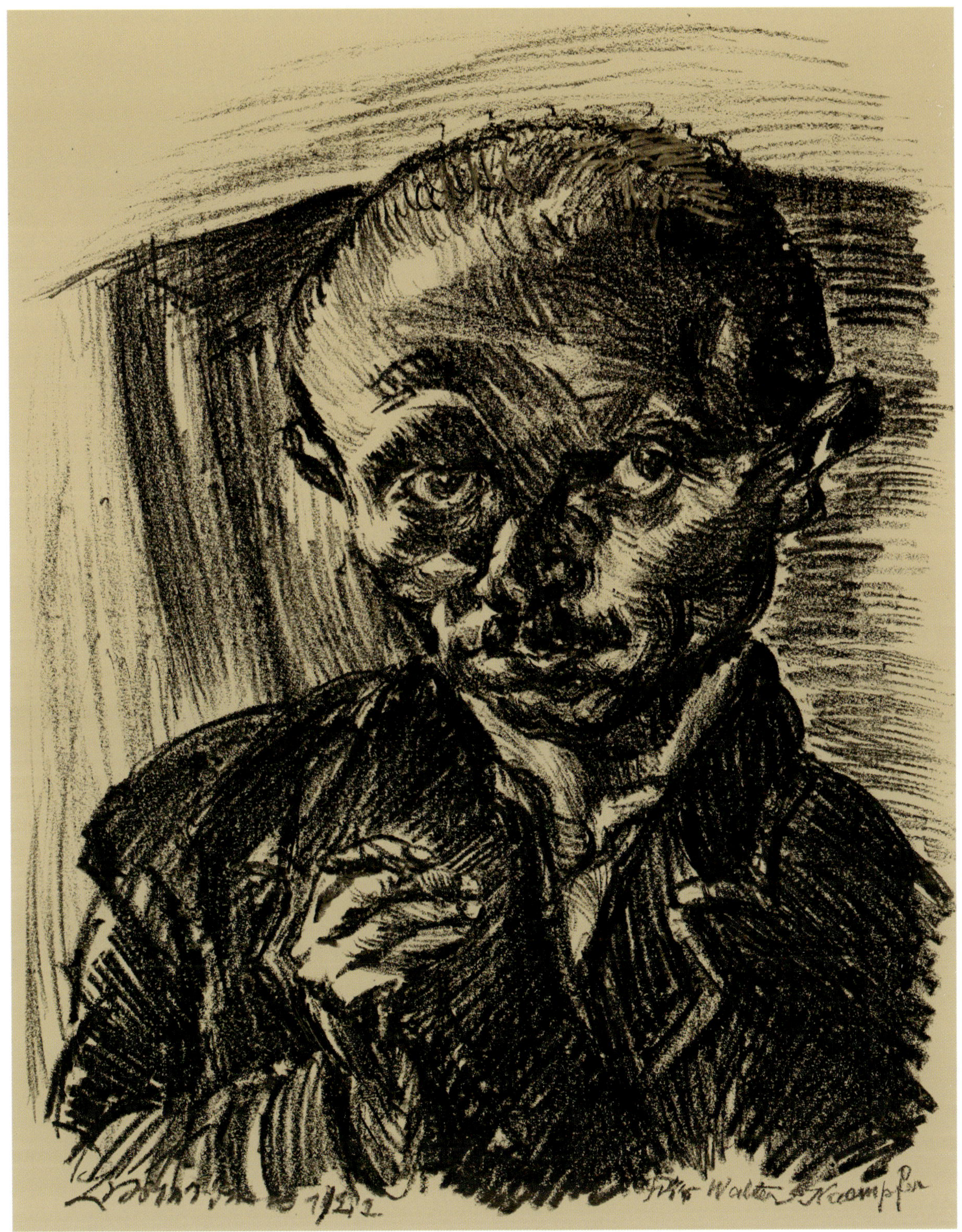

Ludwig Meidner (1884–1966) | *Self-Portrait*
1922 | crayon on paper | 75 x 55 cm
Margaret Fisher Endowment(1997.428); Chicago (IL), Art Institute of Chicago
© Ludwig Meidner-Archiv, Judisches Museum der Stadt Frankfurt am Main
photo: © 2019 The Art Institute of Chicago/Art Resource, NY/Scala, Florence

Meidner was an enemy of the Nazi state as communist, expressionist
and Jew. Monographs about him were selected for destruction in the
Nazi book-burnings of 1933.

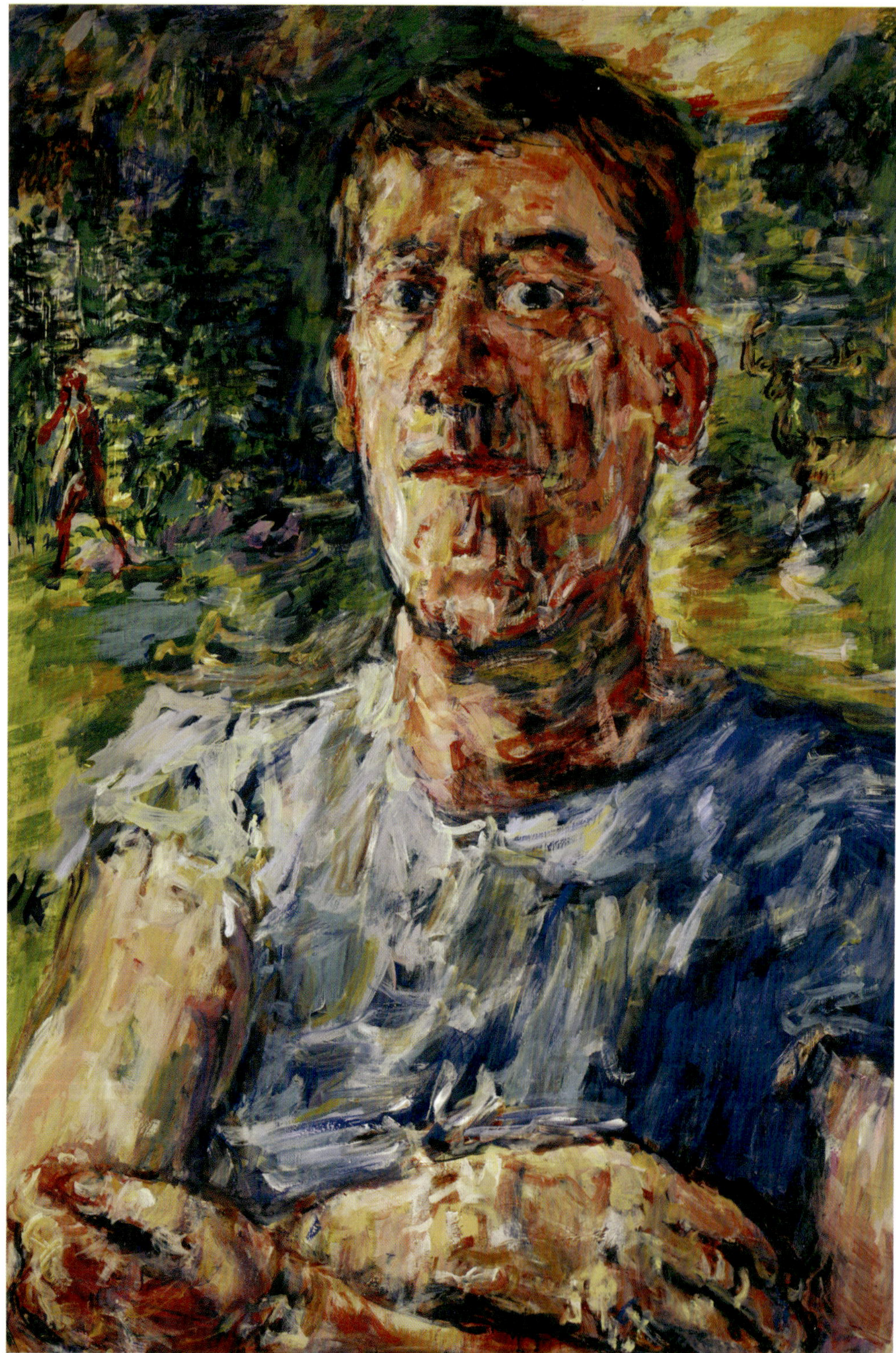

Oskar Kokoschka (1886–1980)
Self-Portrait of a Degenerate Artist
1937 | oil on canvas | 110 x 85 cm
National Galleries of Scotland (on loan from a private collection)
© Fondation Oskar Kokoschka/DACS 2019

Kokoschka took ownership of the 'degenerate' label with
his title. Arms crossed and sleeves rolled up, he is human
and defiant.

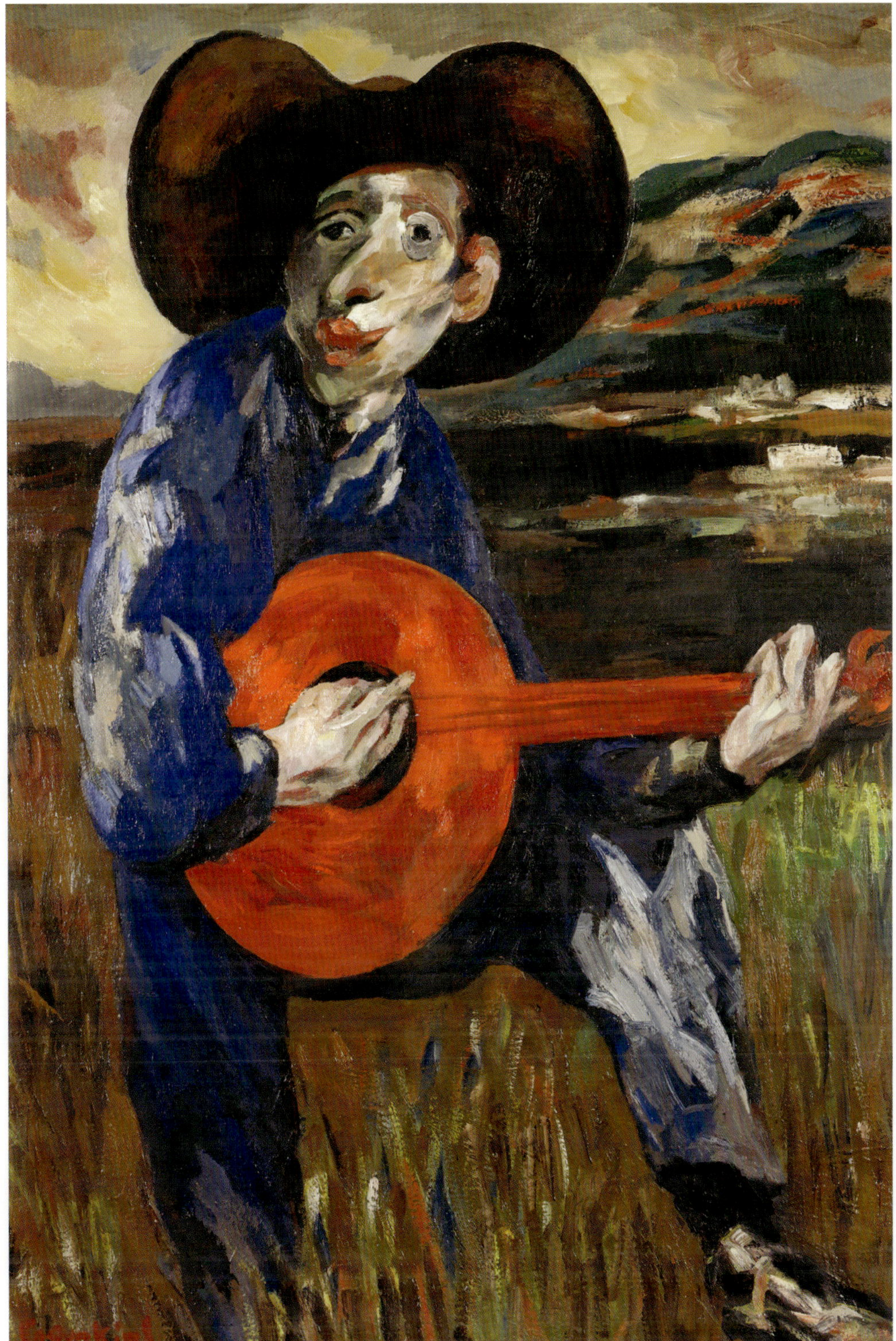

Stanislaw Frenkiel (1918–2001) | *The Guitar Player*
*c.*1980 | oil on canvas | 109 x 75 cm
RWA (Royal West of England Academy) | © Artist's Estate

Made long after his resettlement in Britain, this painting's
free brushwork and colourful subject suggest a lifetime's
distance from the oppression Frenkiel experienced in
Poland and Russia.

months without trial. By the mid-1930s he hid from the authorities and never slept two nights under the same roof. On the streets of Warsaw in the late thirties, he recalled:

> *Armed with sticks and knives, nationalistic students with green ribbons in their lapels attacked Jews and smashed the windows of Jewish shopkeepers […] There was no protection from the police. On the contrary, the police often accused Jews of 'provoking street disorders'.*[5]

The oppression might metamorphose. For Stanislaw Frenkiel the reason for fleeing Poland to Soviet Russia in 1939 was the German occupation and his Jewish background. But there he was imprisoned in a labour camp before being released into the Polish army in 1942. He could not go back to a homeland that was doubly tarnished by the Holocaust and Stalinism.

Artists designated 'degenerate' found eventually they had to leave, stop working or change their art. George Grosz left for the United States even before Hitler took power. Walter Nessler, who was forbidden to paint or teach, made a living as a window dresser but was dismissed when he put a star of David on top of the shop's Christmas tree in solidarity with Jews. He met friends secretly in a back room of a Dresden café: 'We discussed things and showed our paintings which we had done, drawings mostly because they could be easily hidden under mattresses'. When he drew a satirical *Hitler ABC* in 1937 he had to leave the country.[6]

Several leading expressionists withdrew into what was later called 'inner migration'. Erich Heckel and Karl Schmidt-Rottluff both moved into deep countryside. Otto Dix, famous for his depictions of urban nightlife, moved to Lake Constance and said: 'I painted landscapes; that was tantamount

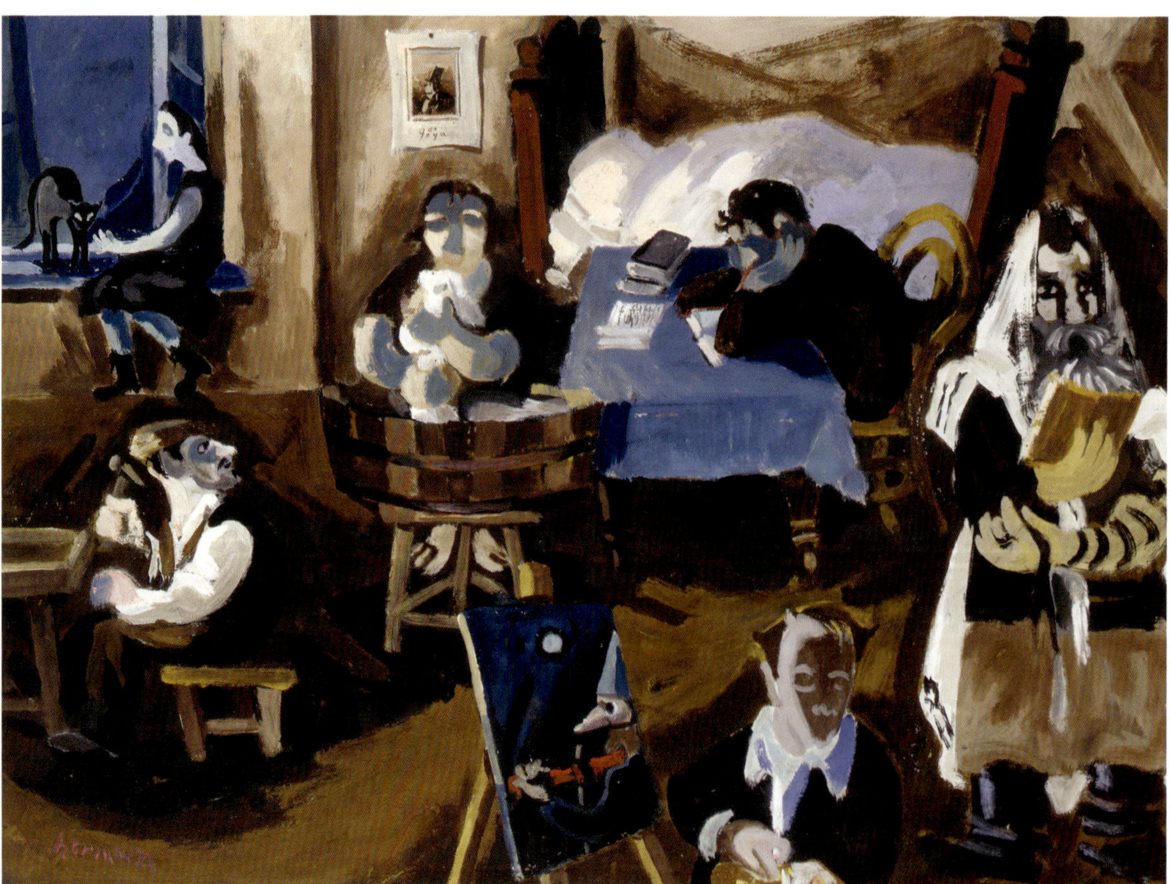

Josef Herman (1911–2000) | *My Family and I*
1941 | gouache on board | 54 x 74 cm
collection of Sir Jeremy and Lady Isaacs | © Artist's Estate/all rights reserved DACS 2019

Herman painted this memory of his home in Warsaw soon after he learned his family was dead. He is at his easel, his mother washing clothes, his father cobbling, his grandfather at prayer.

to emigration'.[7] Nolde, forbidden to paint in 1941, made watercolours on scraps of rice paper in a half-concealed room.[8] Ernst Ludwig Kirchner killed himself.

There were artists (and gallerists, publishers and art historians) who collaborated. Some worked under duress, fearing that they would be victims. However, Joachim Fest has suggested that some experienced a blood-lust: 'a longing for contact with the idealistically misconstrued world of the primitive man of violence – the "noble savage" returned in a barbaric modern guise'.[9] Most culpable were artists such as Josef Thorak, Adolf Ziegler and Arno Breker who – like the architect Albert Speer and filmmaker Leni Riefenstahl – reinforced the Nazi's myth.[10]

As for those who fled, stories of escape could be remarkable. They hinged on luck as well as planning. The Nazi party had crept to power locally; hence the Bauhaus moved to Berlin when Dessau was taken over by the Nazis in 1931 rather than overseas. Those who did not seek to leave immediately in 1933 – hoping and believing all would return to normal – found later departure harder. But those who fled initially to countries where German was understood, such as Czechoslovakia or Switzerland, or even the Netherlands, discovered in due course that only Switzerland was safe. Max Beckmann, dismissed from his teaching post at Frankfurt with 500 of his paintings confiscated, sat out the Nazi period in Amsterdam then left for the United States after the war. Paris was another obvious place to go for artists but few left before war was declared. It was soon occupied and Vichy France surrendered its refugees back to Germany. In August 1940 a group of Americans set up the Emergency Rescue Committee in Marseilles. By the time its agent, Varian Fry, was expelled in September 1941 it had transferred 2,000 people to the United States, including Josef and Anni Albers, Chagall, Dali, Duchamp, Ernst, André Kertész and Fernand Léger.[11]

Emigration was stepwise for many. Those who had chosen Spain soon met with a Civil War that pushed them onwards, for example Arthur Segal, who had been born in Romania and trained in Germany, the painter and gallerist Hans Baruch (alias Jack Bilbo) and Fred Uhlman. The Spanish surrealist Remedios Varo went the other way, to Paris, and then fled occupied Paris to Mexico. The influential German typographic designer Elizabeth Friedlander went to Italy in 1936 but came to Britain when its anti-semitic laws were issued in 1938. Josef Herman used a fake passport in 1938 to get from Poland to Belgium, where he was helped by Permeke, then crossed France to Bordeaux for a ship he hoped would take him to Canada; it landed him in Glasgow. László Moholy-Nagy was a three-fold refugee. He fled Hungary's oppressive regime in 1918 for Germany and the Bauhaus. He then went

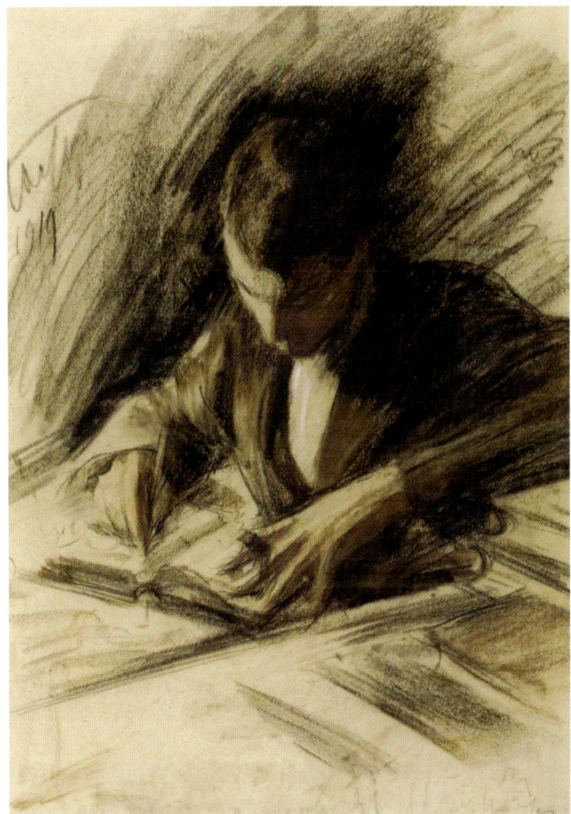

Leonid Pasternak (1862–1945) | *Boris Pasternak Writing*
1919 | chalk on paper | 32 x 26 cm
Tate | photo: © Tate

Pasternak moved his family from Russia to Berlin in 1921 and in 1938 left Germany for Oxford. This swiftly captured portrait shows his son, the future Nobel laureate Boris Pasternak.

to the Netherlands and on to London and in 1937 was invited to found his own teaching institution in Chicago. The photographer Ellen Auerbach emigrated to Palestine in 1933 until Arab unrest made her leave for Britain and then America. Others who moved on over the Atlantic included Mondrian, Gabo and Lotte Jacobi, who opened a successful photographic studio on New York.

The young Jewish artist Willy Tirr waited until late in 1938 to escape Germany. He and a friend posed as English tourists on a walking holiday, wearing tweeds and carrying forged passports, and made it into Holland. He carried a pistol in his knapsack 'just in case'. He was interned in Holland but aided by a German with British citizenship he reached Britain almost at the last moment, in June 1939.[12] Ludwig and Else Meidner also waited until 1939 before escaping to Britain. Even later was Kurt Schwitters. He had remained at home in Hannover until warned that he was liable to be arrested and slipped out to Norway with his teenage son Ernst, a known anti-fascist, on New Year's Day in 1937.

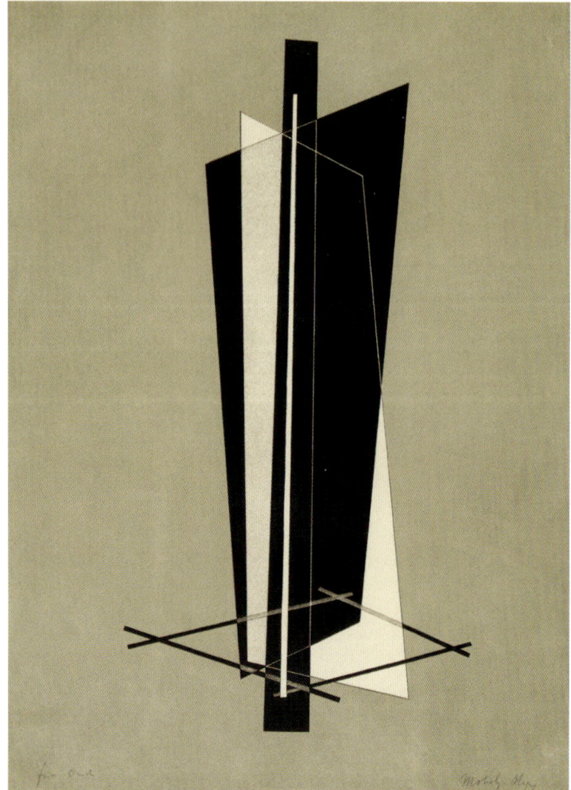

László Moholy-Nagy (1895–1946) | *Untitled*
from *Konstruktionen: Kestnermappe 6*
1923 | lithograph | 50 x 26 cm
gift of Suzette M. Hamill (1947.366.2); Chicago (IL), Art Institute of Chicago
photo: © 2019 The Art Institute of Chicago/Art Resource, NY/Scala, Florence

The Bauhaus artist and designer Moholy-Nagy was in London only
briefly before going to establish a new institution in Chicago but
was a charismatic presence.

On the invasion of Norway in April 1940 they
escaped by icebreaker for Edinburgh.

Few who had seen the interior of a concentration
camp had any chance to get away, but some did.
Erich Kahn was permitted to leave Welzheim on
condition that he emigrated. Ernst Eisenmayer was
sent to Dachau after being caught trying to escape
from Austria but his younger brother had arrived in
England with the *Kindertransport* and his guardian
sponsored Ernst's release to Britain in April 1939.[13]

It is thought some 200 Jewish professional
painters and sculptors were murdered in the camps,
and more died in the wider persecution.[14] While
many went unrecognised, others are familiar
names today: the pioneering abstract painter Otto
Freundlich, who was interned in France on the
declaration of war and deported after the surrender
to an extermination camp, and the French painter-
poet Max Jacob, who died in transit to Auschwitz.
The Russian-born expressionist Chaïm Soutine,
whose paintings reached an auction record of
$28 million in 2015, went into hiding in Vichy

France and died from a perforated ulcer that
was not treated soon enough.

Some of the most powerful paintings express-
ing the situation for Jewish artists were by Felix
Nussbaum, an artist of the New Objectivity movement, who was a refugee and ultimately a victim.
He was studying at the Berlin Academy when the
Nazis came to power. He stayed in Italy, then went
to Paris and finally he and his wife, the Polish painter Felka Platek, moved in with friends in Brussels.
After the occupation of Belgium in 1940 they went
into hiding but both were murdered in Auschwitz
a month before Brussels was liberated. His parents,
brother, sister-in-law and niece were killed too.[15]
Many Jewish refugees in Britain would bear the
knowledge that their families were murdered,
including Hilda Goldwag from Austria, Georg
Mayer-Marton from Hungary and Josef Herman
and Jankel Adler from Poland.

Refuge in the United Kingdom was far from
automatic. While it was possible to travel without
a visa, the Aliens Order of 1920 required anyone
who wished to stay to have a work permit or
means of support. The rules were tightened rather
than relaxed in 1938 as anti-semitic oppression
escalated: the 'Aryanisation' policy, seizure of
Jewish property, increased violence, the *Anschluss*
that made Austria subject to Nazi laws in March,
the Sudeten annexation of September and *Kristallnacht* in November. Migration was increasing. Of
the 80,000 would-be refugees who came to Britain
from January 1933 to September 1939, 50,000
arrived after March 1938. Britain imposed new
standards, preferring: 'distinguished persons,
i.e. those of international repute in the field of
science, medicine, research or art' or 'industrialists
with a well-established business.' The agreement
in November 1938 to the *Kindertransport*, a programme created by British charities to rescue children while leaving their parents behind, was a final
flourish of asylum before war was declared.[16]

For all the escapes that were successful, thousands must have failed. People with a disability
were unlikely to be permitted residence, and others
who could not pay their way were forced to move on.
Among known cases is that of the textile designer
Otti Berger, who taught at the Bauhaus, set up her
own textile company, developed intricately beautiful
woven patterns and pioneered plastic fabrics. As a
Jew she was forced to give up her company in 1936.
She fled to London and hoped to follow her mentor
Ani Albers to the United States but could not organise her departure despite the offer of work at
Maholy-Nagy's new institution in Chicago. In
Britain, lacking contacts, unable to speak English
and hampered in learning it by deafness, she was
without support. In 1938 she returned to her family
in Croatia. They were transported to Auschwitz
in 1944 and killed.[17]

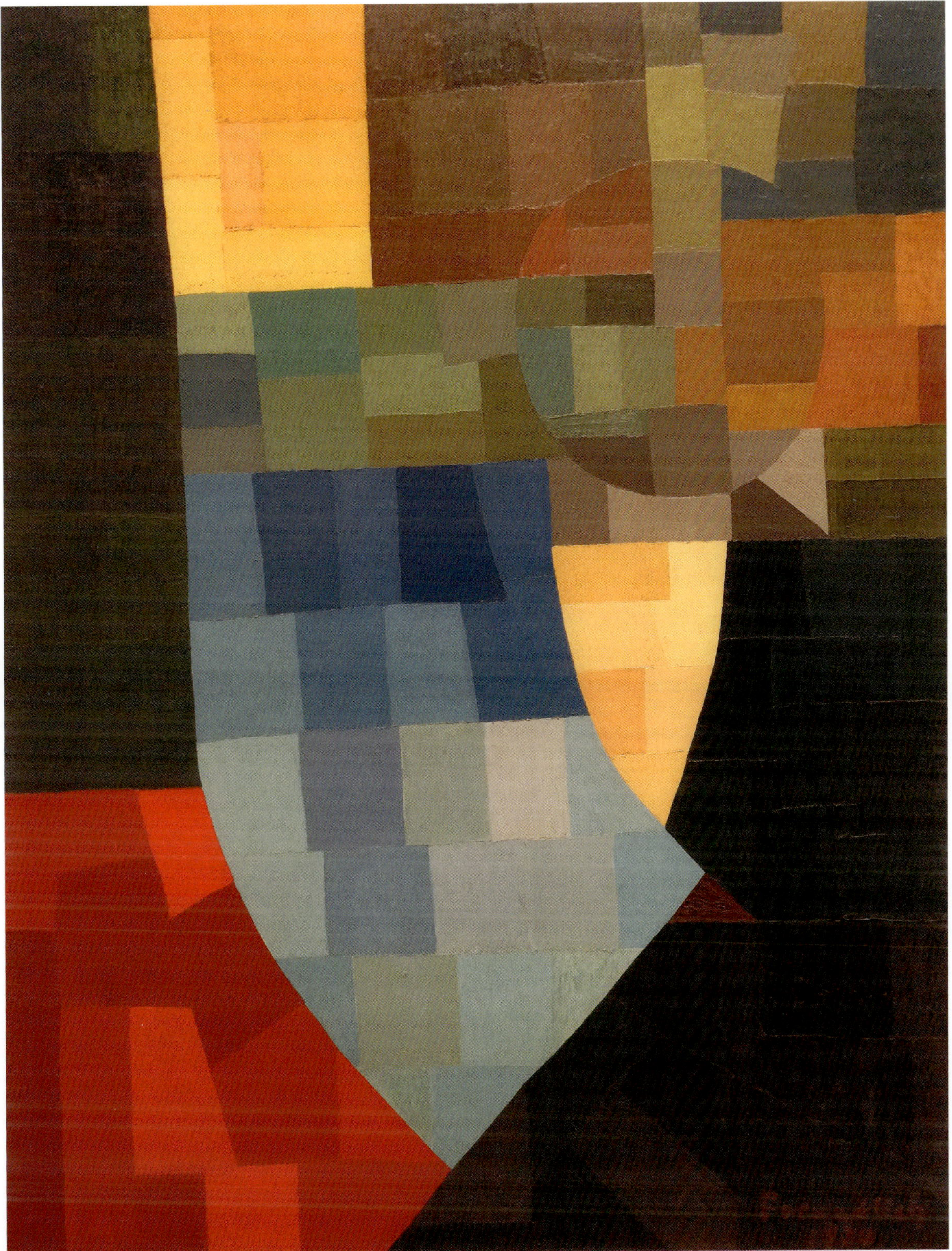

Otto Freundlich (1878–1943) | *Komposition*
1930 | oil on canvas | 147 x 133 cm
Donation Freundlich, Musées de Pontoise

Freundlich was a pioneer of abstract painting and design who lived
in Paris from the early 1920s. He was arrested for his Jewish heritage
and murdered on arrival at Majdanek concentration camp, aged 64.

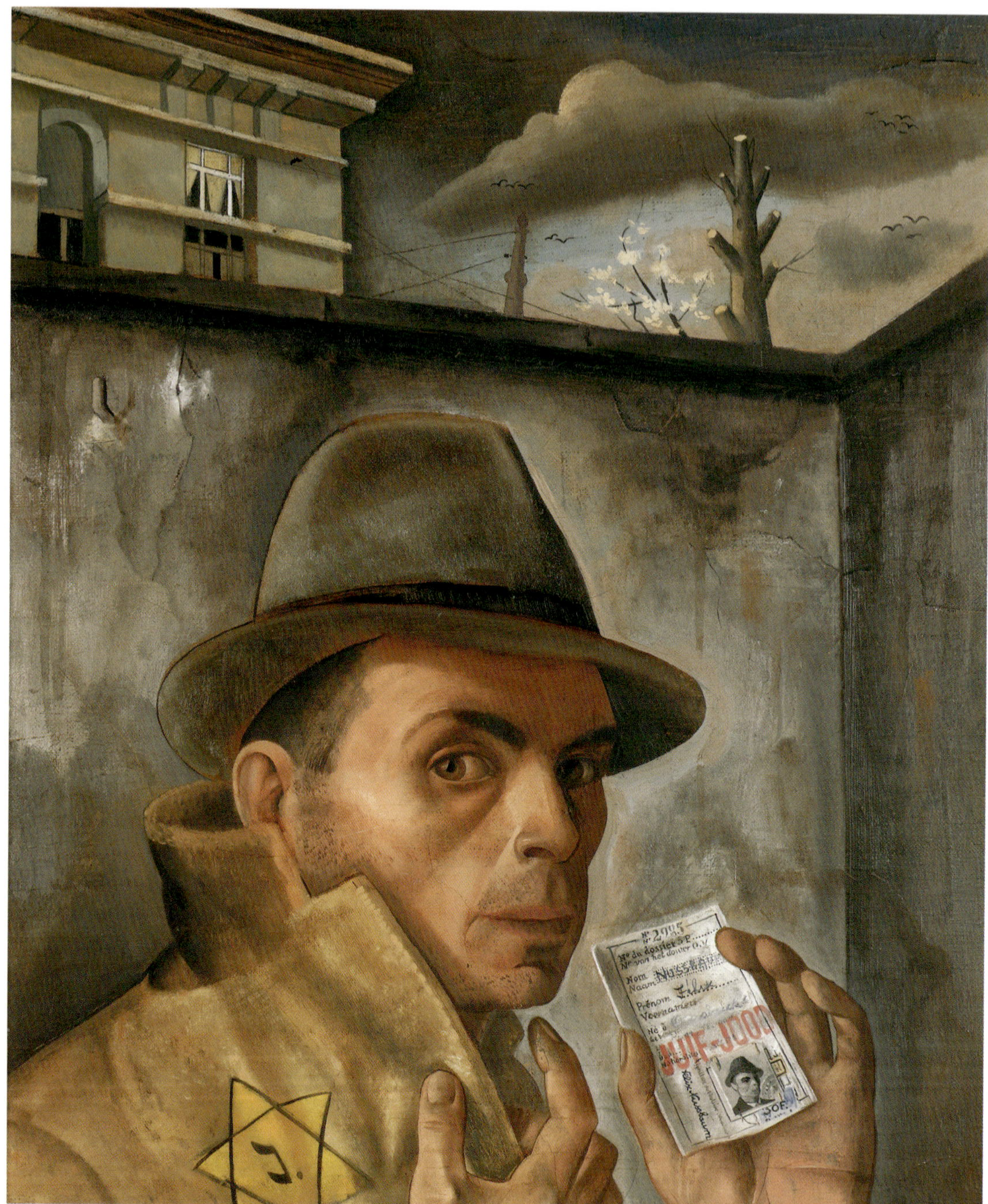

Felix Nussbaum (1904–44)
Self-Portrait with Jewish Identity Card
1943/4 | oil on canvas | 56 x 49 cm
Felix-Nussbaum-Haus Osnabrück, loan from the Niedersächsische
Sparkassenstiftung | photo: Museumsquartier Osnabrück, Felix-Nussbaum-Haus

Nussbaum painted this vivid memory of the oppression he had
lived under in Germany while in hiding in Brussels, to which he
had escaped in 1937. He was murdered at Auschwitz in 1944.

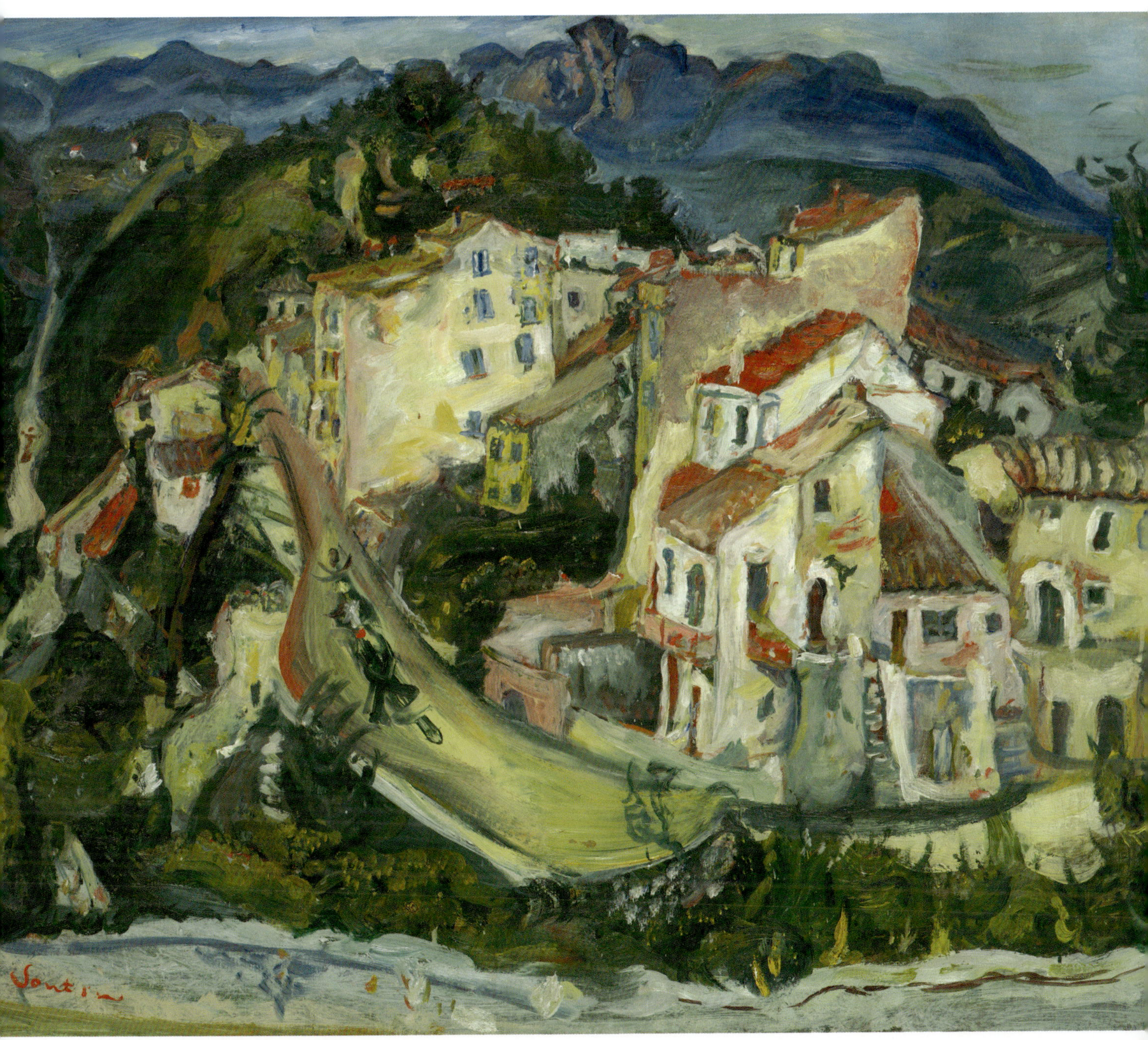

Chaïm Soutine (1893–1943) | *Landscape at Cagnes*
*c.*1923 | oil on canvas | 60 x 73 cm
Charles H. and Mary S.F. Worcester Collection (1947.114);
Chicago (IL), Art Institute of Chicago
photo: © 2019 The Art Institute of Chicago/Art Resource, NY/Scala, Florence

Soutine grew up in what is now Belarus and studied in Vilnius but
aged 20 moved to Paris. After a period of intense poverty he became
commercially successful in the early 1920s and painted often at Cagnes
on the Côte d'Azur. He went into hiding after the German invasion.

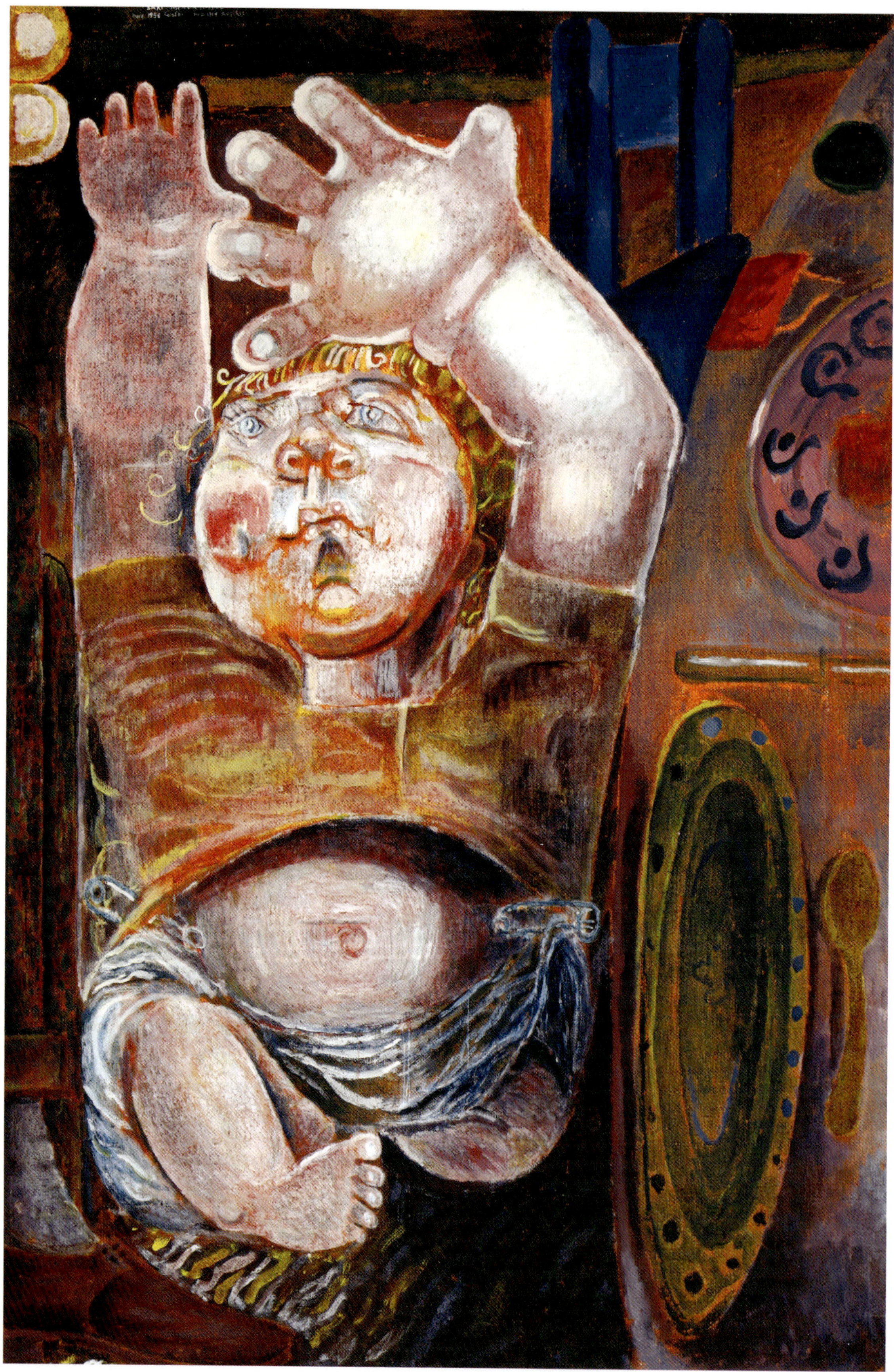

The thirties émigrés
reception and survival

WHAT WAS IT LIKE TO BE AN ARTIST WHO LANDED in Britain in the 1930s? The immediate problem for most was securing a living. They had to show means of support but few managed to bring much with them. To make it worse the earlier arrivals of 1933–6 found a period of recession. With no government scheme to bring them to safety, they needed luck, money, connections, resourcefulness and determination.

The first help was from organisations like the Jewish Refugee Committee, the Academic Assistance Council, the Quakers and the Plymouth Brethren. Refugee artists helped them raise funds, for example Heinz Worner organised the Artists Aid Jewry Exhibition at the Whitechapel Gallery. Support was given to artists specifically by the Artists' International Association, the Artists' Refugee Committee and the Free German League of Culture. Fred and Diana Uhlman were key figures in both the latter organisations, set up in 1937–8 and run from their address in Hampstead. Uhlman had been a lawyer in Germany but as a socialist and Jew he left for Paris in 1933 where, unable to practise, he took up painting influenced by the childlike vision of artists such as Utrillo and Rousseau. Moving on to Spain he met the wealthy Englishwoman Diana Croft, who helped him get to London. They created networks of supporters and took people into their home, including John Heartfield and the art historian Francis Klingender.[1] They also helped the Czech painter Friedrich Feigl and Helmuth Weissenborn, who had lost his teaching position in Leipzig for being married to a Jew. The *Kindertransport* scheme helped a few art students young enough to qualify for it: one was

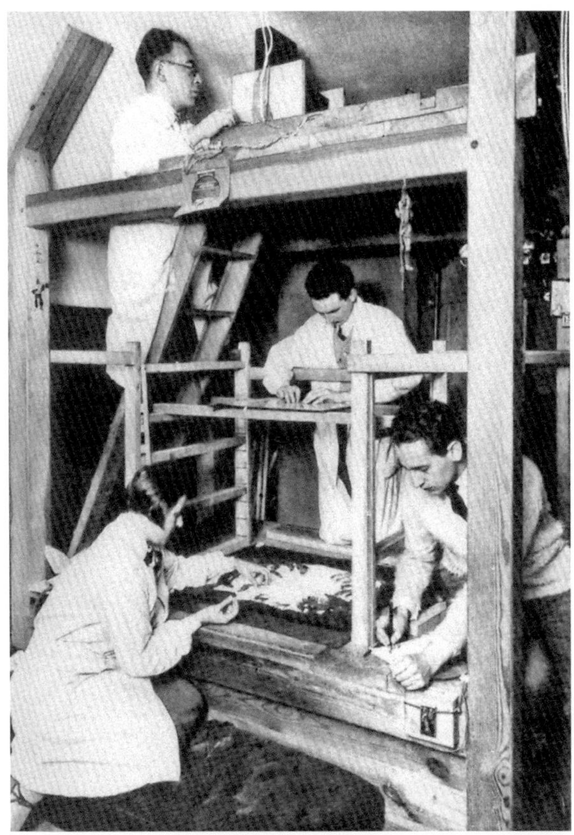

Lotte Reiniger (1899–1981) working on her pioneering silhouette animation films with her husband Carl Koch, Walter Türck and Alexander Kardan.
Wikimedia Commons | © Christel Strobel, Primrose Film Production

Susan Einzig, who had attended the Breuer school of design at 15.

Personal contacts were vital. Piet Mondrian left Paris in 1938 when Ben Nicholson sent him a formal letter of invitation; Winifred Nicholson found him a place to stay in Hampstead.[2] Maholy-Nagy was encouraged to come by the critic Herbert Read, who acted as a guarantor for artist refugees, as did Kenneth Clark. Ludwig and Else Meidner were aided by Augustus John. Willi Soukop was invited to Dartington by a woman who met him in Vienna. Business connections could be equally important. The Bauhaus-trained designer Margarete Heymann (later Grete Marks) came with help from Heals in 1938 after she was forced to relinquish her ceramics factory. The designer Hugo Dachinger was sponsored by an English firm who employed him as a window dresser in Vienna. Jan Le Witt and Jerzy Himmelfarb from Poland brought their graphics company Le Witt-Him sponsored by their English clients, the Victoria and Albert Museum and Lund Humphries. Even with work, however, continued residence was not assured; the animator Lotte Reiniger and her husband came to England in

---

Heinz Koppel (1919–1980) | *Sari*
1959 | tempera and oil on canvas | 153 × 102 cm
Koppel family | © Artist's Estate

Heinz Koppel, a refugee from Berlin and Prague in the 1930s, brought a German expressionist vision and a powerful artistic integrity to Britain. He painted this remembrance of his daughter Sari after she had died in a tragic accident.

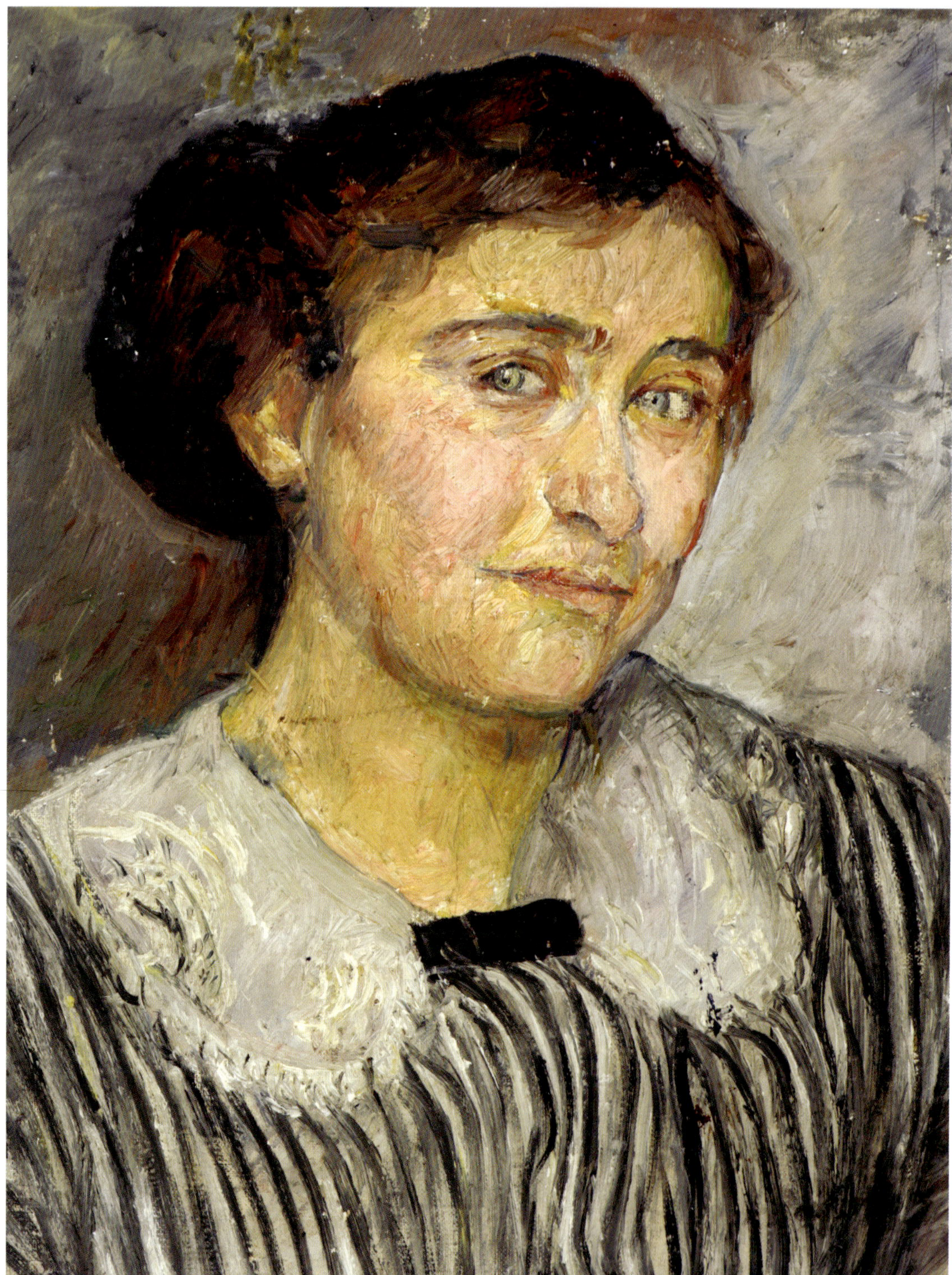

Adèle Reifenberg (1893–1986)
Portrait of the Artist's Sister-in-Law, Elise Reifenberg
*c.*1930 (undated) | oil on canvas | 46 x 36 cm
Ben Uri Collection; presented by Leinster Fine Art 1991 | © Artist's Estate

Reifenburg studied in Weimar and taught in Berlin art schools.
She moved to London with her husband Julius Rosenbaum in
1939 where they ran a private painting school. Her sister-in-law
was an anti-nazi novelist by the pen-name Gabriele Tergit who
also came to London.

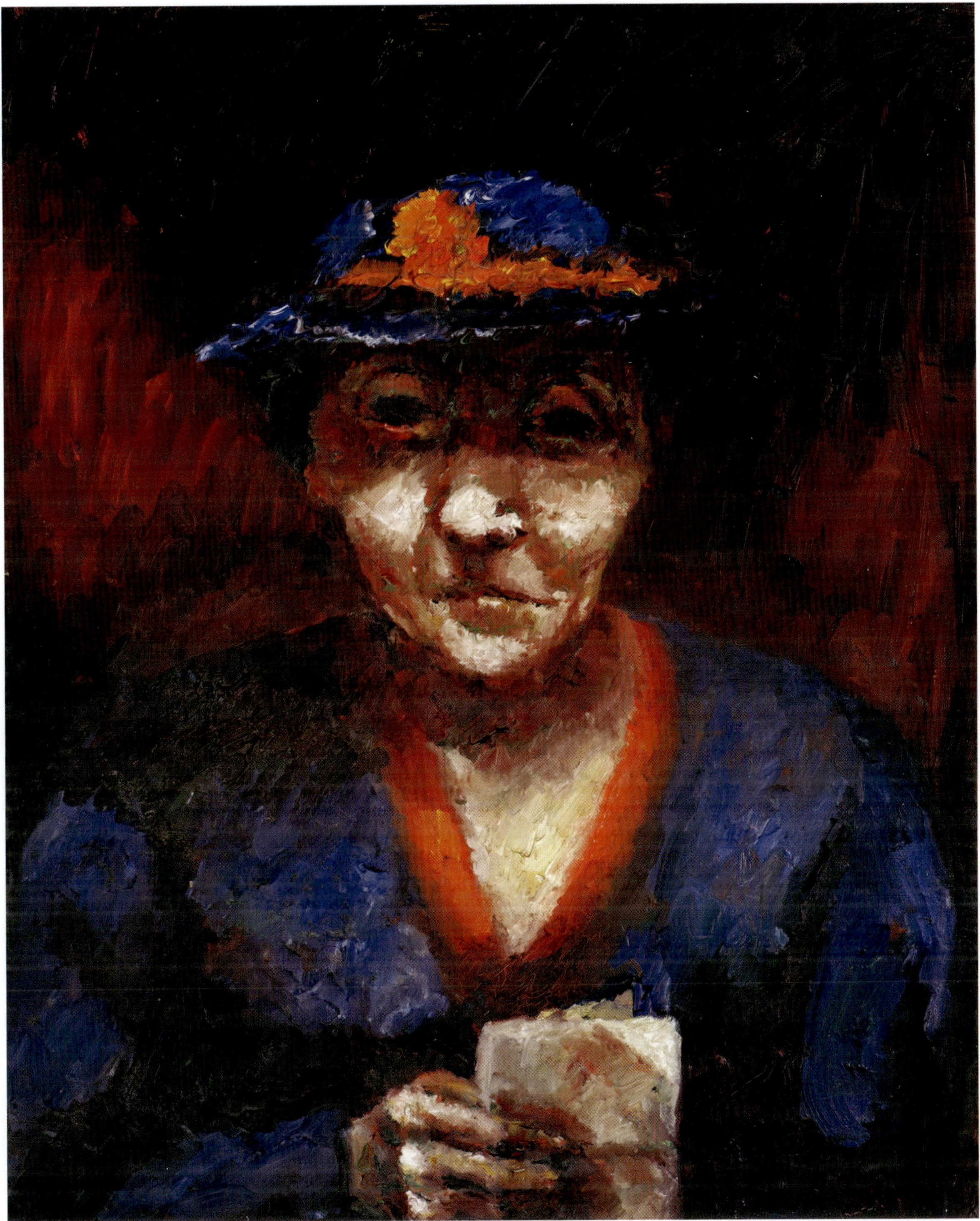

Else Meidner (1901–1987) | *Woman with Hat*
*c.*1950 | oil on canvas | 82 x 67 cm
Ben Uri Collection; acquired with the assistance of Ethel Solomon 1950
© Ludwig Meidner-Archiv, Jüdisches Museum der Stadt Frankfurt am Main

Else Meidner, who was encouraged to study art by Käthe Kollwitz
and had a successful exhibition in Berlin in 1932, worked as a servant
for an elderly woman in London. She and her husband Ludwig lived
in poverty.

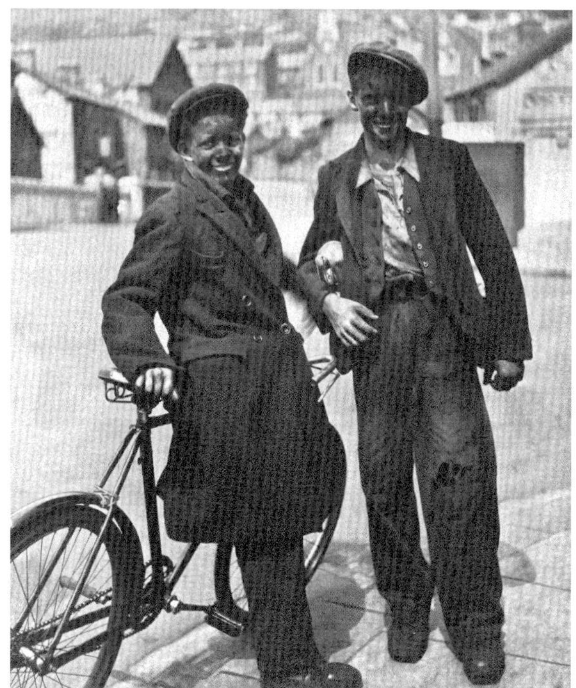

Edith Tudor Hart (1908–1973) | *Two Young Miners*
*c.*1935 | photograph
National Library of Wales, Aberystwyth | © Estate of Wolfgang Suschitzky

Tudor Hart went with her husband, who was a doctor, to
the Depression-hit Rhondda Valley during the mid-1930s and
submitted photographic essays to numerous magazines. A striking
quality in her images was short depth of field: pin-sharp subjects
and backgrounds out of focus.

1936 but could not extend their visas and went on
to France, Italy and even back to wartime Germany
before settling in London in 1949.[3]

British family relationships gave rights to some.
Peter de Francia had grown up in Paris with an
English mother and left his studies in Brussels
when the invasion began. The Belgian painter and
architect Willi Rondas also had an English mother
and joined the British army after being evacuated
from Dunkirk with the Belgian army. New family
connections were made: Uhlman married Diana
Croft, and in Vienna in 1933 Edith Suschitzky
married a young English doctor, Alexander Tudor
Hart. She helped later to bring her brother and
mother to Britain. In Dresden Walter Nessler met
an English dancer, Prudence Ashbee, and having left
claiming it was a two-week holiday they married.[4]

Refugee organisations helped people obtain
work permits. For women these were often as maids:
the photographer Inge Ader and the painter Else
Meidner both did domestic work. Moholy-Nagy
took on a poster for the London Underground,
photographs of Oxford for John Betjeman, a window display for Simpson's in Piccadilly and special
effects for Alexander Korda's film *Things to Come*.

John Heartfield sold his photomontages to Stefan
Lorant's *Lilliput* and *Picture Post*, though his
devotion to Stalin ruled him out for many publishers and he scraped a living. The sculptor and
printmaker Bettina Adler worked at a button
factory in Merthyr Tydfil.[5] Julius Rosenbaum,
who had trained in Paris, Munich and Berlin
before being forbidden to paint, made a living
as a decorator and his wife Adèle Reifenberg
gave private tuition. Jacob Bornfriend became
a diamond cutter.

One of the most productive fields artistically
was photography. Portrait photographers who set
up in Britain included Inge Ader, Rolf Mahrenholz,
Lucia Moholy and Gerty Simon. 'New Objectivity'
photographers whose images offered a contrast with
existing British photography included Bill Brandt,
Felix H. Mann and pioneers of magazine photo-
essays such as Kurt Hutton (originally Hübschmann)
and Gerit Deutsch, who provided over 50 for *Picture
Post* from 1938 to 1950. Oher émigré photographers
at work were Eric Auerbach, Bertl Gaye, Lotte
Jacobi, Elsbeth Juda, Lotte Meitner-Graf, László
Moholy-Nagy, Otto Salomon (alias Peter Hunter)
and Kurt Schwitters' son Ernst. Many did innovative work. Edith Tudor Hart saw photography
as a weapon in the fight against injustice and her
witness to Depression-era communities appeared
in *The Geographical Magazine*, *News Chronicle*,
Picture Post, *Lilliput* and *Design for Today*.[6]
Her brother Wolfgang Suschitzky recorded life
around the bookshops of Charing Cross Road,
symbolic of intellectual freedom. However, Gerty
Simon exemplifies how these photographers might
be forgotten. In 1934 the *Sunday Times* called
her the 'most brilliant and original of the Berlin
photographers' and she had two exhibitions in
her first two years in Britain, yet she was barely
remembered until her archive was donated to the
Wiener Library in 2016. Her portrait subjects included Einstein, Lotte Lenya and Kathe Kollwitz
in Germany and Kenneth Clark, Peggy Ashcroft,
Aneurin Bevan and Paul Nash in Britain.[7]

If refugee photographers were appreciated,
how were other artists received in pre-war Britain?
It was a time when progressive artists were eager
to explore modernism and internationalism. The
numbers of continental émigrés and the high pro-
files of Gabo, Mondrian and Kokoschka constituted
a significant injection of energy. Frances Spalding
has said: 'By the end of the 1930s, London, or more
specifically Hampstead, had become the centre
of an international avant-garde.'[8] Nevertheless,
there was hostility or at least indifference in other
quarters. A wave of interest in expressionism in the
early 1920s had petered out and the influence of
the Bloomsbury Group, *Horizon* magazine and the
surrealists was for the school of Paris. German art
was not much understood. John Willett summed up:

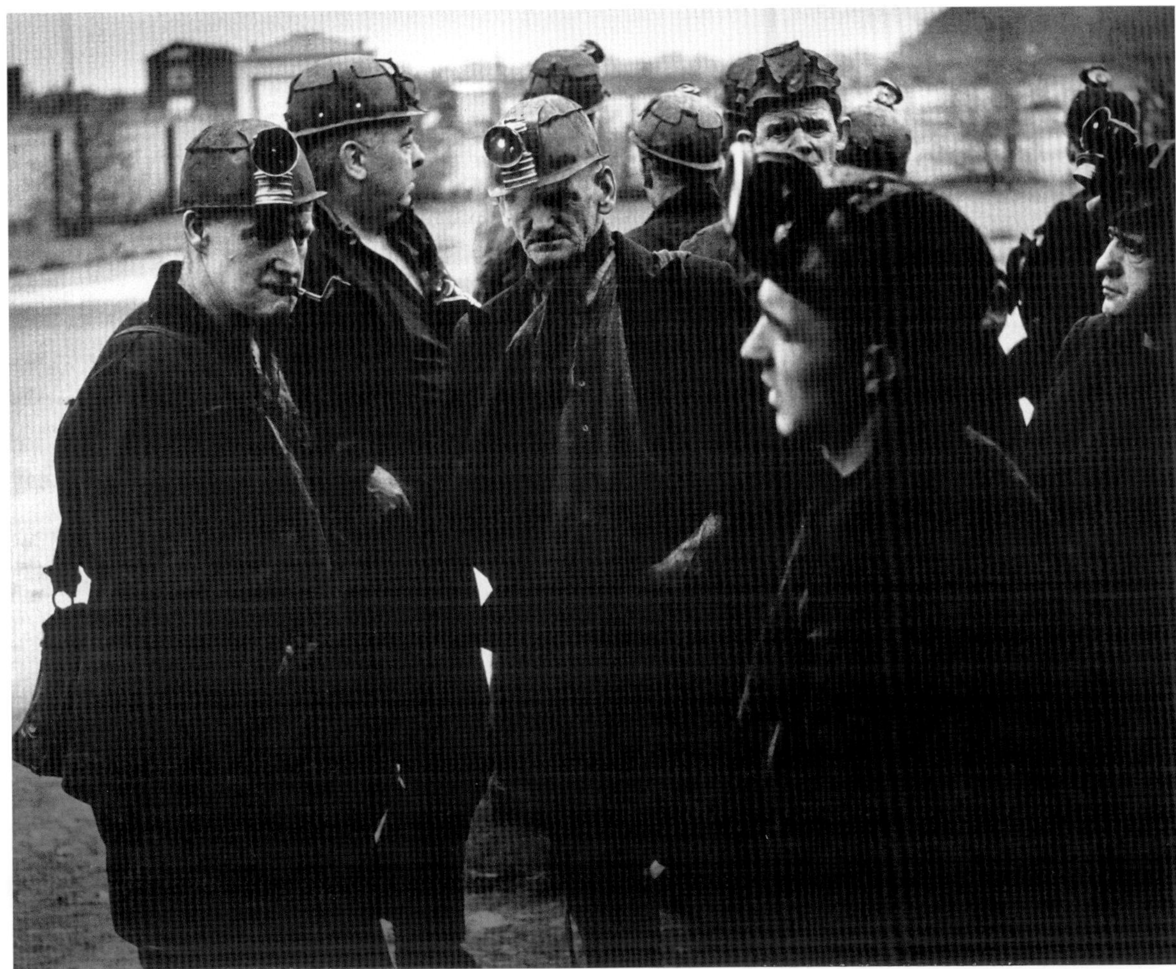

Wolfgang Suschitzky (1912–2016) | *Miners at Shilbottle Colliery*
1952 | photograph
National Library of Wales, Aberystwyth | © Estate of Wolfgang Suschitzky

Austrian-born Suschitzky was brought to Britain by his sister Edith
Tudor Hart. He worked for many publications documenting British
life. He later made documentaries and feature films.

*The fact that the resident art-lovers were not
merely ignorant of the development of Central
European art since – well, certainly since the
mid-nineteenth century and possibly even since
Dürer's time – but positively resistant in most
cases to its more recent movements, made the
life of even the most eminent of its exponents
difficult indeed.*[9]

German artists felt the need to state their case in
Britain and to defy the *Reichskulturkammer* back
home. The visual arts section of the Free German
League of Culture had more than a hundred members; Kokoschka became its president. Herbert Read
was another champion. A year after the 'Degenerate
Art Exhibition' of 1937 he organised a rebuttal
in the form of 'Twentieth Century German Art'

with 270 exhibits by many of the same artists.
The Chamberlain Government was uneasy at too
much profile for the émigrés while it was appeasing
Germany and some critics were unsympathetic.
Raymond Mortimer wrote:

*People who go to see this exhibition are only
too likely to say: 'If Hitler doesn't like these
pictures, it's the best thing I've heard about
him.' For the general impression made by the
show on the ordinary public must be one of
extraordinary ugliness.*[10]

Nevertheless, the mission to educate was pursued.
A Penguin survey was published: *Modern German
Art* by Oto Bihalji-Merin writing under the pseud-
onym Peter Thoene. In 1942, an exhibition in an

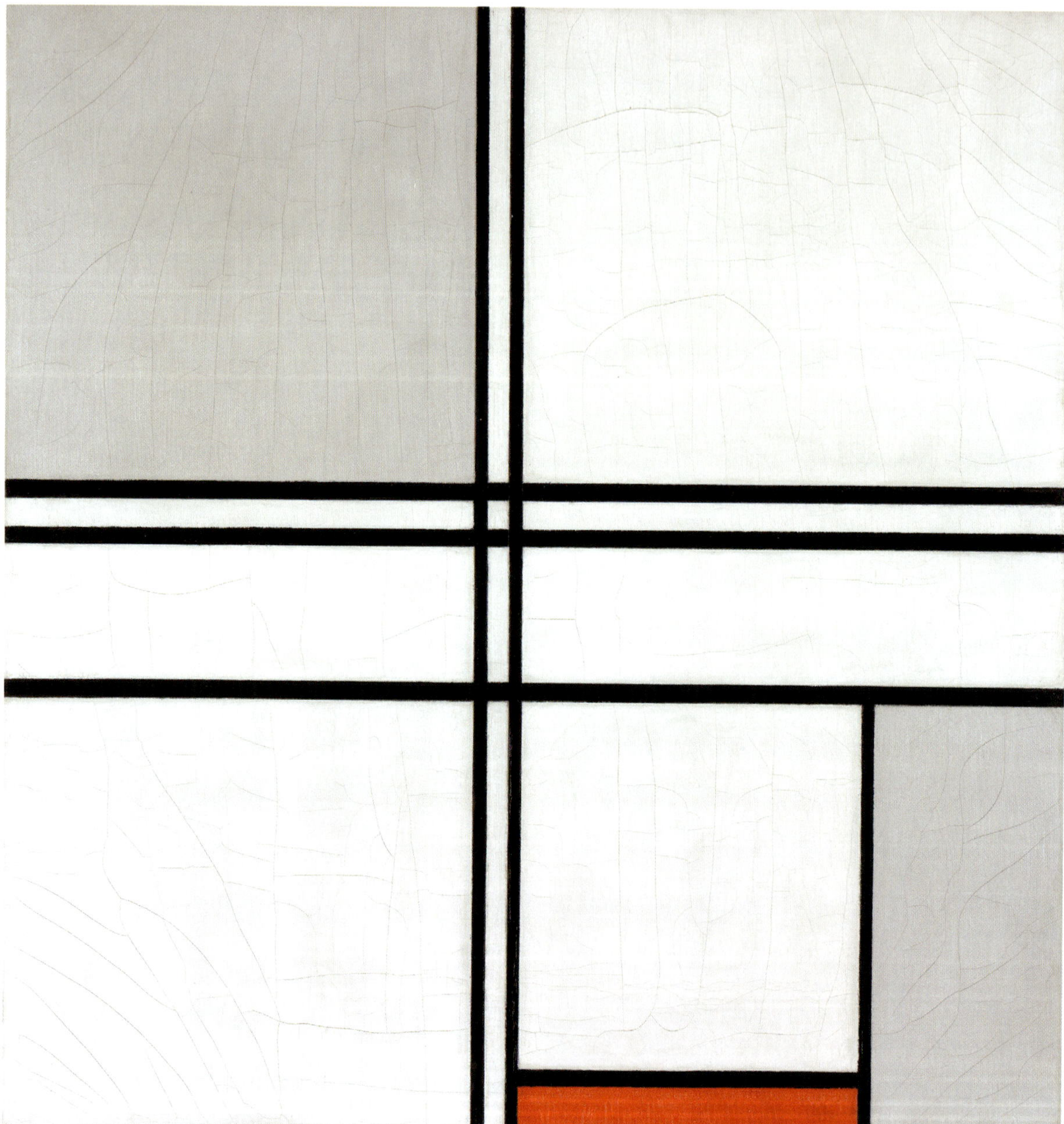

Piet Mondrian (1872–1944) | *Composition (No. 1) Gray-Red*
1935 | oil on canvas | 57 x 56 cm
gift of Mrs Gilbert W. Chapman, Art Institute of Chicago

Mondrian's geometrical compositions represented international art
of the highest importance coming to Britain in 1938.

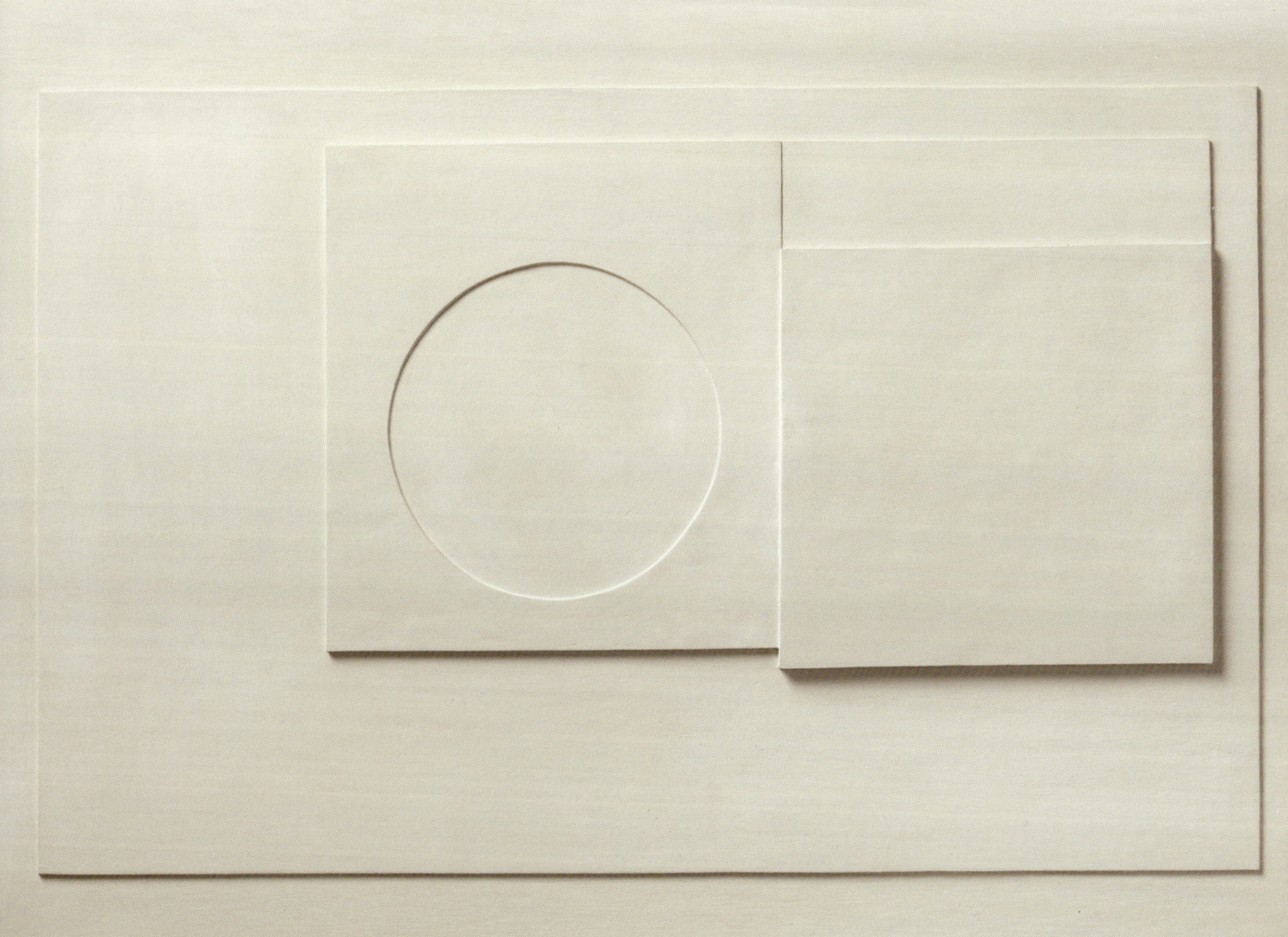

Ben Nicholson (1894–1982) | *1935 (white relief)*
1935 | oil on carved and built-up wood | 54 x 80 cm
British Council Collection | © Angela Verren Taunt/all rights reserved DACS 2019
photo © British Council

Nicholson had met Mondrian and seen his geometrical abstracts in
1932 and began making his white reliefs shortly afterwards. Their
relationship intensified when Nicholson helped Mondrian to escape
to Britain.

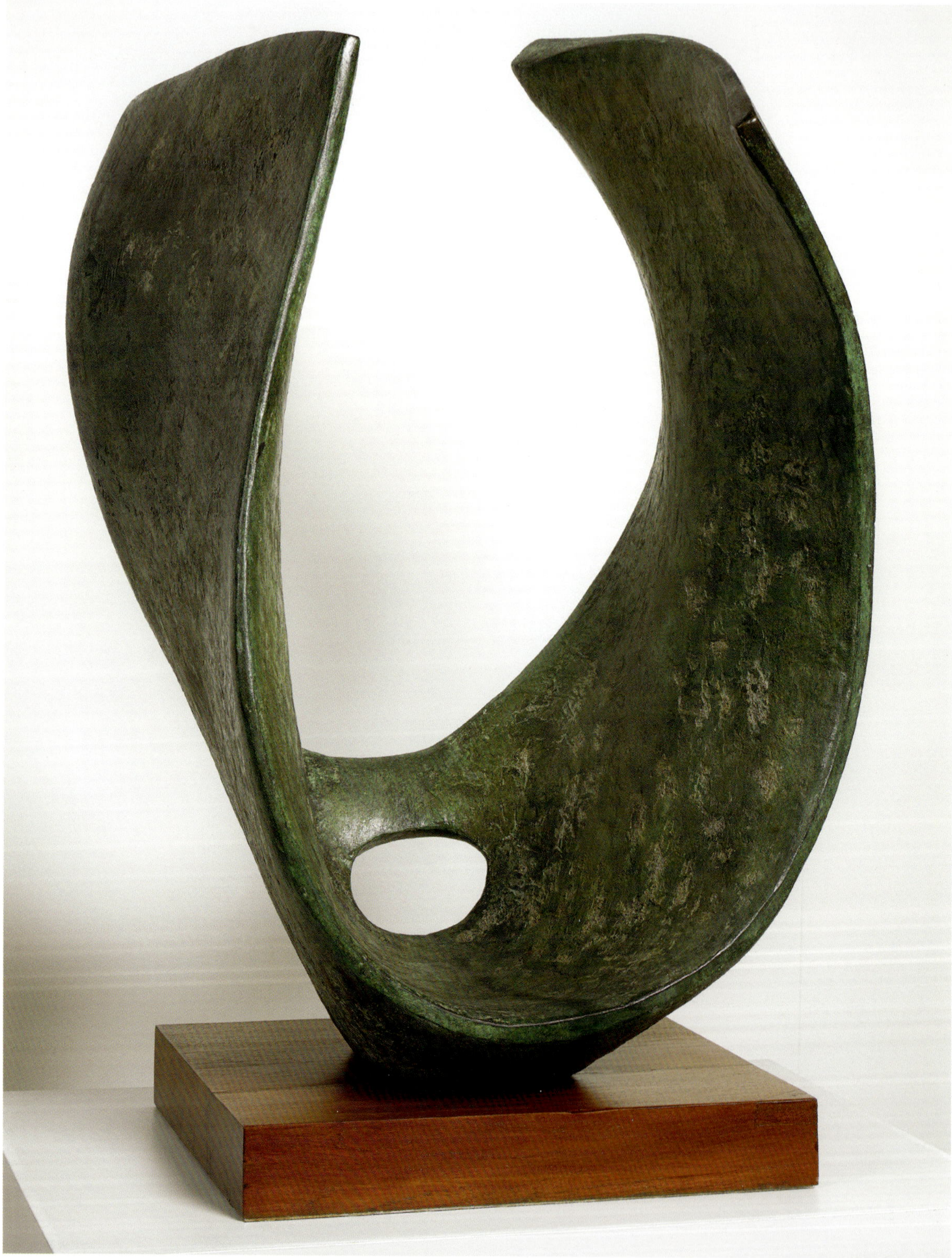

Dame Barbara Hepworth (1903–1975) | *Curved Form – Trevalgan*
1956 | bronze on wood base | 68 x 100 x 63 cm
British Council Collection | © Barbara Hepworth/Bowness | photo: © British Council

Hepworth was closely associated with émigré modernists Naum Gabo
and Piet Mondrian. Gabo moved with her and Ben Nicholson to
St Ives during the Second World War.

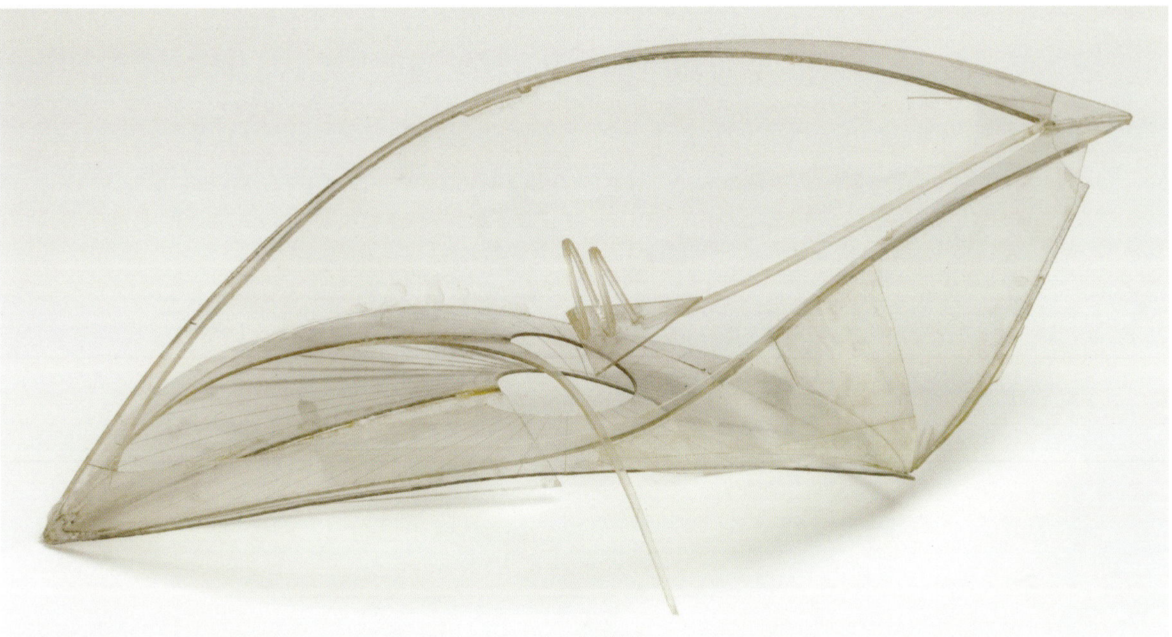

Naum Gabo (1890–1977) | *Model for 'Spiral Theme'*
1941 | plastic | 6 x 17 x 11 cm
Tate | The Work of Naum Gabo | © Nina & Graham Williams | photo: © Tate

The Russian Constructivist spiral theme developed by Gabo proved influential for many artists, including Barbara Hepworth, Peter Lanyon and Wilhelmena Barns-Graham.

empty shop in Regent Street was titled 'Allies Inside Germany'.[11] Some artists sought to alert the public to the realities of Hitler. Josef Flatter produced a touring exhibition in 1938 of cartoons based on quotations from *Mein Kampf.* They were prescient and horrifying, some showing ovens and poison gas, yet they were maligned as 'Jewish propaganda' or the 'atrocity propaganda' discredited after the last war.

The émigré artists congregating in Britain represented enormous diversity: post-Impressionists, expressionists, abstract artists, constructivists; and Mondrian, who was creating new forms unrelated to the outside world but capable of inspiring transcendent responses. Critical to professional engagement with them was the circle of modernist artists and critics in Hampstead. Herbert Read was a central figure, seeing it as a moment in which British art could regain international significance. His network included the émigré architects Walter Gropius and Marcel Breuer, the continental artists Moholy-Nagy, Gabo and Mondrian and forward-looking British artists Paul Nash, Henry Moore, Barbara Hepworth, Ben Nicholson, Edward Burra and Tristram Hillier.[12]

Hepworth and Nicholson had travelled together in France in 1932 and visited nearly all the major modernists. Shortly afterwards Nicholson was in Paris again and met Mondrian and Moholy-Nagy and moved into the creation of his white reliefs in late 1933. This Parisian group transferred to Hampstead: Maholy-Nagy in 1935, Gabo in 1936 and Mondrian in 1938. Meanwhile, in 1936, 'Abstract and Concrete' curated by Nicolette Gray brought them all together in Britain's first international exhibition of abstract art, shown in Oxford, London, Liverpool and Cambridge.[13]

Gabo's influence was critical. He and other Russian Constructivists had opened up sculptural forms, literally, by piercing them to make the absences part of the whole, something carried forward by both Hepworth and Moore. The group published *Circle* in 1937 to promote the pro-abstraction side in the debates on modernism. Gabo's influential essay 'The Constructive Idea in Art', argued that geometric shapes were naturally connected to emotions. He inspired artists to embrace creativity that would advance society through harmony and beauty in contrast to everyday disorder. The ideas were fundamental for Hepworth and Moore in particular. Gabo's curved and ovoid forms, and his use of cords in sculpture, were transferred into many of Hepworth's sculptures of this time and later.

When war was declared on 3 September 1939, no immigrants from enemy countries were allowed entry and temporary visas were invalidated.

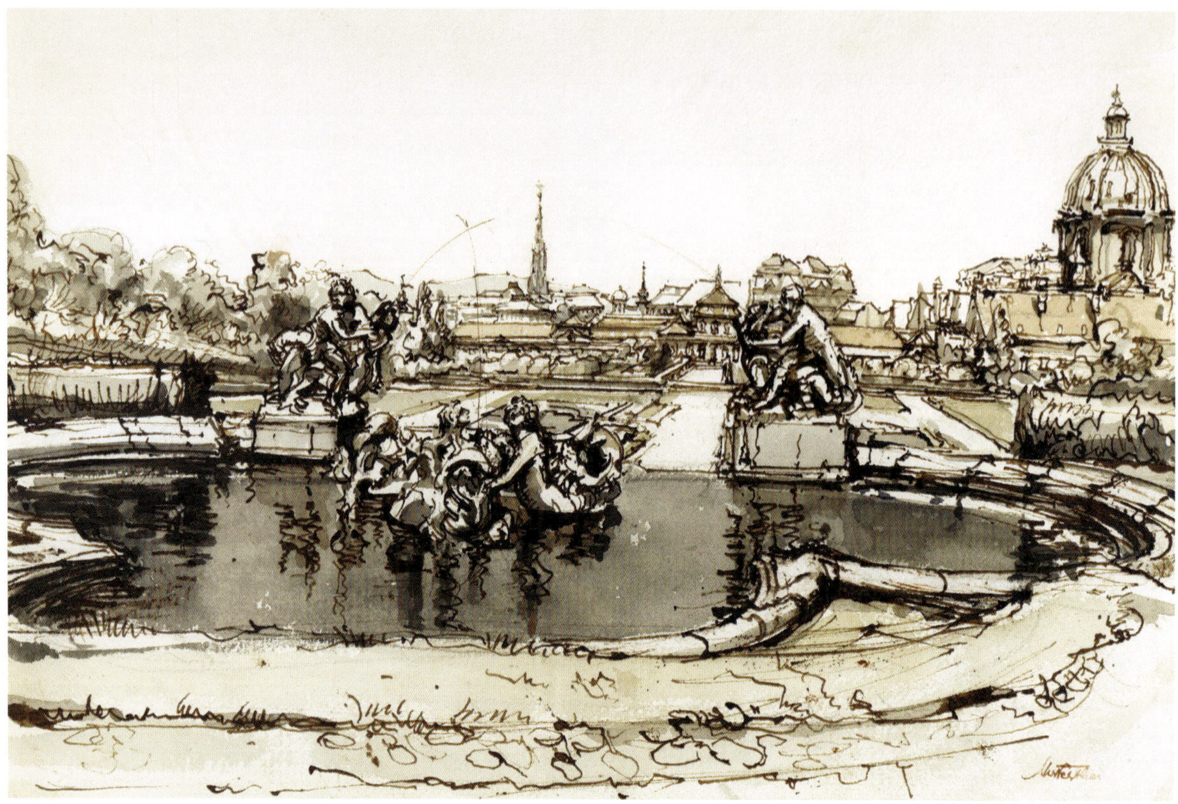

Marianne von Werther (1901–1984)
View from the Belvedere, Vienna
1970 | ink and wash on paper | 38 x 56 cm
RWA (Royal West of England Academy) | © Artist's Estate

By no means all the artists who arrived were of the avant garde.
The Czech artist Marianne von Werther, who had studied in Vienna,
captured classical architecture through drawings.

Tribunals were set up to classify 73,000 refugees
for internment – A for high risk, B for those likely
to be loyal and C for those about whom the government was satisfied. The vast majority were C – about
66,000. Only 569 were deemed a significant risk
and interned. But as the Nazis advanced and Italy
joined the Axis concerns grew that a 'fifth column'
might be at work and internment was extended to
almost all German, Austrian and Italian men. It
encompassed people who had made their lives in
Britain for up to six years, though some were by-
passed, for example Oskar Kokoschka, who had
become a Czech citizen, and Heinz Koppel, whose
family had Cuban passports.

Men were picked up by the police wherever they
could be found. When Walter Nessler was arrested
it was days before he learned why or could tell his
family. Many were deeply angry. The anti-fascist
artist Jack Bilbo, who had arrived in 1936, said:

> *I, who had suffered so much from the Nazis,*
> *whose father was forced by them to commit*
> *suicide, whose mother was most probably in*
> *their hands and for all I knew murdered [...]*
> *I, who had sacrificed everything in my fight*
> *against them, was now a Nazi suspect myself.*[14]

The project was kept secret from the public. Most
internees were sent to the north-west and then the
Isle of Man. Some were shipped to Canada or Australia until the *Arandora Star* was torpedoed in July
1940 carrying 1,200 internees, of whom 479 died.[15]

It is hard not to hear echoes of the concentration
camps, but internment was very different. The
better camps, most famously Hutchinson on the
Isle of Man, which housed 1,400 men in Victorian
boarding houses, became inadvertent centres of
self-help with courses, lectures, language studies
and concerts. Internment was odious but artists
might continue working, which they could not in
their homelands.[16] Schwitters, detained on arrival,
completed up to 300 pieces while interned, both
scintillating portraits on pieces of composite ceiling
material or parts of tea-chests and 'merz' collages

of porridge, linoleum and scraps. The shortage of materials resulted in inventions: the theatre designer Samson Schames made mosaics from bombardment debris, others scraped images onto windows and printed with a laundry mangle; Hugo Dachinger painted on broadsheet newspapers using toothpaste and pigments gathered from ash, mud and plant sap. In due course the Artists' International Association began supplying art materials, people were given space to work and exhibitions were held.[17]

Nevertheless, many found it painful. Martin Bloch could not bring himself to create, though in due course he painted a surrealist scene of the absurdity of camp life, in which herrings on the table turned into mermaids.[18] Artists at Hutchinson published a petition for release with help from Kenneth Clark. (Ludwig Meidner declined to sign as he felt safer without worries about money or survival.) The signatories were an impressive roster of continental artists: Blensdorf, Charoux, Georg Ehrlich, Hermann Fechenbach, Karl Felkel, Paul Hamann, Fritz Krämer, Herbert Markiewicz, Hermann Roessler, the Schwitters, Fred Solomonski, Erich Stern, Fred Uhlman and Hellmuth Weissenborn. They wrote:

We came to England because we believed that here we would find that liberty again which we had lost, and because we saw in her the last bulwark, the last hope for Democracy in Europe. We are asking our British colleagues and friends and all who are interested in art to help us obtain our freedom again [...] The tensions under which we exist here, the sense of grievous injustice done to us, the restlessness caused by living in close proximity with thousands of other men [...] prevent all work and creativity. [...] We want to create something that lives, something that perhaps, beyond the bounds of war, could be of the greatest use to this country. This has always been the mission of Art.[19]

Not all the artists were at Hutchinson. Margarete Klopfleisch, Pamina Liebert-Mahrenholz and Erna Nonnenmacher were sent to Holloway women's prison at first, where Liebert-Mahrenholz made sculpture from bread.[20] Walter Nessler was at Huyton; Bloch, Fritz Kormis, Hugo Dachinger and Samson Schames were at Sefton on the Isle of Man; at nearby Onchan were Bilbo, Henrion, Eugen Hersch, Klaus Meyer and Hermann Nonnenmacher. Others moved around included Alva (Siegfried Solomon Alweiss), Erich Bischof,

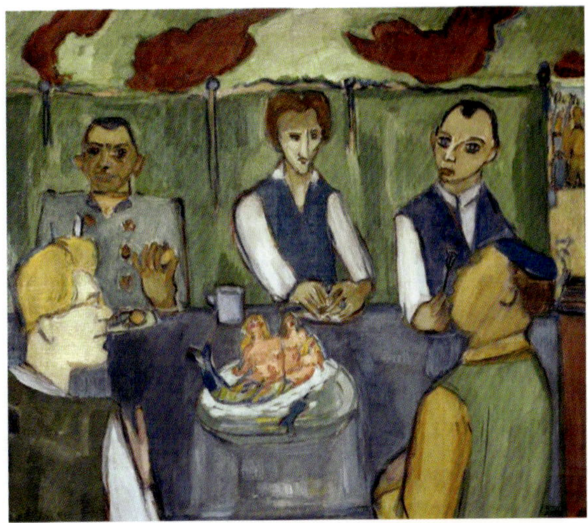

Martin Bloch (1883–1954) | *Miracle in the Internment Camp*
1941 | oil on canvas | 67 x 76 cm
private collection | © The Martin Bloch Trust

Bloch painted a self-portrait (bottom right) with Walter Nessler (centre) and Fred Kormis (bottom left) in the canteen tent of his internment camp. One of the herrings they had come to hate is transforming into objects of desire.

Ervin Bossányi, Theodor Kern, Kurt Lade, Reinhold Nägele, Carlo Pietzner, Albert Reuss, Henry de Roessingh, Julius Rosenbaum, Arthur Segal, Erich and Günter Wagner, Erich Wolfsfeld and Richard Ziegler. Transported to Canada were Theo Balden, René Graetz, Heinz Worner and Paul Feiler (even though he had been to an English boarding school and the Slade School of Art). Sent to Australia were Georg Teltscher and Hein Heckroth.[21]

Internment ended as it became clear that civil liberties must be respected and few internees were Nazis. Releases were haphazard, sometimes absurd: the file of the artist Peter Fleischmann (later Midgley) had been mislaid and as there was no record of his internment it was decided he could not be released.[22] Heartfield was allowed to leave on grounds of ill health. Dachinger was released in January 1941 after a campaign by the Artists' Refugee Committee: he showed 40 of his newspaper drawings at the Redfern Gallery in April, titled 'Art Behind Wire'. The art historian Kurt Hinrichsen, who had also been interned, concluded that despite the frustrations, artists at least had found themselves intellectually at liberty: 'Their artistic impulses and convictions had not been censored or curtailed. In 1940, German and Austrian art, strangled on the Continent, survived and developed in British internment camps.'[23]

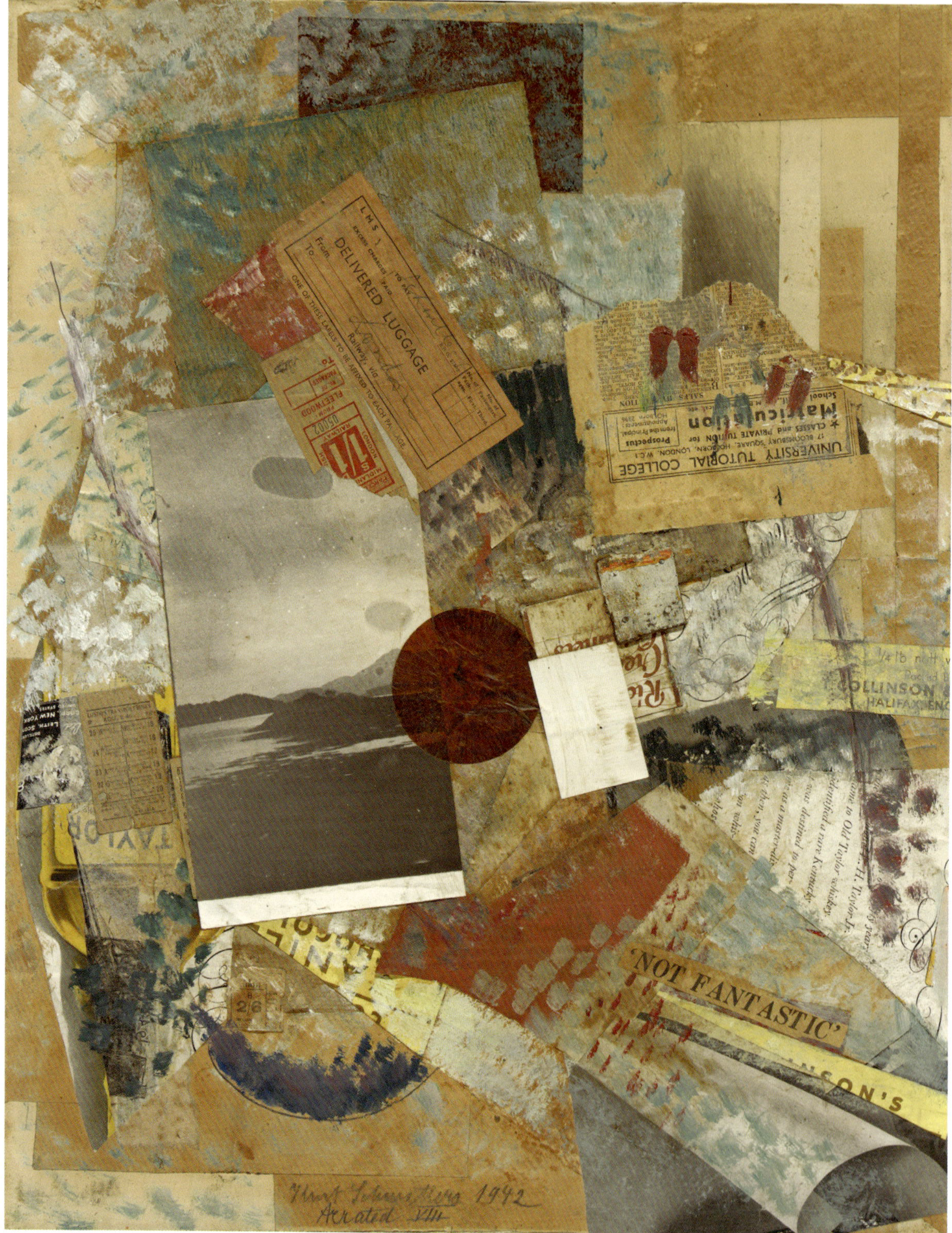

Kurt Schwitters (1897–1948) | *Aerated* VIII
1942 | collage, wood and paint on paper on canvas | 50 x 40 cm
Robert A. Waller Fund (1959.19); Chicago (IL), Art Institute of Chicago
photo: © 2019 The Art Institute of Chicago/Art Resource, NY/Scala, Florence

▶ **Kurt Schwitters** (1897–1948) | *Fred Uhlman*
1940 | oil on canvas | 70 x 45 cm
Hatton Gallery, University of Newcastle upon Tyne
photo: © Tyne & Wear Archives & Museums/Bridgeman Images

Schwitters had been making his innovative, Dadaist 'merz' or
rubbish works since the Great War. He continued them in internment
and afterwards using found materials.

Schwitters was a skilled painter as well as an innovative maker
of 'merz'. He painted stunning portraits of his fellow internees in
1940–1, including artist, writer and refugee supporter Fred Uhlman.

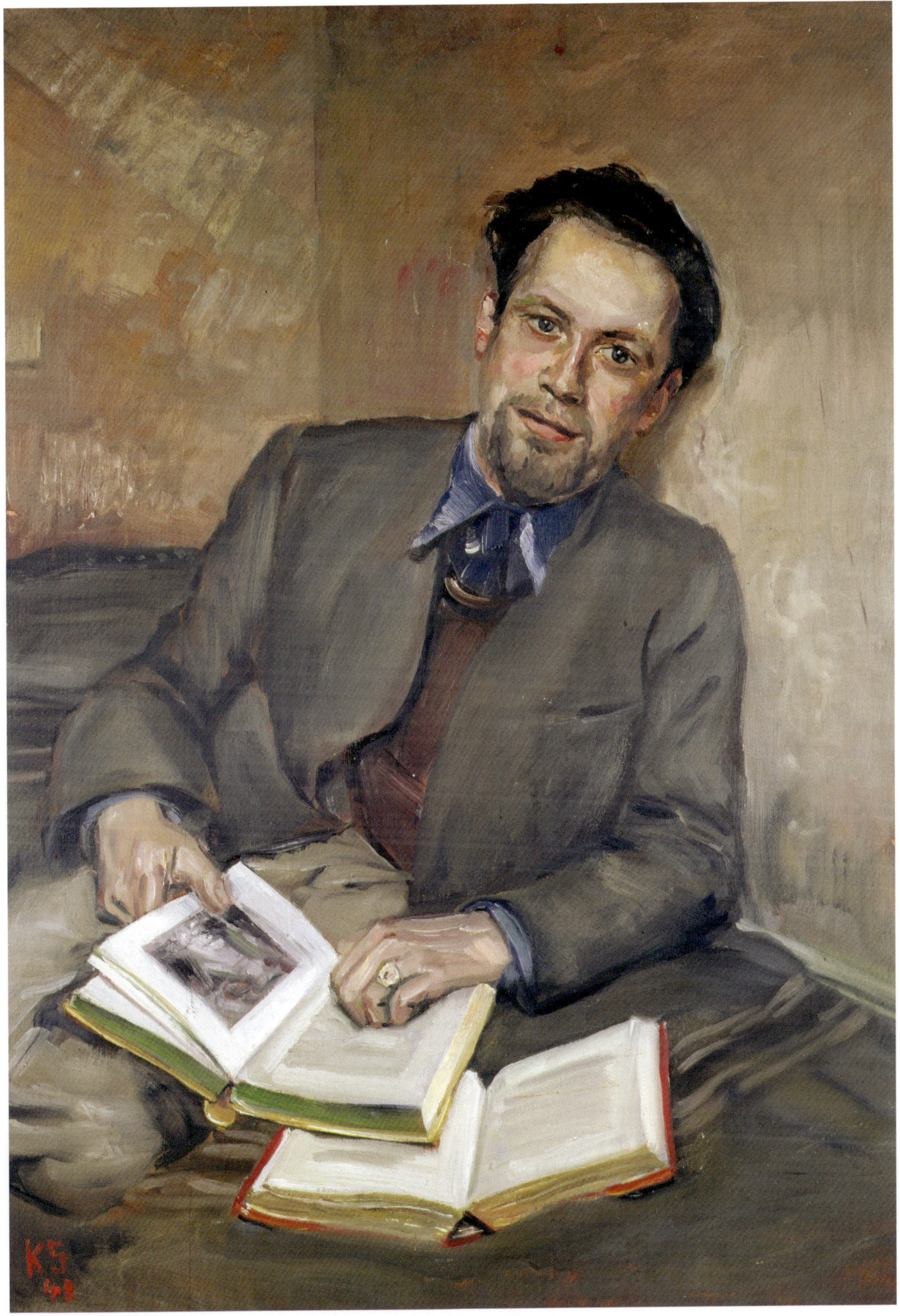

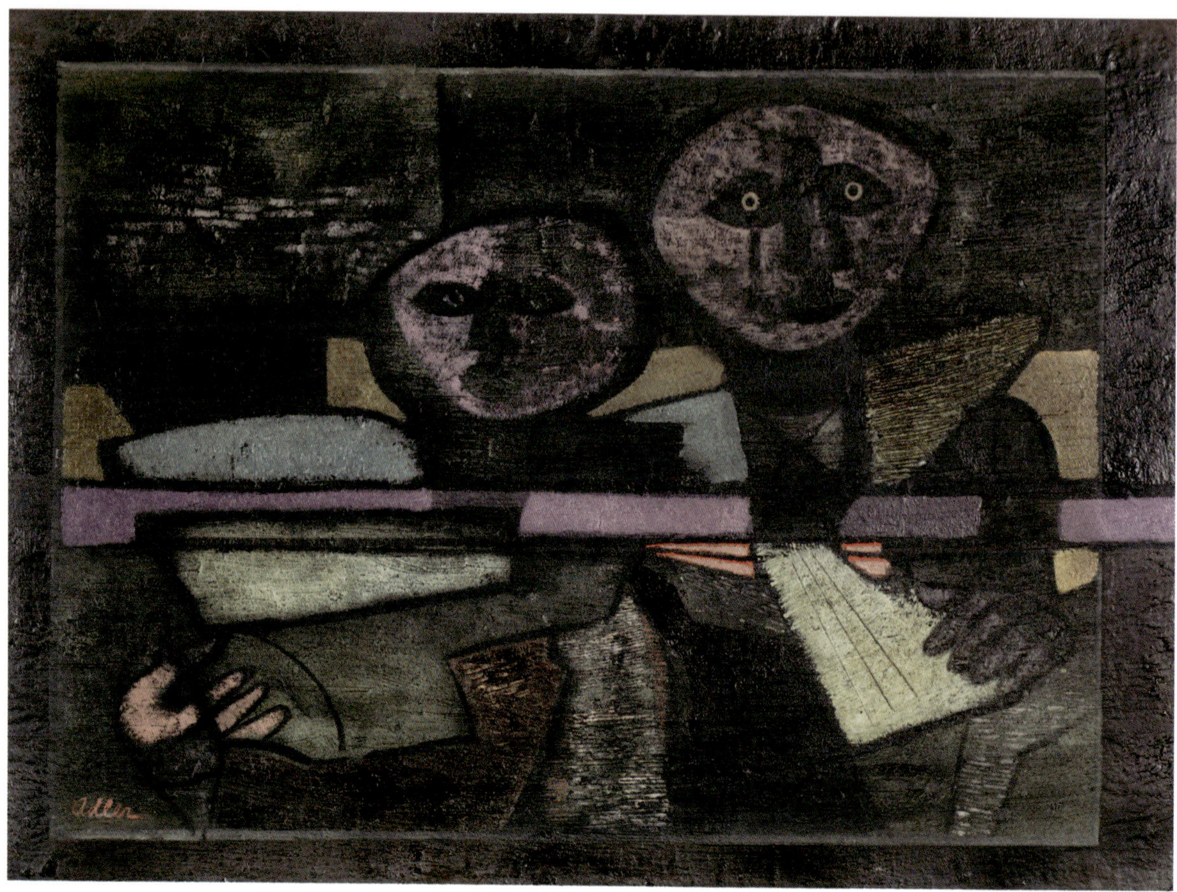

Jankel Adler (1895–1949) | *Orphans*
1941 | oil and gesso on panel | 57 x 79 cm
Tate | © DACS 2019 | photo: © Tate

Adler painted *Two Orphans* in 1942 as a double portrait after he
and Josef Herman had learned from the Red Cross that their families
were dead. The two figures bear heavy packs and wait at a barrier
in the darkness.

The émigré achievement

THE IMPACT OF THE 1930S ARTIST REFUGEES ON British life would unfold over several decades, but first came the war effort. Those from enemy states were precluded from sensitive duties such as working on camouflage or as Official War Artists but there were many jobs to be done. Lucie Rie was a fire watcher and worked in an optical instrument factory.[1] Henrion produced exhibitions for the British and American governments and Wolfgang Suschitzky made public information films. Ludwig Meidner was a mortuary caretaker and sketched corpses after air raids to assist identification.[2] German-speaking artists could be valuable: Elizabeth Friendländer forged German papers and document stamps and contributed to black propaganda while Richard Ziegler, who had exhibited with Dix and Grosz before coming to Britain in 1937, published excoriating caricatures of the Nazis in his book *We Make History* under the pseudonym Robert Ziller.[3] Josef Flatter merged artistry and close-up experience of Nazism in cartoons air-dropped over Germany:

> *The moving force was hatred, it took concrete shape before my eyes. And my hatred of those responsible for the wanton cruelty done to so many innocent victims was boundless. I went about in the shape of my adversaries. I crept into their skin.*[4]

Some artist refugees saw action. Several Polish artists were in the military in exile and Franta Belsky joined the Czech army. When German and Austrian nationals were permitted in the Pioneer Corps, several artists joined up: Walter Nessler served at D-Day and Willy Tirr trained commandos and took on bomb disposal. Tirr later transferred to the Intelligence Corps and the denazification programme and the surrealist René Halkett conducted denazification at the prisoner of war camp for German officers at Bridgend and translated at the Nuremberg trials.[5] Georg Adams-Teltscher drew maps for the army, free to play his part at last.

In art, the influence of the émigrés was all the greater for pre-war British insularity. Although a few young artists might have studied in Paris, in general appreciation of current European art was limited by the costs and difficulties of travel, the absence of international art in exhibitions and the lack of colour publications. The émigrés filled a void, connecting British art to traditions and innovations from a wider sphere. Many of them were richly cosmopolitan. Marie-Louise von Motesiczky had studied art in Vienna, the Hague, Paris and Berlin and at Max Beckmann's masterclasses in Frankfurt. Before he arrived in London in 1937, Heinz Henghes had grown up in Hamburg, run off to America at 17, met Brancusi in Paris and spent time in Italy. Willi Rondas from Brussels had qualified in architecture in Paris, practised in the Belgian Congo and studied painting with Dufy and Berard. Some personal histories were breathlessly international: the French-born sculptor Michael Werner grew up in Austria, attended university in Berlin (where he organised an anti-Nazi youth movement), continued his degree at Oxford, left to study with the surrealists in Paris and returned to England in 1938.[6] It was a worldliness reflected in the personalities of many refugees. As Daniel Snowman wrote:

> *Virtually all were precisely the kind of people who would have got into severe trouble with the Nazis had they stayed: expressive, questing personalities, independent-minded, inclined to dissent, interested in alternative arguments – the kind of people who have always found it difficult to flourish in an authoritarian or strictly hierarchical environment.*[7]

As the war drew to an end the émigrés began to ask how they would forge their futures. Many found it hard to refocus creatively. After mind-numbing work in a lampshade factory and making bundles of kindling, when Pamina Liebert-Mahrenholz finally returned to painting it was with diminished output.[8] Edith Tudor Hart, now known to MI5 as a handler of KGB spies, took a job as a housekeeper and destroyed her photographic catalogue. The traumas of oppression, flight and loss caught up with many. The cartoonist 'Vicky', Victor Weisz, who had produced anti-Nazi cartoons so courageously in Berlin, committed suicide in 1966. The sculptor Jussuff Abbu, once flamboyant and charismatic but classed as 'degenerate', saw his health break down in post-war London.[9]

Some artists tackled the inhumanity through their work. Ludwig Meidner began a series titled 'Suffering of the Jews in Poland' and said: 'I am compelled evermore, perpetually to think about the destiny of my brothers.'[10] Georg Mayer-Marton painted an image of desolate hardship after learning that his parents had been among 5,000 Jews from Győr deported to Auschwitz. Josef Herman described how Jankel Adler brought him a painting as a gift: 'There were two orphans in the picture; after a while I realised that one was me and the other was himself'.[11] Having distanced his art from politics, Kokoschka felt compelled to address events in an

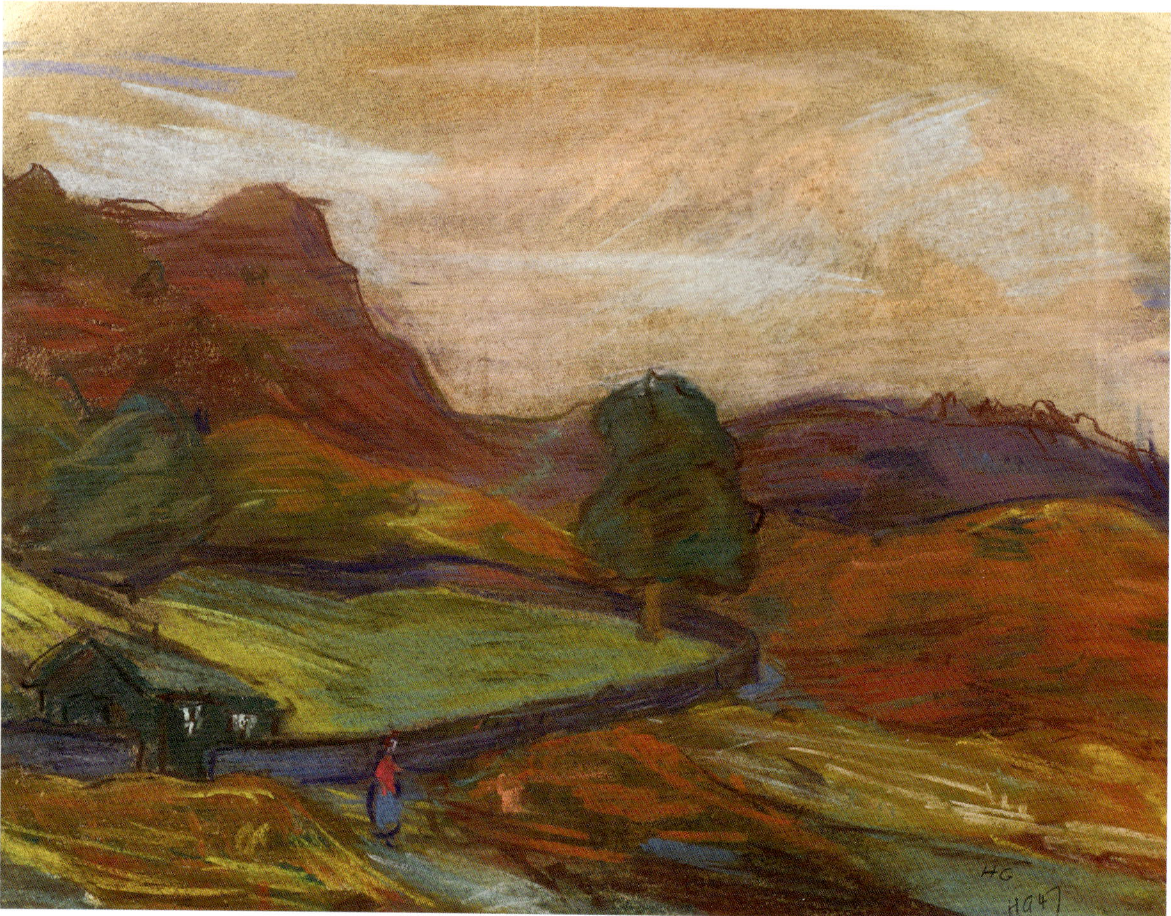

Hilde Goldschmidt (1897–1980) | *Cottage in the Valley*
1947 | pastel on paper | 35 x 50 cm
Ben Uri Collection | © Artist's Estate

From 1942 to 1950 Hilde Goldschmidt retreated to a wood in Cumbria
where she painted in a hut with Kurt Schwitters as a neighbour. She
had come to London in 1939 from a cosmopolitan life as a student
of Kokoschka and visitor to Paris and New York.

allegorical style that absorbed the British tradition
by referencing Hogarth's satirical narratives.[12]

A host of cosmopolitan exiles went back to
newly liberated France, Czechoslovakia, Poland
or Scandinavia. However, there was no question
of the kind of repatriation programme seen after the
Great War. The dilemma for those from German-
speaking nations was that each city square, each
institution, would remind them of the poison it had
brimmed with in the last 12 years.[13] As a result, most
wished to assimilate into Britain, especially if they
were Jewish. The most frequent exceptions were
the communist enemies of Hitler, who thought
of themselves as temporary exiles and preserved
their German culture ready to return. Theo Balden
(born Otto Koehler), who had been arrested for
communist activity in 1934, went to the German
Democratic Republic. John Heartfield was refused

asylum in Britain and entry to West Germany as
an outspoken communist so also went east.[14] A
few Jewish artists returned in search of German
culture: Hilde Goldschmidt went back to Austria
and Ludwig Meidner quit his years of poverty in
Britain for better recognition in West Germany,
though his wife Else stayed.

Those for whom any sense of belonging in one
place was shattered might look for opportunities
in America or seek a more reflective life elsewhere.
Moholy-Nagy and Mondrian had gone west before
the war and now the expressionist stage designer
Samson Schames left for New York, the surrealist
photographer Grete Stern for Argentina. The sculptor Anna Mahler, who had been awarded the *grand
prix* in the 1937 World Exhibition in Paris, went
restlessly to California at the end of the war, to
London in 1964, to Italy, then back to London.

Ernst Schwitters returned to Norway, his first place of refuge when he was 17; Henry de Buys Roessingh went on to Portugal. Some made peace with their homelands only in their final years, including Kokoschka, who had gained a British passport and refused the Austrian government's attempts to woo him back until 1978. Peter Potworowski went home to Poland in 1958 and died four years later. Richard Ziegler and Frederick Könekamp both returned to Germany shortly before they died. The Austrian sculptor Mary Durasova-Kopova (Duras) settled in Prague but became a refugee again in 1968 and went back finally to Austria.

Yet notwithstanding the churn of post-war movement, huge numbers stayed. Many of them shared characteristics complementary to those in Britain: willingness to cross traditional cultural frontiers, communicativeness, ideological agnosticism, tough professionalism in contrast with the British love of amateurism and the embrace of feeling, not understatement and 'good taste'.[15] They had increasing influence in the coming years and brought, in the words of Margaret Garlake:

deeply held beliefs in the social role of art,
the nature of artistic practice and the balance

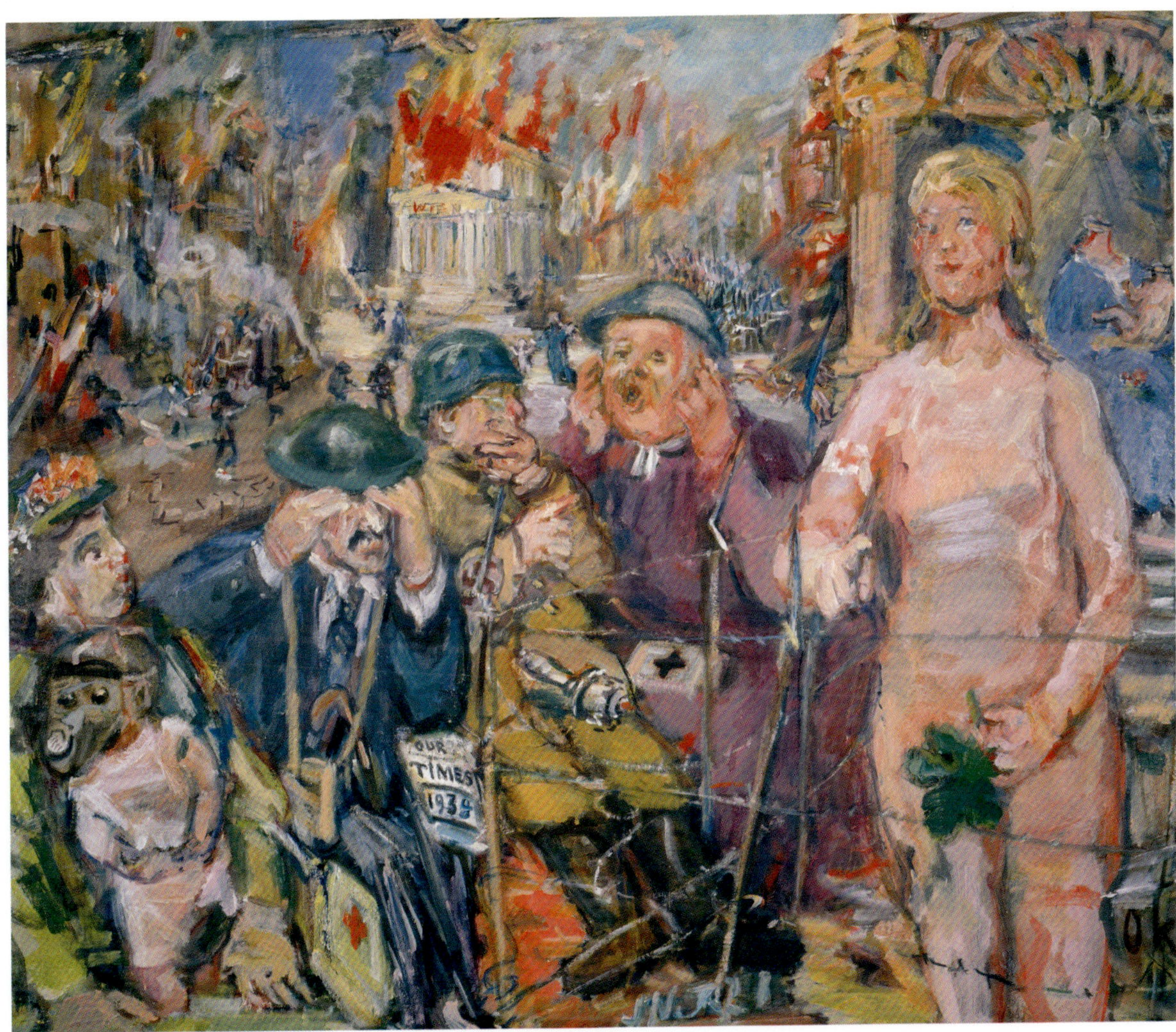

Oskar Kokoschka (1886–1980) | *Anschluss – Alice in Wonderland*
1942 | oil on canvas | 63 x 74 cm
Wien Museum on loan from VIG | © Fondation Oskar Kokoschka/DACS 2019

Austria personified as the naked truth is behind barbed wire with a headless Madonna and child. On the other side are three figures: stateman, soldier and priest, who see, speak and hear nothing of the evils on the crowded square or Vienna town hall aflame. Kokoschka donated the proceeds from the painting to educate Austrian children in Britain.

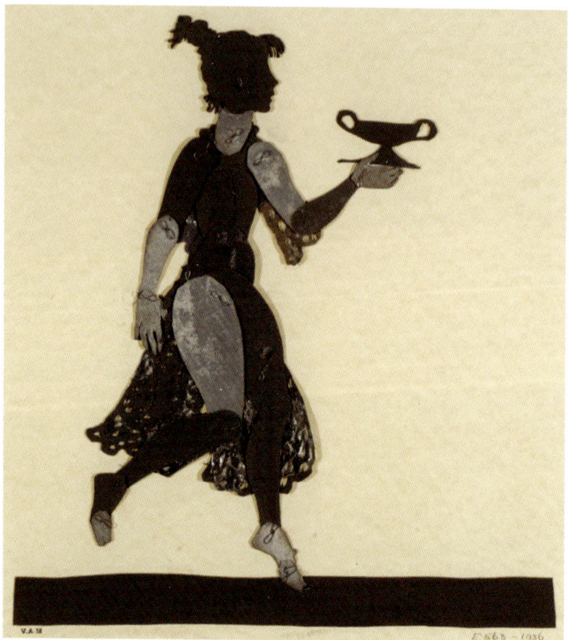

Lotte Reiniger (1899–1981) | *Pygmalion's Servant*
1935 | card, lead sheet and wire | 27 x 24 cm
Victoria and Albert Museum, London; given by Miss Lotte Reiniger
© DACS 2019 | photo: V&A

This articulated silhouette was for a central character in the short
animated film *Galathea*. The photograph shows the back of the
card figure with the flat pieces of lead used to keep it in place.
The subtlety of movement Reiniger achieved with such figures
is breathtaking even now.

*between tradition and modernity that were
either ahead of thinking in this country or
sufficiently distinctive to act as models
for change.*[16]

Many of the contributions were individual, artist-
by-artist additions to the visual culture of the
nation. Lucie Rie established herself as one of the
finest studio potters in post-war Britain. Among
her protégés was the teenage migrant Hans Coper.
The sculptors Benno Elkan and Fred Kormis completed vast numbers of portrait busts, medals and
public sculptures. Hans Feibusch revivified the
mural movement, training assistants and completing schemes in public buildings across the nation.
He was among the artists who contributed to the
Festival of Britain in 1951, which became a public
showcase for refugee artists, among them Josef
Herman, Siegfried Charoux, who made a relief
of a family looking into the future across the
Thames and Peter László Peri, who produced a
concrete wall-sculpture, *Sunbathers*.[17] The *Jewish
Chronicle* noted:

*It has long been England's policy to give
asylum to refugees, and its hospitality has*

*enabled them to make their contribution to
the stream of British culture. A glance through
the lists of architects and designers shows how
many refugees have been employed at the South
Bank. Each has doubtless added something
of his own to a trend of design that is having
a great influence on future work in England.*[18]

Artistic influence came about through presence
and contact as much as public visibility. Individual
artists could be powerful influences on those who
got to know them. A few cases stand for a multitude. Josef Herman combined personal charisma
with a direct connection to the Belgian expressionists. The first British artist influenced by him was
Joan Eardley, whose expressive paintings of wild
coastal landscapes and children in the Glasgow
tenements echo his bold style and his commitment
to working life and working people. They met
as soon as Herman arrived in Glasgow in 1940,
when Eardley started as a student at the school
of art. They saw one another frequently for three
years. Christopher Andreae argues: 'Even though
Herman left Glasgow in 1943, his encouragement
of Joan and example to her has probably not been
emphasised enough.'[19]

Herman moved to the South Wales mining
village of Ystradgynlais in 1944, where Will
Roberts became an informal pupil, acknowledging later that Herman encouraged him to take up
painting seriously. His glowing landscapes of farms
and tinplate works while expressive of a different
personality owed much to Herman's technique and
vision.[20] The Welsh Committee of the Arts Council
organised a touring exhibition for Herman in 1948
and when its curator, David Bell, wrote the first
survey of Welsh art history shortly afterwards he
emphasised how Herman had made audiences
look seriously at miners and their communities:

*He has made of the South Wales scene
something which has never been made before.
He has, in fact, recreated it in a European
idiom and in a language which has a wider
significance than the locality itself.*[21]

Two outstanding British painters of the mid-
twentieth century, Robert Colquhoun and Robert
MacBryde, were linked to European modernism by
Jankel Adler: in Düsseldorf Adler had known Otto

Fred Kormis (1897–1986) | *Girl Looking Up*
1966 | fibreglass | 108 x 52 x 74 cm
RWA (Royal West of England Academy) | © Artist's Estate

Fred (originally Fritz) Kormis fled Germany when he was banned
from working in 1933. He made emotive public sculptures including
a monument to prisoners of war, in Gladstone Park, London.

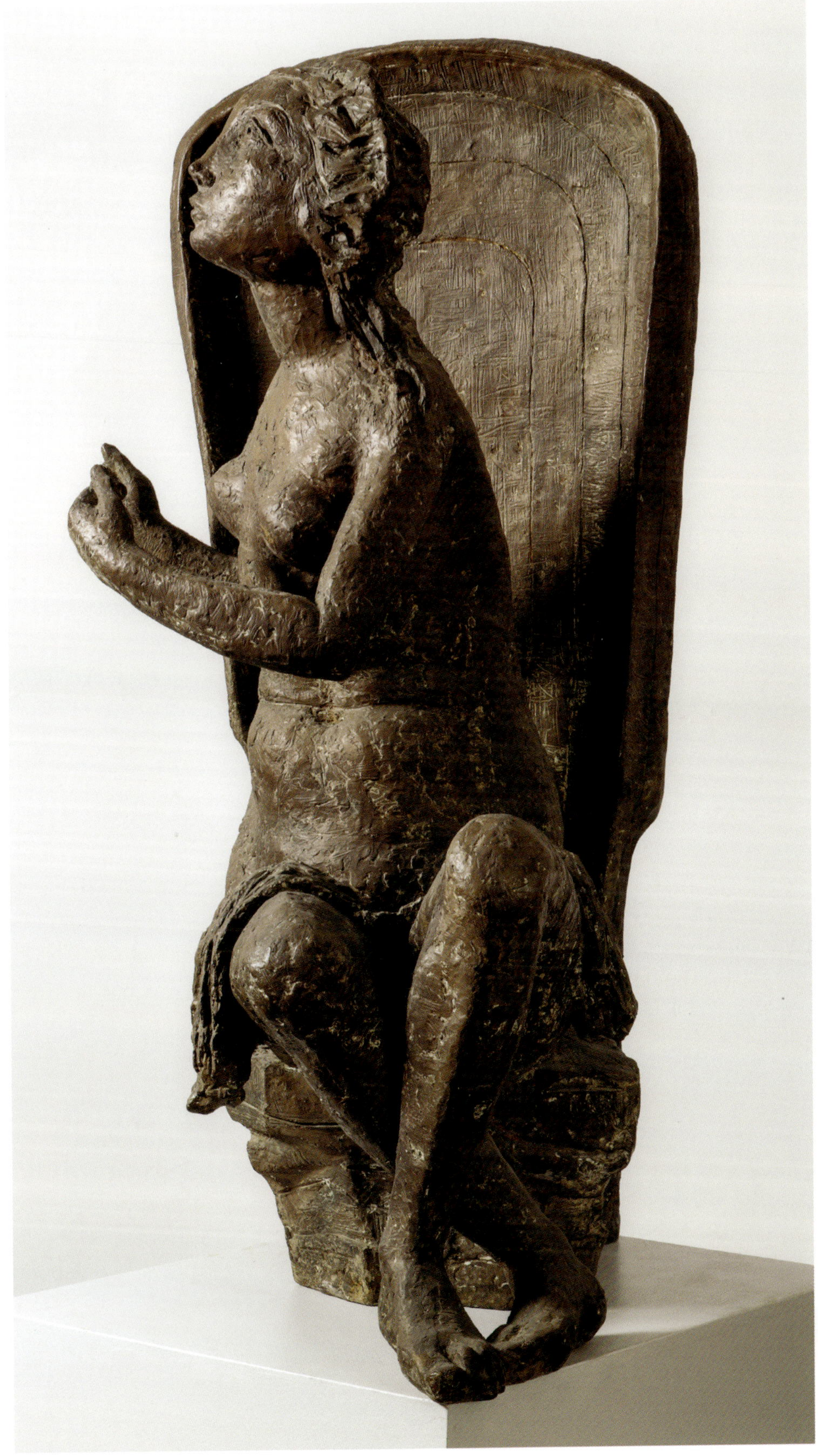

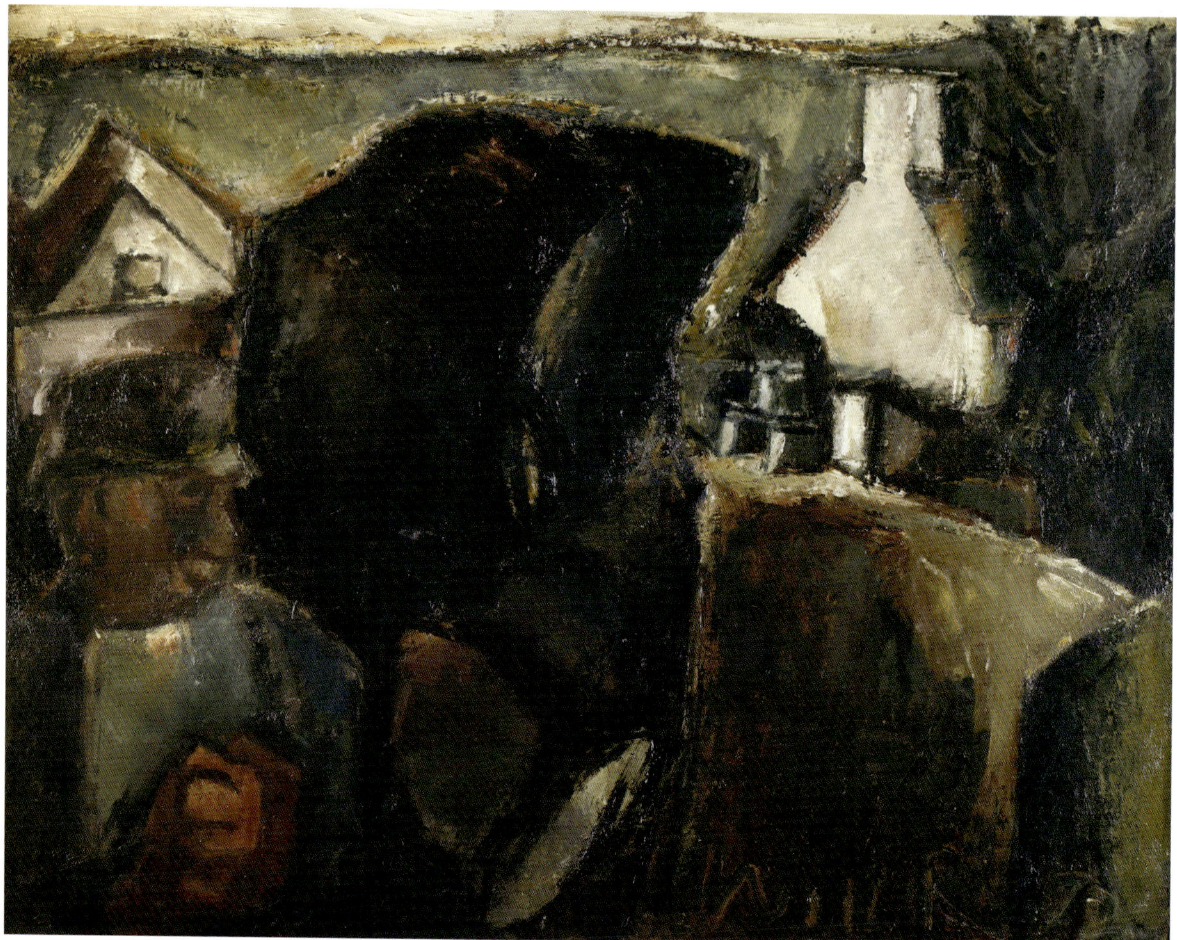

Will Roberts (1907–2000) | *Tyn-y-waun, Cimla*
1972 | oil on board | 73 x 95 cm
National Library of Wales, Aberystwyth | © Artist's Estate

Roberts painted the farms and industry around the Neath Valley where he lived, not far from his initial mentor Josef Herman in the Swansea Valley.

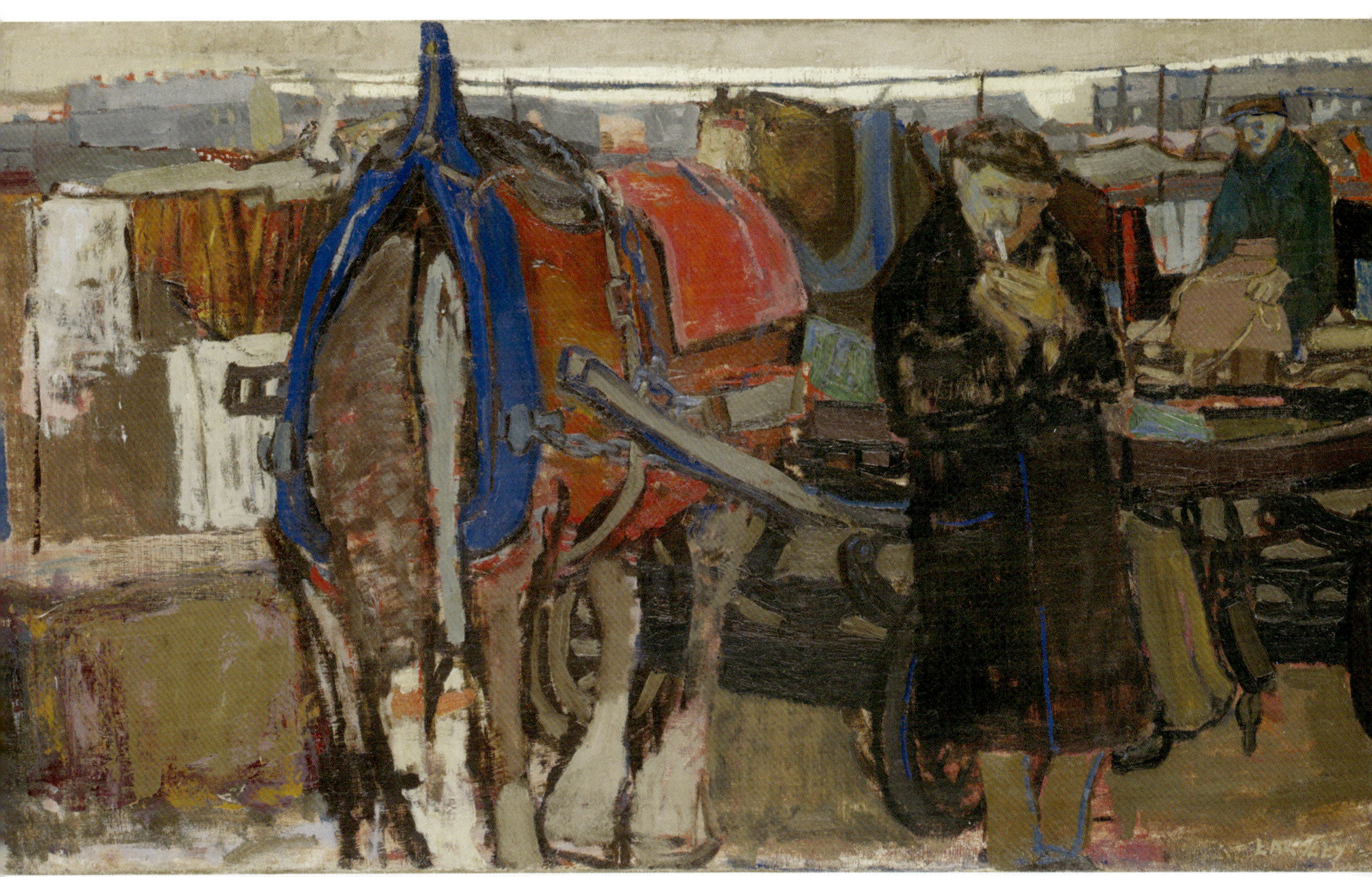

Joan Eardley (1921–1963) | *A Carter and His Horse*
*c.*1950 | oil on canvas | 70 x 119 cm
Government Art Collection | © Estate of Joan Eardley/all rights reserved DACS 2019
photo: © Crown copyright: UK Government Art Collection

Eardley's rich colour and interest in working people chimed with
Josef Herman's.

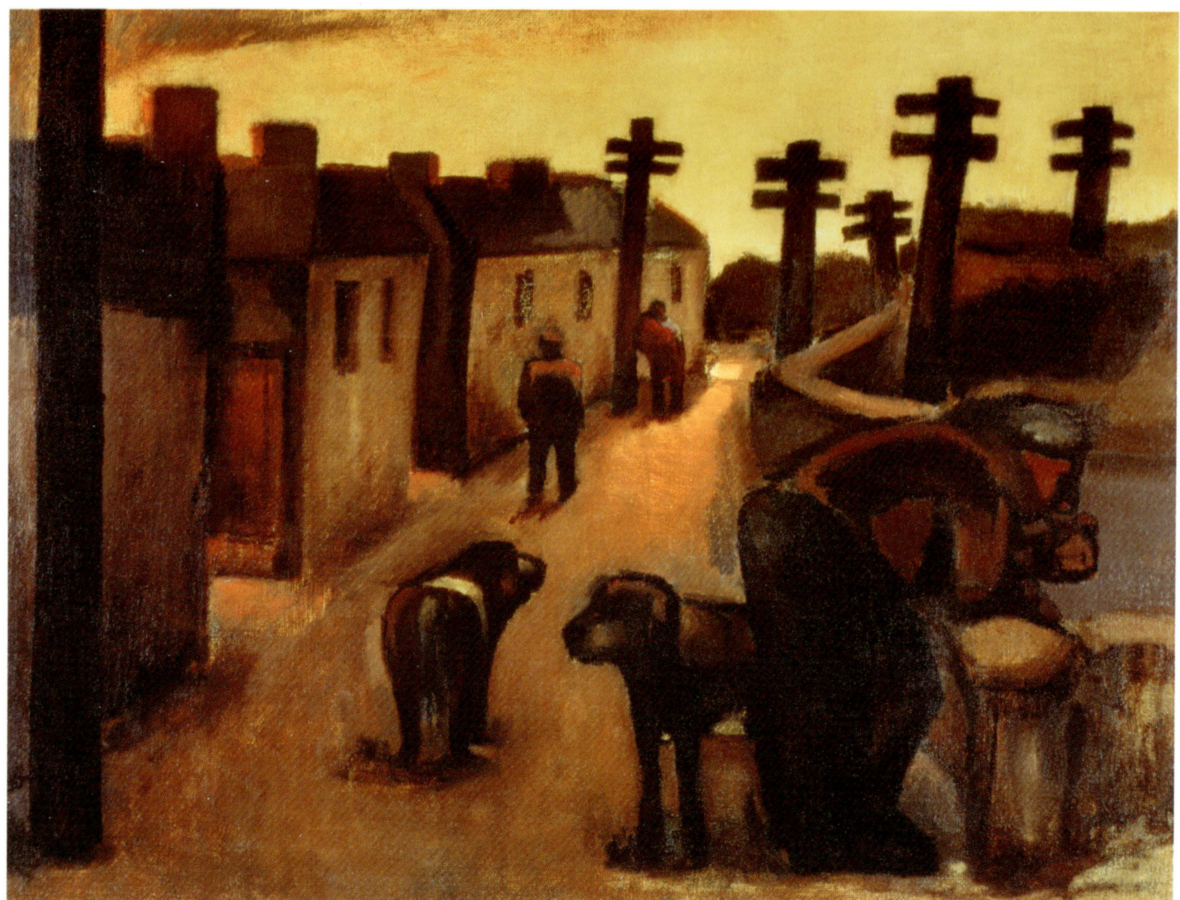

Josef Herman (1911–2000) | *Evenfall, Ystradgynlais*
1948 | oil on canvas | 76 x 101 cm
New Walk Museum and Art Gallery, Leicester | © Artist's Estate/all rights reserved
DACS 2019 | reproduced courtesy of Leicester Arts & Museums Service
photo: © Leicester Arts & Museums/Bridgeman Images

Josef Herman was deeply moved by the enfolding hills and strong
community of Ystradgynlais in 1944 and remained there for 12 years.
He recalled it in paintings for the rest of his life.

Dix and shared a studio with Paul Klee and in
Paris he knew Hayter and Picasso. Colquhoun and
MacBryde met Adler first in Glasgow when he was
evacuated there in the Polish army, then in 1943
they took a house together in London. Both of them
referred to Adler as 'the Master'. Their painting
almost immediately took on characteristics shared
with his in the choice of figure subjects, expressive
use of colour and flattening of forms, transforming
from a neo-romantic idiom to 'a richer eclecticism,
a less parochial style, and more humanistic subject
matter.'[22]

Heinz Koppel had a personal impact even when
his work confounded wider audiences. His widow,
Pip, said: 'I think the European element confused
them, which was too strange, too strong at that
time'.[23] A *Times* review of his exhibition at the
Beaux Arts Gallery was headlined 'Mr. Heinz

Koppel, a Painter with Too Many Ideas'.[24] He
spent 12 years from 1944 living and working
at a workers' educational settlement in Merthyr
Tydfil as a resident artist, appointed on Cedric
Morris's recommendation after his studio in
London was bombed out. Students from Cardiff
School of Art heard about Koppel and were
mesmerised when they came to find him. The
path of one of them, Ernest Zobole shifted from
a Bonnard-inspired post-Impressionism to an
expressionism of fractured, multiple perspectives.
The mature painter Esther Grainger was equally
captivated. Several local youngsters from his classes
went on to be professional artists or art teachers.
The painter John Uzzell Edwards recalled visiting
aged 14: 'My father took me up to Dowlais and
we walked in and I just saw this room full of
people working, and the most amazing paintings.

I knew straight away it was the real thing.'[25]

Perhaps a negative case study should be considered too, in which expected influence never reached fruition. Oskar Kokoschka was internationally renowned as Austria's greatest living painter but perhaps because his teaching was overseas, no direct impact was specially apparent.[26] He committed himself to British citizenship and yet he was awarded a CBE rather than the knighthood some expected; he had retrospectives in Switzerland and New York but no exhibition at the Tate until 1962; and his work was bought for British public collections only after his death in 1980. It is an indication that interest in figurative, expressive painting was muted, especially once abstraction, Pop and conceptual art began to dominate.

Teaching did allow other émigrés to have influence. In the United States, institutions were built around émigré professors, for example Moholy-Nagy at Chicago's institute of design, Josef and Ani Albers at Black Mountain College and some 75 émigrés at the School for Social Research in New York.[27] They were more dispersed in Britain: George Him at Leicester, Mayer-Marton and Koppel at Liverpool, Willy Tirr at Leeds and Heinz Henghes at Winchester. Peter Potworowski energised staff and students at Bath Academy of Art as a senior artist who had studied in Poland and with Fernand Léger in Paris. Kenneth Armitage wrote: 'He came from an outside world, from a longer timespan; he brought a foreign flavour and his values and approach were different'.[28] The émigré teachers were especially concentrated in London: for example Hermann and Erna Nonnenmacher at Morley College, Susan Einzig at Camberwell and Chelsea, Kalman Kemeny at Hammersmith, Henrion at the Royal College, Klaus Meyer as

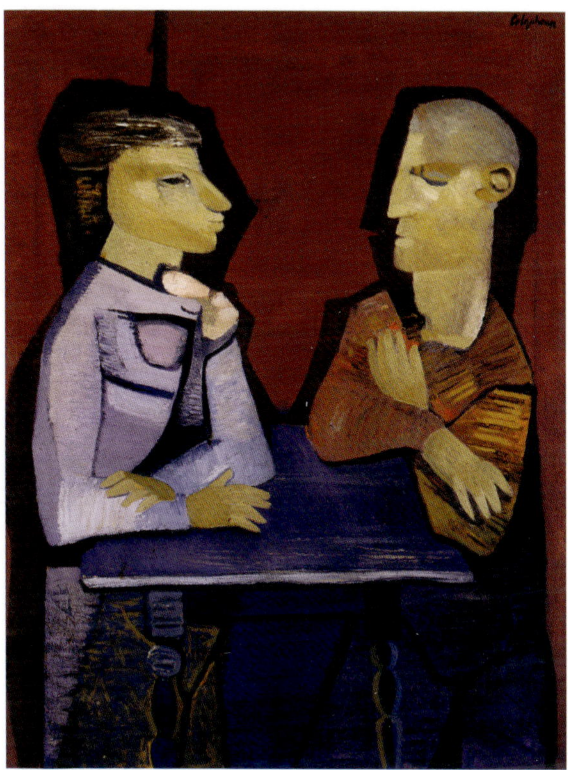

Robert Colquhoun (1914–1962) | *The Students*
1947 | oil on canvas | 77 x 61 cm
British Council Collection | © Artist's Estate/Bridgeman Images
photo: © British Council

This double portrait by Colquhoun of himself with his partner Robert MacBryde shows strongly the influence of Jankel Adler.

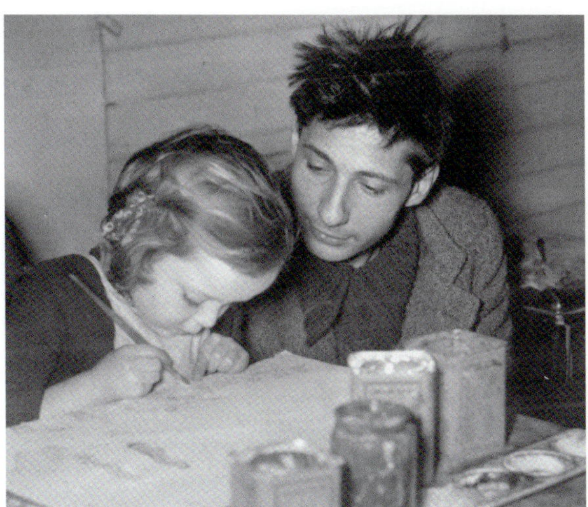

Heinz Koppel was 25 when he began teaching both adults and children in the workers' educational settlement at Merthyr Tydfil.

head of art at Kilburn, Helmuth Weissenborn at Beckenham and Ravensbourne. George Adams (previously Georg Adams-Teltscher) brought progressive Bauhaus design to the London College of Printing.[29] Willi Soukop taught at Guildford and at Chelsea then ended his career as Master of Sculpture at the Royal Academy Schools. He was an important mentor for his Guildford student Elisabeth Frink, fighting for her to have a place at Chelsea against the judgement of the principal.[30]

Perhaps because it was difficult to obtain posts or because they valued freedom, artists also taught independently. Having run an art school with Karl Schmidt-Rotluff in Berlin, Martin Bloch set up the School of Contemporary Painting in London from 1936–9 with Roy de Maistre before taking a post at Camberwell after the war, where Gillian Ayres was among his students. In north London Paul Hamann and Hugo Dachinger put on life classes and Elsa Fraenkel taught art. Arthur Segal ran his 'Painting School for Professionals and Non-Professionals' for forty years with a focus on art as therapy. Frederick Könekamp built a group of artists around himself at Cotllwyd in West Wales.

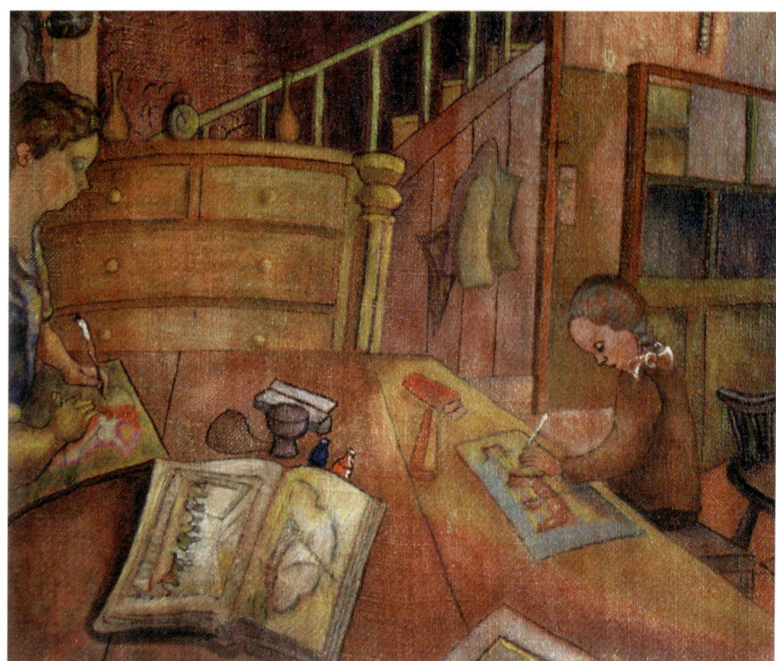

Frederick Cooper (1901–1955) | *Untitled* | oil on canvas | 30 x 40 cm
private collection | © John F. Cooper

'Mr Cooper', an unemployed miner, was a student at Heinz Koppel's painting classes in the workers' settlement. His son John F. Cooper also attended and became an artist and teacher. This picture shows two companions painting across the table.

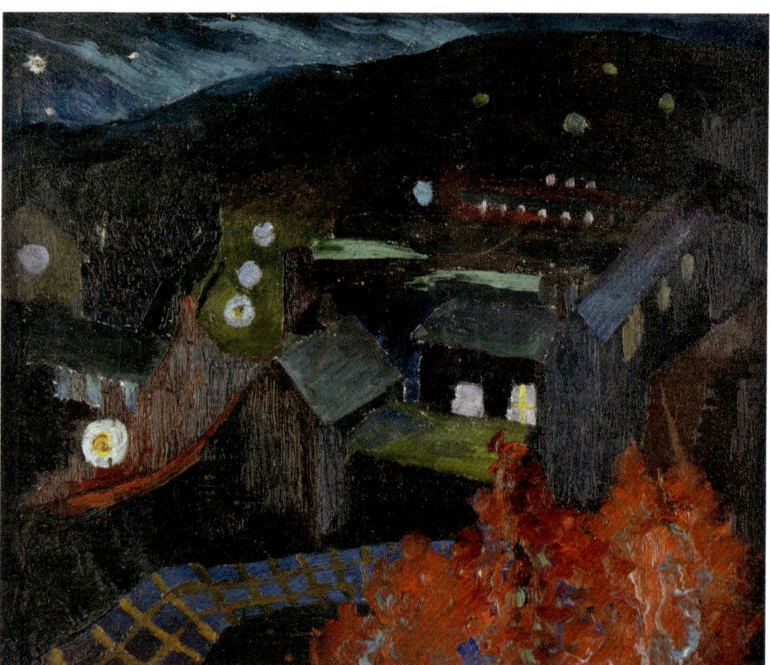

Esther Grainger (1912–1990) | *Pontypridd at Night*
1953 | oil on board | 38 x 50 cm
National Library of Wales, Aberystwyth | © Artist's Estate

This painting was a response by Grainger to Heinz Koppel's vision. She said that his painting 'is neither in the French tradition nor the English tradition, but stems from German expressionism, which even now the English find difficult. But the pictures are wonderful.'

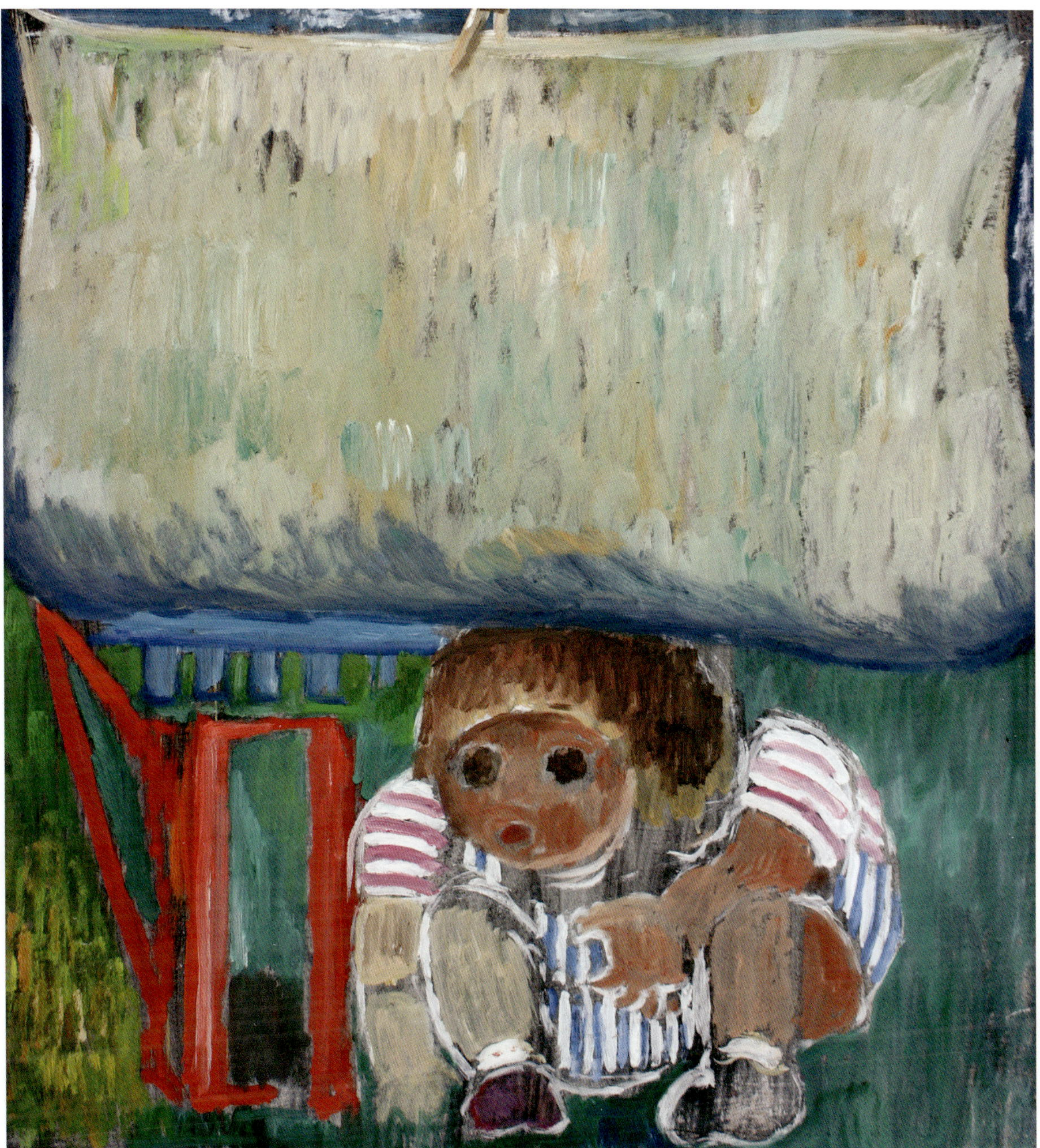

Heinz Koppel (1919–1980) | *In the Backyard (Ruth)*
1955/6 | oil on hardboard | 78 x 71 cm
private collection | © Artist's Estate

Koppel would often challenge artists to consider 'how would a child
see it' and he was fascinated by the world of children as a subject.
His daughter Ruth is looking out from under billowing laundry.

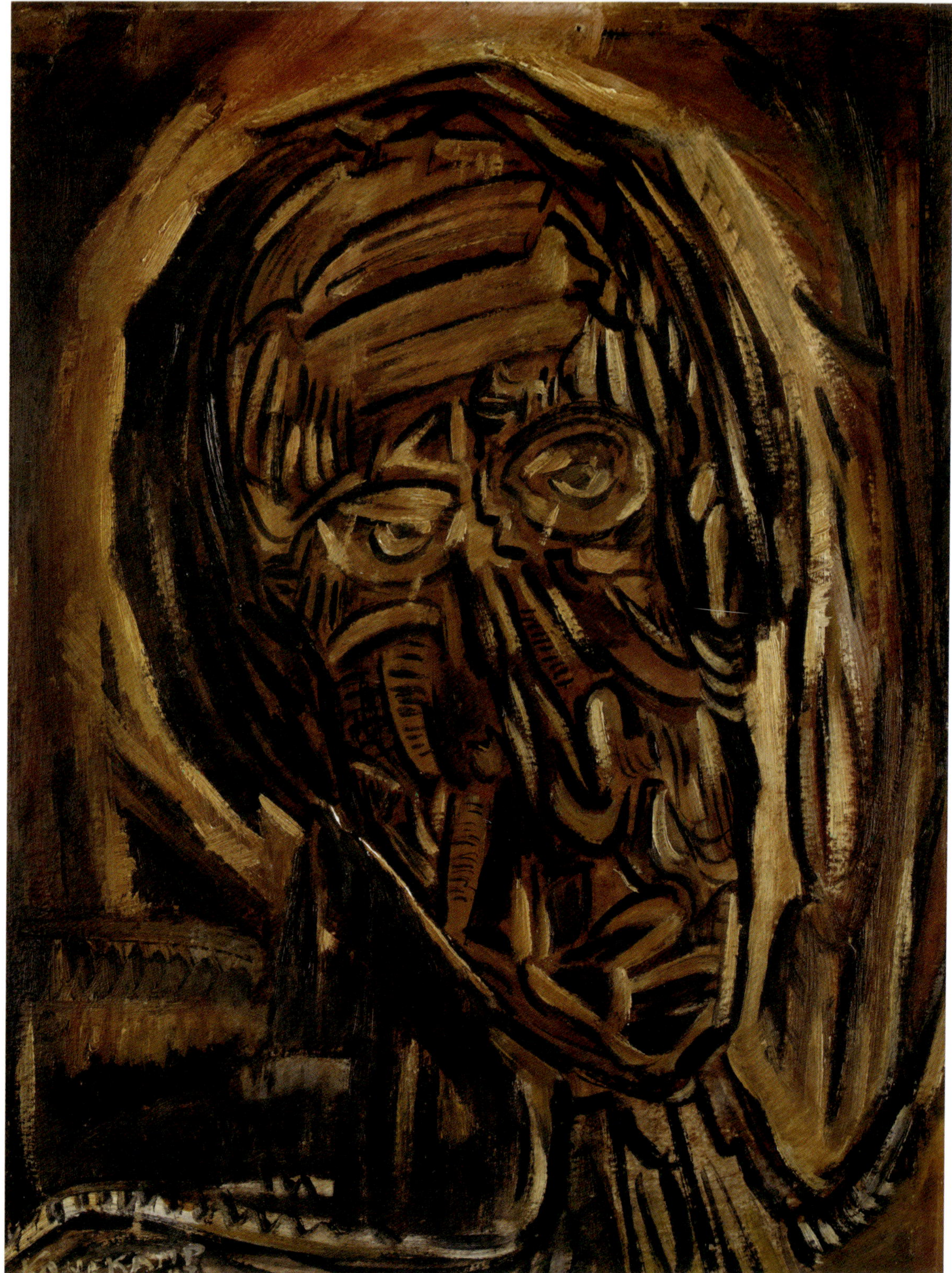

Frederick Könekamp (1897–1977) | *David James Jones (Gwenallt)*
*c.*1945 | oil on board | 40 x 37 cm
National Library of Wales, Aberystwyth | © Artist's Estate

Könekamp's was the kind of German expressionist art that British audiences found challenging. He was under threat as a socialist in Germany and came to Britain in 1935.

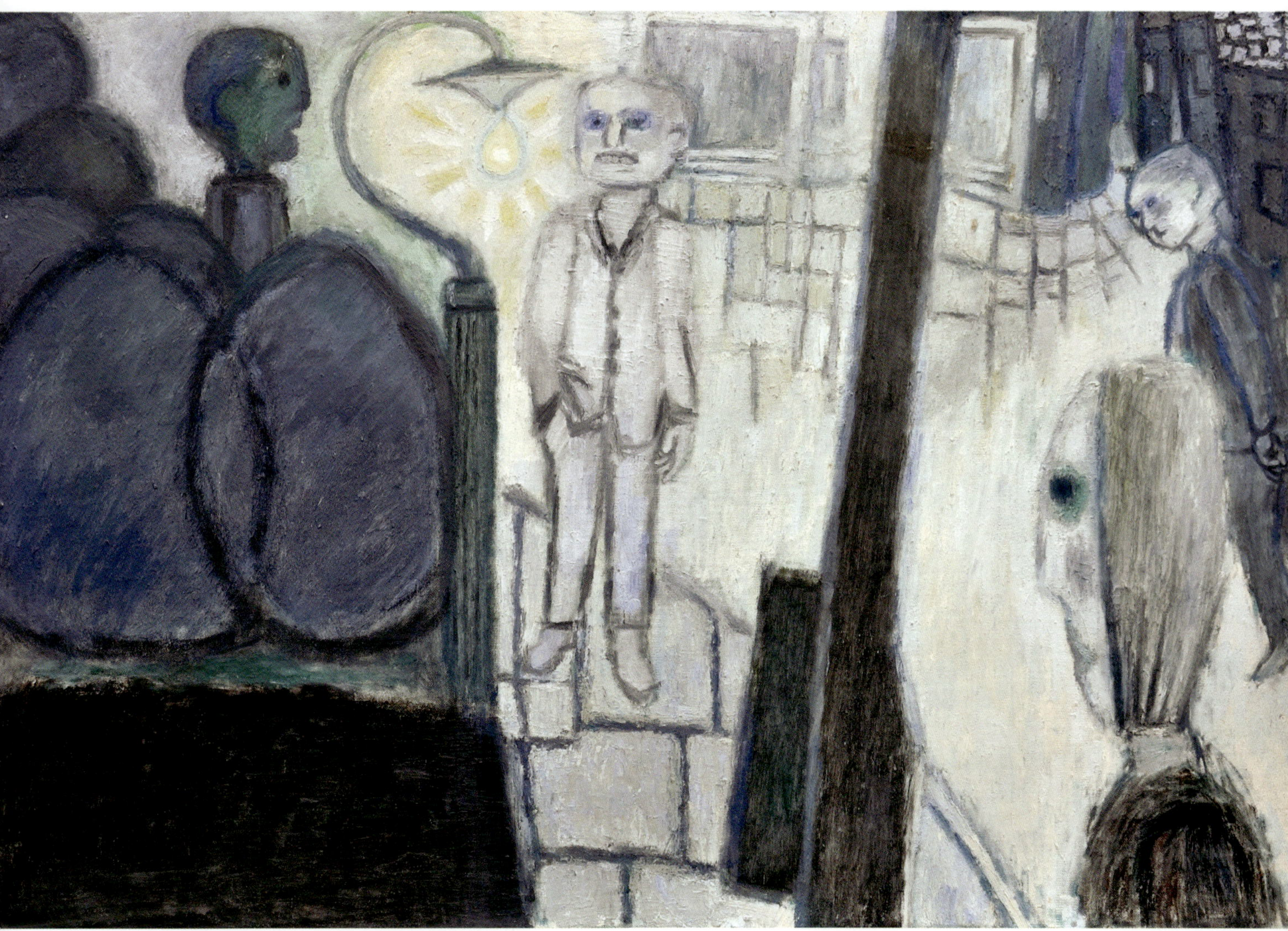

Ernest Zobole (1927–1999) | *Untitled*
*c.*1960 | oil on canvas | 80 x 122 cm
private collection | © Artist's Estate

Zobole was one of the most distinctive artists in Wales from the 1960s
to the 1990s, capturing a unique vision of his home in the Rhondda
Valley that gained much from Koppel.

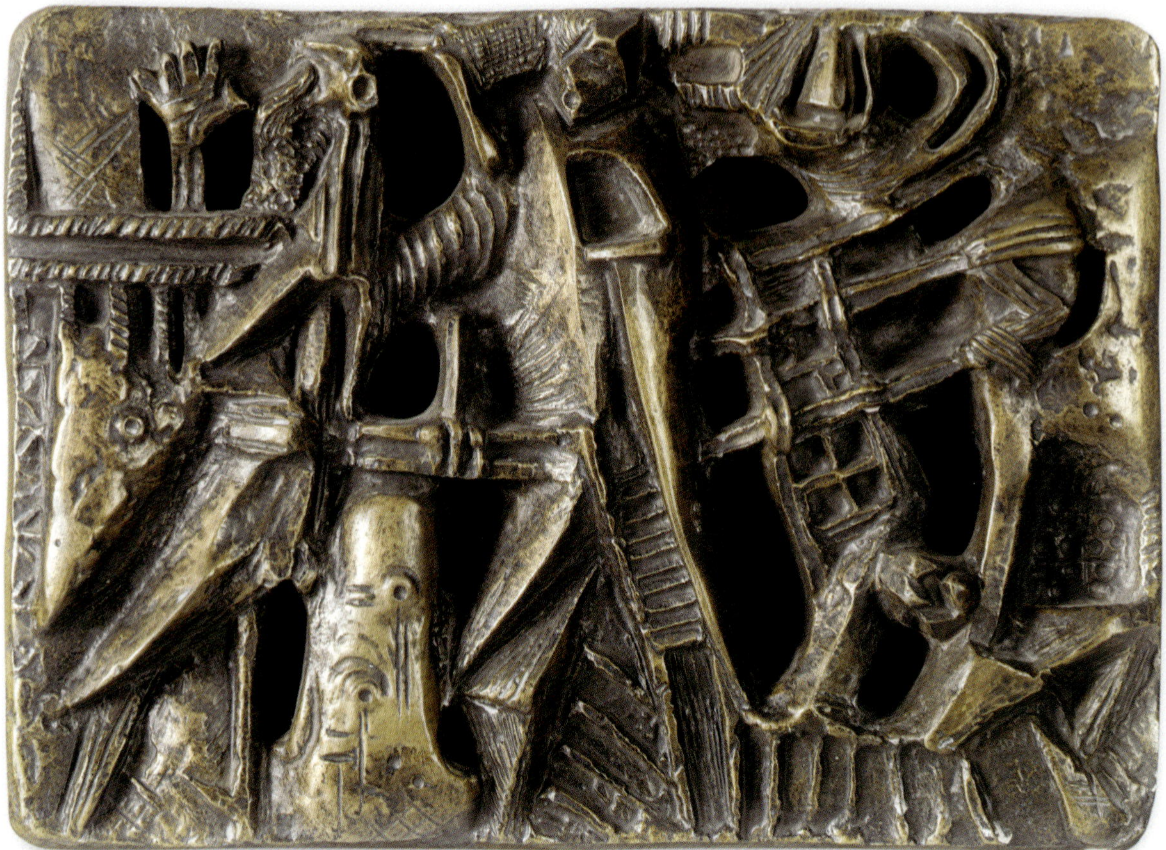

Willi Soukop (1907–1995) | *Struggle*
1983 | bronze on wood | 22 x 28 x 8 cm
RWA (Royal West of England Academy) | © Artist's Estate

Soukop taught at Dartington and other schools as well as London art
colleges from 1935. The distorted and dynamic figuration of this piece
can be related to the work of his student Elisabeth Frink.

Was there any lasting impact of the émigrés
on British art? Some substantial changes in British
practice can be identified – the impact on architecture, on art history and on British art publishing,
for example through the establishment of Phaidon
and Thames and Hudson. The commercial galleries
of London were transformed by names such as
Annely Juda, Gustav Delbanco and Andras Kalman.
Art history and conservation were also radically
professionalised.[31] In the production of art itself,
Naum Gabo's decade in Britain was critical. It was
influential first in Hampstead (alongside the briefer
presence of Moholy-Nagy and Mondrian) and then
in St Ives. For the duration of the war Gabo moved
to Cornwall where his intellectual approach to
Constructivism and sensitivity to form helped
to create the St Ives School – not only Hepworth
and Ben Nicholson, with whom he had moved
from London, but Peter Lanyon, John Wells and
Wilhelmina Barns-Graham. Frances Spalding says:
'His presence, together with that of Hepworth and
Nicholson, transformed the small town into a vital
centre for modern art. It was here that modernist
and native traditions merged, abstractions combining with a sense of place.'[32]

Another influence was 'slow-burn' but powerful:
that of Kurt Schwitters. He had only one solo show
during his exile, at Jack Bilbo's private gallery.[33]
He lived in hardship after internment, then moved
to the Lake District. With a stipend from MOMA in
New York he was able to spend the last year before
his death working on his 'Merzbarn', a recreation of
his pivotally influential collaged environment, the
'Merzbau', but this time in a Cumbrian barn. Tom
Ambrose has written: 'Although Schwitters was not
forgotten he had been neglected; one of the most
individual and pioneering artists of the twentieth
century had been allowed to die largely unrecognised
in poverty and exile.'[34] Schwitters died the day after
he was granted British citizenship in 1948. Later,
his influence could be seen in Pop Art, Conceptual
Art and installation; in fact it was the Pop Artist

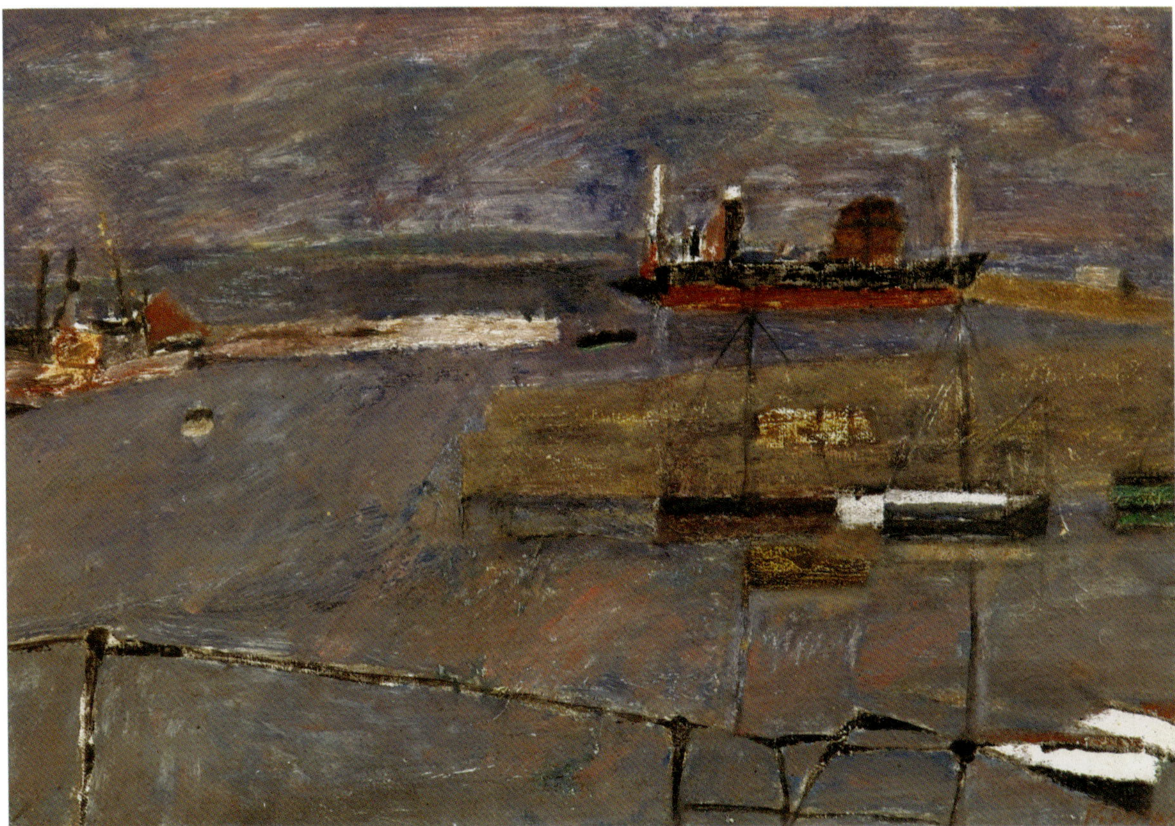

Peter Potworowski (1898–1962) | *Newlyn Harbour*
1954 | oil on canvas | 30 x 45 cm
RWA (Royal West of England Academy) | © Artist's Estate

Potworowski had a lifelong interest in the sea after working on a
merchant ship between Marseilles and North Africa. His retrospective
exhibition in Poland was destroyed in transit during the German
invasion of 1939.

Richard Hamilton who arranged that part of the
Merzbarn should be rescued for posterity.[35]

Photography in Britain was reshaped. Duncan
Forbes wrote of the émigré photographers and
illustrated publishers who entered Britain in the
1930s: 'Bringing with them skills honed working
for Europe's vibrant illustrated press, they transformed the manner in which visual reportage was
both produced and consumed in Britain. What is
now described as the British documentary tradition
was substantially formed and developed by these
photographers and editors.'[36] The impact was
there in portrait photography too, and in the later
work of Bill Brandt in emotive, surreal landscape
photography.

Margaret Garlake has argued that refugee sculptors brought about a shift in attitudes by bringing
a tradition of narrative public works to post-war
redevelopment, particularly in housing schemes,
shopping centres, hospitals, schools and colleges.[37]
Artists such as Siegfried Charoux, Georg Ehrlich

and Franta Belsky led the way. From his first UK
public commission in 1948, Charoux took reflective public sculpture far beyond traditional statuary.
Belsky produced playful works such as *Joyride* at
Stevenage and a fountain on the South Bank. In
the new enthusiasm perhaps 2,000 public sculptures
were erected between 1945 and 1986 in a wave of
post-war reconstruction and new towns that drew
in Elisabeth Frink, Barbara Hepworth, Henry
Moore, Victor Pasmore and many others.[38]

Finally, it is worth referencing the boost to
British animation from émigré artists Lotte Reiniger
and János Halász. Reiniger, whose *The Adventures
of Prince Achmed* of 1926 was the world's first
feature-length animation, came to Britain with her
husband and collaborator Carl Koch in 1936 and
made films for John Grierson at the GPO film unit.
She returned permanently to Britain in 1949 and
produced a dozen films with paper-cut figures in
stop-motion on the multiplane animation table
she invented.[39] Among those who worked with

her was Jane Phillips, who went on to establish the Caricature Theatre. Halász (later John Halas), who had established the first animation studio in Hungary, also arrived in 1936. As Halas and Batchelor he and his wife made public information films during the war and afterwards feature-length animations including *Animal Farm*. Britain has remained a leading centre for creative animation.

John Rothenstein's *British Art Since 1900*, written in 1962, surveyed the 100 artists he considered most important in the last six decades. Two continentally trained refugees were included, Josef Herman and Uli Nimptsch, but equally important was the visibility of British artists for whom contact with the 1930s émigrés was influential, among them Colquhoun, Freud, Frink, Hepworth, Lanyon, MacBryde, Moore and Nicholson. (Pissarro and those he influenced were also included.) Significantly, though, David Herman sees a failure in the postwar period to notice Jewish artists, citing Herbert Read's *Contemporary British Art* in 1951, which dealt with three artists who were Jewish to 67 who weren't, and Kenneth Clark's two-volume autobiography, which did not mention a single Jewish artist.[40] This does seem extraordinary in the nation of Bomberg and Gertler, Epstein,

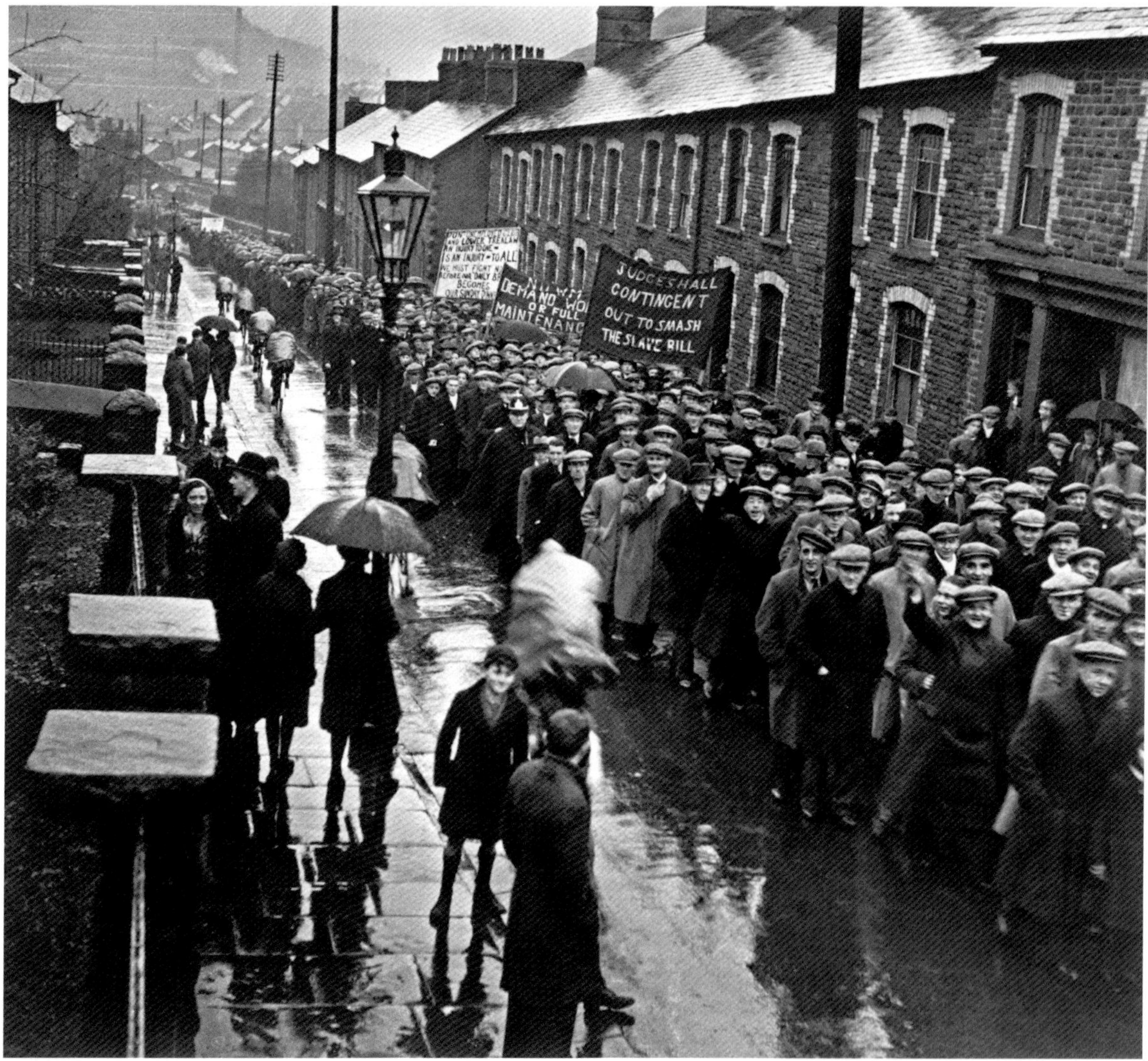

Edith Tudor Hart (1908–1973) | *Demonstration in the Rhondda*
c.1934 | photograph
National Library of Wales, Aberystwyth | © Estate of Wolfgang Suschitzky

A Depression-era Rhondda demonstration has banners referring to the 'slave bill', a name given to the Unemployment Act 1934 which sought to move the unemployed into work camps.

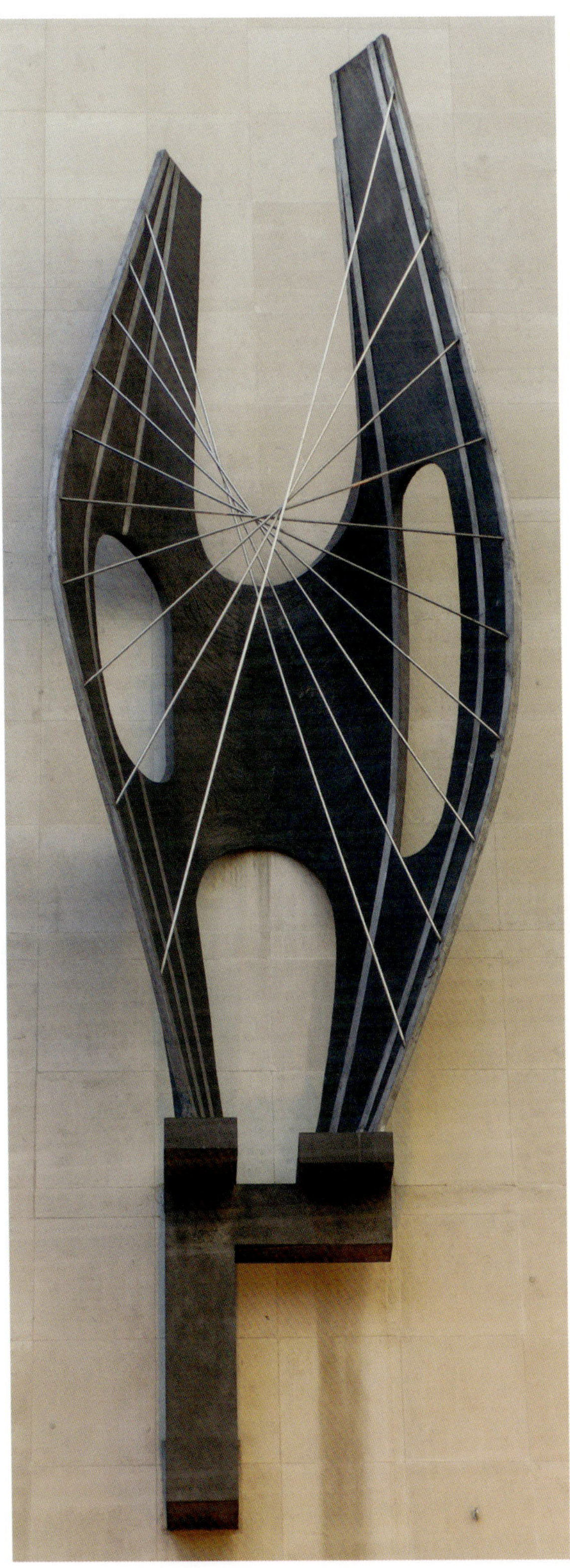

Barbara Hepworth (1903–1975) | *Winged Figure*
1963 | aluminium with stainless-steel rods | 3.8 m high
John Lewis, Holles Street, London | photo: Justinc, Wikimedia Commons

Hepworth was among the prominent creators of public sculpture in the post-war period. The form of *Winged Figure* recalls Gabo's strung spirals.

Herman, Freud and Auerbach.

Many of the artist refugees from totalitarian Europe made long, happy and constructive lives. For all its narrow-mindedness and lack of generosity at times, and the knowledge that it could have saved more lives than it did, Britain still gifted refugees conditions that were the polar opposite to those of fascism. Fred Uhlman reflected in his autobiography about his adopted home: 'If tolerance, kindness, political maturity and fairness are the touchstones of civilisation, Great Britain is the most civilised nation on earth'.[41] That view from 1960 may still be an aspiration.

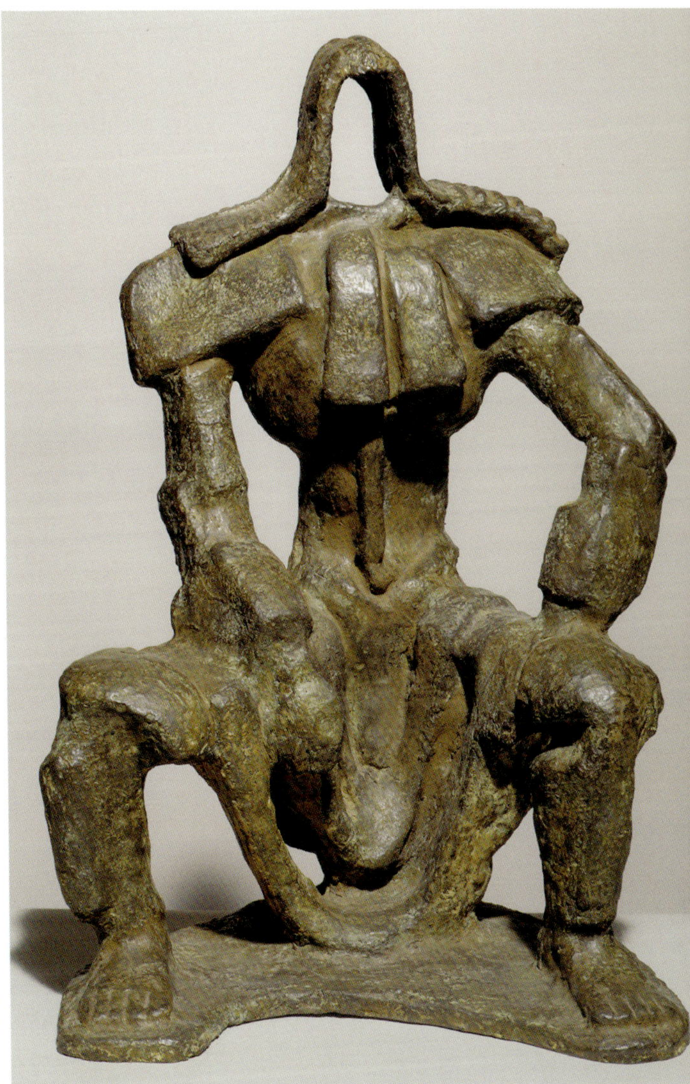

Siegfried Charoux (1896–1967) | *Civilization: The Judge*
1962 | bronze | 49 x 33 x 27 cm
Tate | © Langenzersdorf Museum/Estate of Siegfried Charoux | photo: © Tate

Charoux wrote: 'The "Judge" represents Justice (jurisprudence and jurisdiction) in that inhuman form mankind all over the world now tolerates: drapery and an obsession for punishment.'

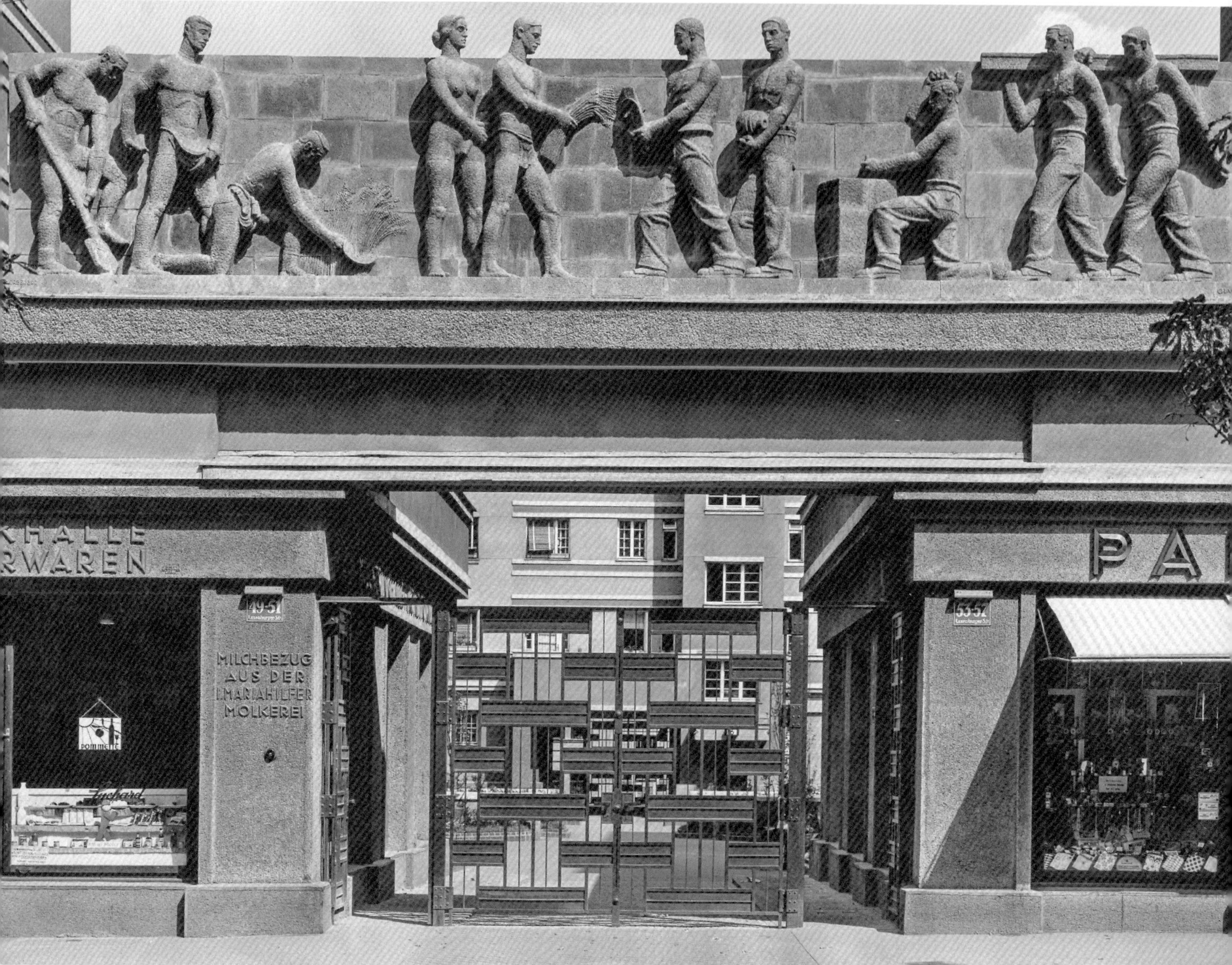

Siegfried Charoux (1896–1967) | *Worker Frieze*
1931 | ceramic | approximately 2 x 8 m
Zurcher-Hof, Vienna | photo: Martin Gerlach Junior (1879–1944), *c*.1931,
courtesy of Langenzersdorf Museum

This frieze commissioned by the city for a new apartment complex in
Vienna was Classical in inspiration and modern in style. Agricultural
workers of the ancient world on the left meet construction workers
from the right. Charoux would bring a similar approach to public
art in British development projects.

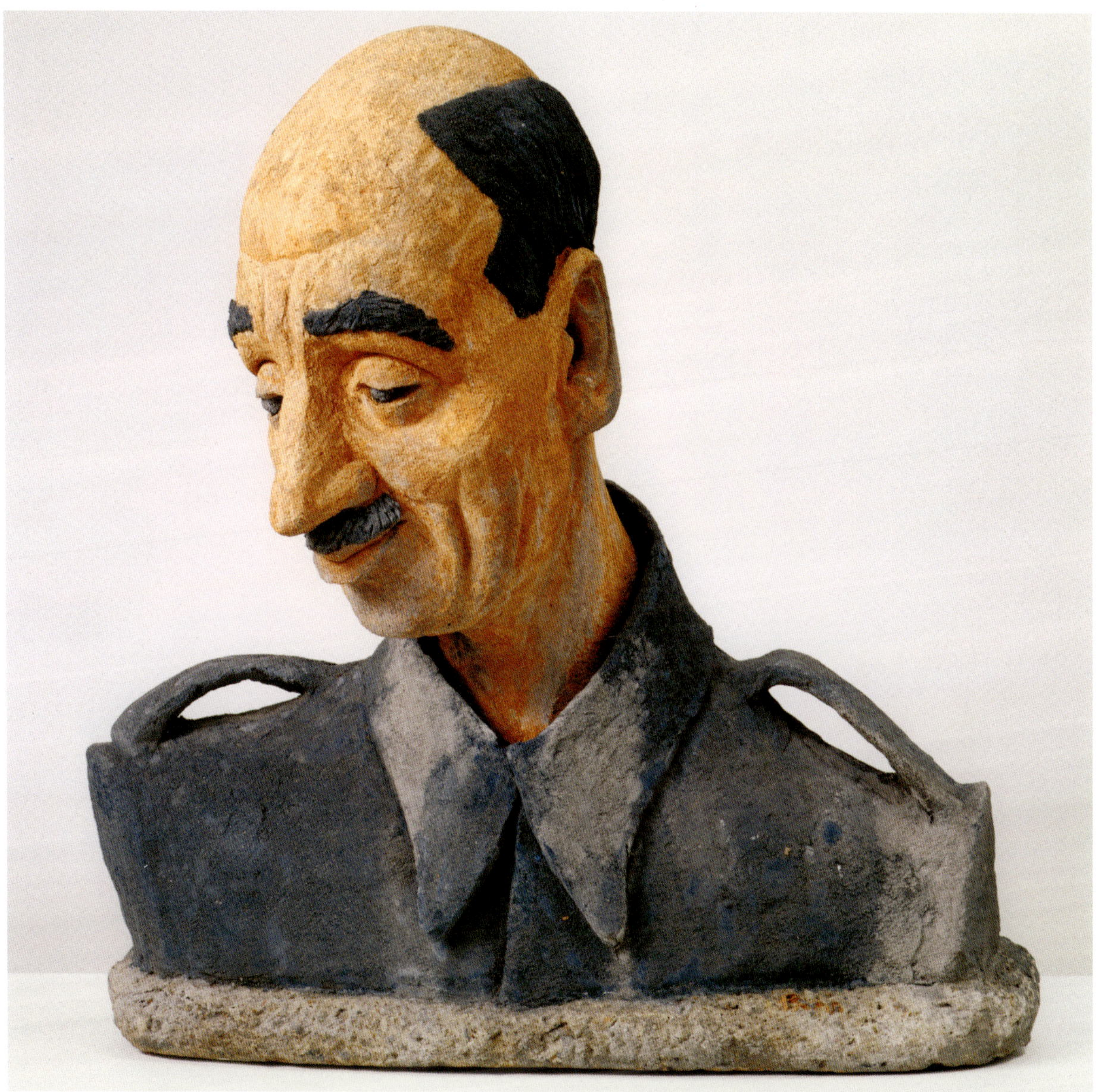

Peter László Peri (1899–1967) | *Mr Collins from the A.R.P.*
1940 | painted concrete | 67 x 68 x 40 cm
Tate | © The Estate of Peter László Peri/all rights reserved DACS 2019 | photo: © Tate

Peri and his English wife had been arrested in Berlin as communists
and came to Britain in 1933. In 1929 he had turned from abstract,
Constructivist sculpture to representational figures concerned
with workers' culture.

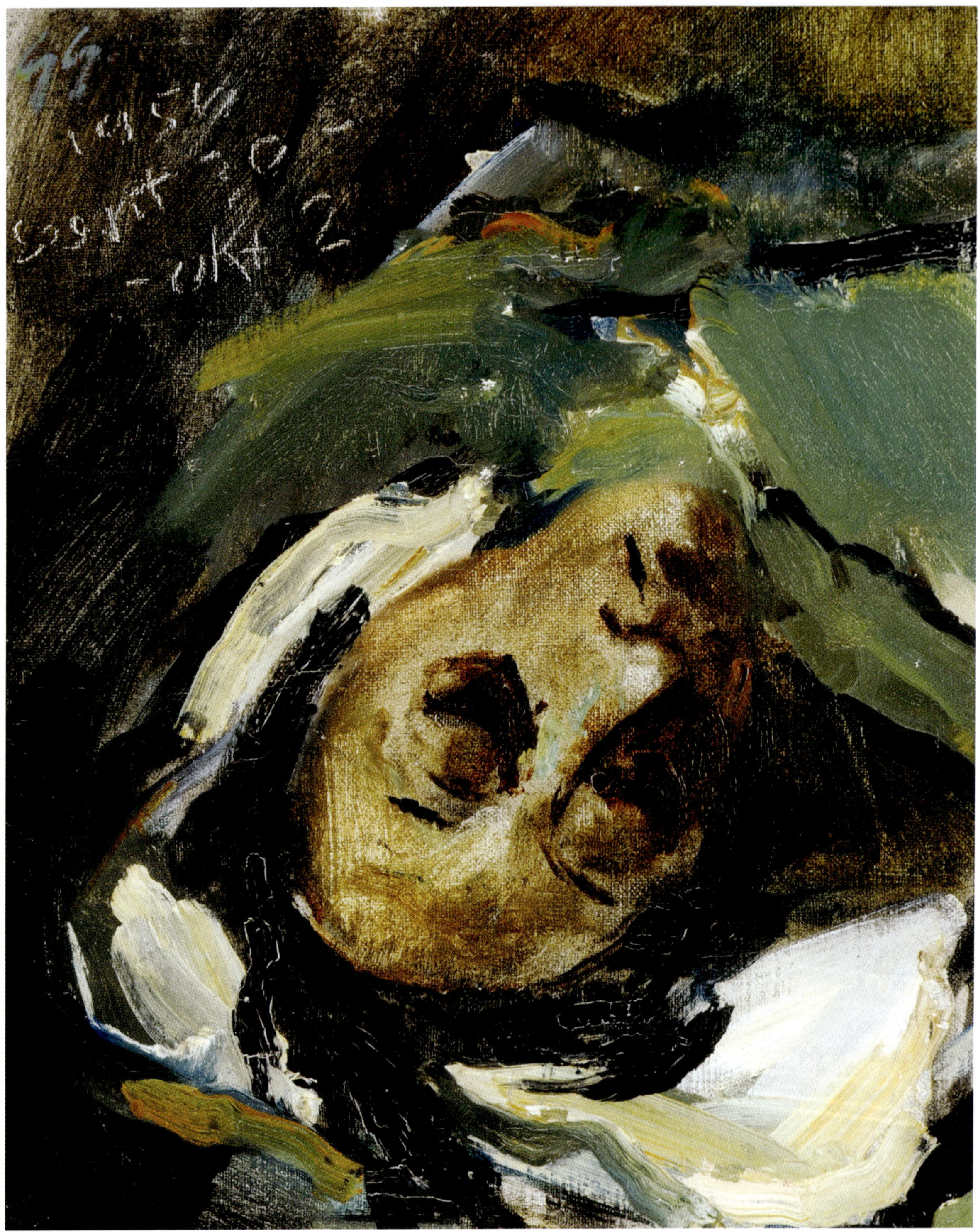

György Gordon (1924–2005) | *Mother on her Deathbed*
1956 | oil on canvas | 36 x 29 cm
Gift of the Estate of György Gordon, 2017, University of Leeds Art Collection
© Artist's Estate

Gordon's mother died in the year of the Hungarian Uprising, 1956.
His portrait of her on her deathbed suggests his anger at personal and
public worlds turned upside-down. His exposure of feeling and free
handling of paint were influenced by the expressionism of Soutine.

Continuing crises

ARTIST REFUGEES MAY NOT BE RECOGNISED FOR years after their arrival, and patterns of influence take time to emerge. Knowing who has come and how they have contributed inevitably gets harder nearer to the present. Nevertheless, some stories can be narrated of individual artists and the crises that drove them to leave home.

The peace after the Second World War was an uneasy one as power blocs vied for dominance. Poland and Czechoslovakia found themselves in the Soviet bloc. The sculptor Franta Belsky stayed in Prague after demob from the Czech army to study and undertake commissions. The communist take-over in 1948 determined him to settle in Britain where he had a long career in public sculpture. Some in the Polish army in 1939 had seen Stalinism close-up, having crossed into Russia and immediately been arrested. The mural painter Adam Kossowski nearly died in a labour camp before Russia joined the Allies and he was released into the army; Stanislaw Frenkiel had a similar experience. Marian Kratochwil, Zdzislaw Ruszkowksi and Aleksander Żyw were among those who found their way to Britain to rejoin the Polish army and then sought refuge as they saw their country subsumed into the Soviet bloc; Marian Bohusz-Szyszko came having been a prisoner of war in Germany.[1] Many of these artists taught in British colleges, Frenkiel as director of art at London's Institute of Education.

The defeat of Japan in the Pacific theatre also unleashed ideological clashes. In China the civil war ended in 1949 with the creation of the People's Republic. Many people associated with the former government left quickly. Li Luan-Chai went with his family to Taiwan and studied art with Li Chung-sheng. He started making abstract drawings in 1956 influenced by Chinese philosophy, calligraphy and colour, seeking to recapture the quality of Chinese porcelain and ancient cave paintings. Ten years later he arrived in London where he began to exhibit photography, abstract and conceptual art. In 1968 he moved to Cumberland, buying a farm from his friend Winifred Nicholson which he turned into a gallery that showed the work of other artists, including Andy Goldsworthy, David Nash and Bill Woodrow. His own work was acquired for several British public collections, including Tate. Chien-Ying Chang and Cheng Wu Fei had both studied and taught in China before coming to study at the Slade School of Art in 1947 with

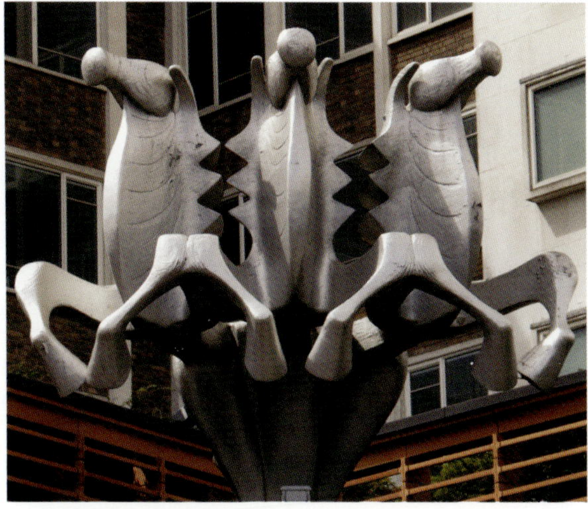

Franta Belsky (1921–2000) | *Triga*
1958 | cast aluminium
Caltex House, Knightsbridge, London | photo: Tony Hisgett, Wikimedia Commons

Belsky settled in Britain as a result of the 1948 Communist coup, where he made a significant contribution to public sculpture.

support from the British Council. Following the communist victory they heard news of purges, labour camps and the ill-treatment of two of their friends who had returned. They married in Britain in 1953. Both exhibited work in Chinese idioms.[2]

Along the Iron Curtain, liberal movements that tested Soviet domination created refugees from Hungary and Czechoslovakia. After 6,000 Soviet tanks rolled into Hungary on 4 November 1956, 3,000 people died in street fighting, thousands were arrested and hundreds were executed. An estimated 200,000 refugees fled. Among those who came to Britain were the illustrator Victor Ambrus, prolific stamp designer Julian Vasarhelyi (said to have designed 7,500 stamps for 165 countries), docu-mentary film maker Robert Vas and painter György Gordon. The first film made by Vas in Britain was *Refuge England* (1959), which followed an immi-grant from Hungary trying to understand his new home with no English and little money. Gordon had recently graduated from the Academy of Fine Arts in Budapest and escaped with his 7-year-old daughter to Austria and onwards to the United States. He was immediately interned as a suspected communist and returned to a prison in Austria while his daughter was left in a refugee camp. They reached Britain in 1957, where Gordon learned the language and six years later secured a lectureship at Wakefield College of Art. His paintings were fluid and expressive, many of them concerned with mourning or the vulnerability of the human body. He had major exhibitions in Wakefield, Leeds, the National Portrait Gallery and, in 1992, post-communist Budapest.[3]

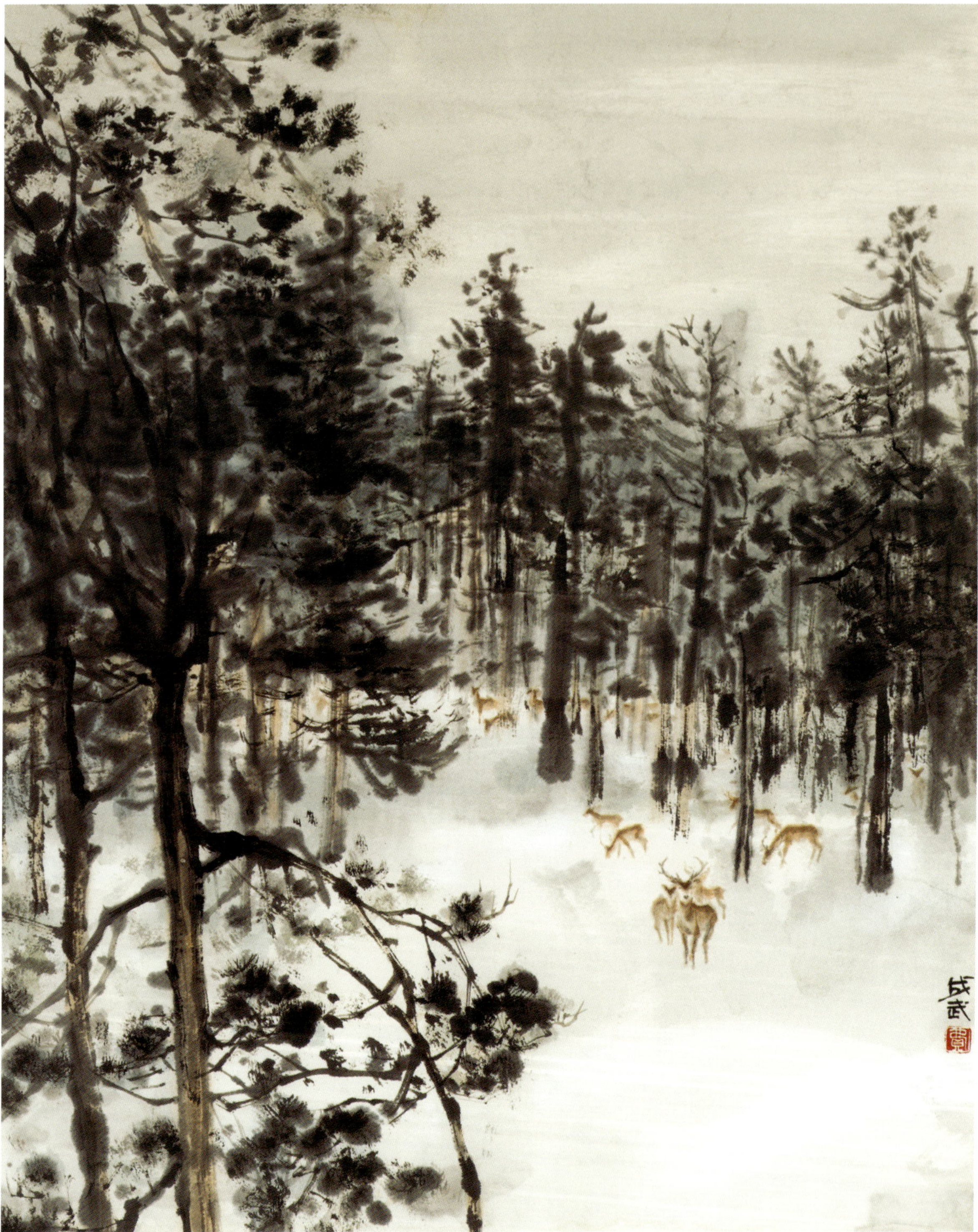

Cheng Wu Fei (1914–2004) | *Snow Forest*
1965 | watercolour | 52 x 44 cm
RWA (Royal West of England Academy) | © Artist's Estate

Cheng Wu Fei was one of the Chinese artists who feared the new
communist regime. The Cultural Revolution of the late 1960s would
prove disastrous to many artists who remained in China.

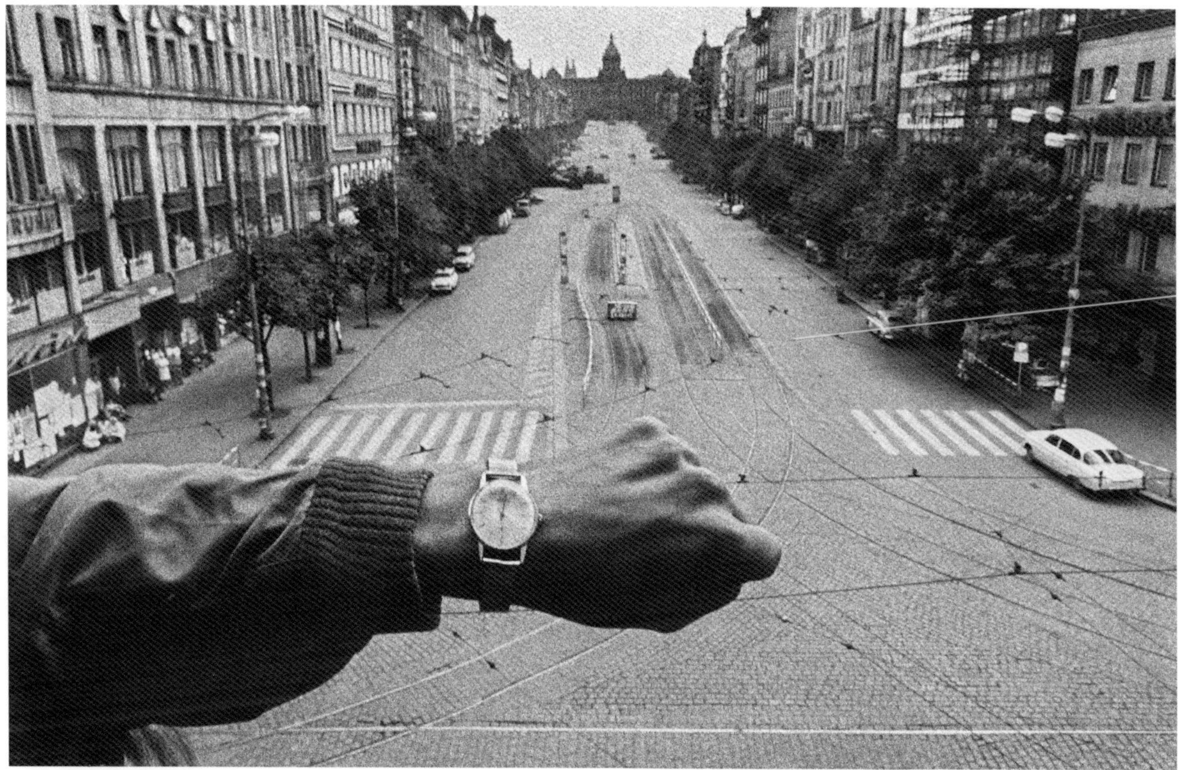

Josef Koudelka (b.1938)
Czechoslovakia. Prague. August 1968. Warsaw Pact troops invasion
1968 | photograph | 23 x 36 cm
© Josef Koudelka/Magnum Photos

Koudelka had never photographed a major event until he found
himself in the middle of the Soviet invasion and compelled to
record it. This image shows Wenceslas Square abandoned.

The Prague Spring seemed almost a reprise of
1956. After Alexander Dubček initiated reforms in
1968 the Warsaw Pact sent in massed troops. Some
300,000 people left the country. The painter Jiri
Borsky came to Britain, becoming a British citizen
in 1975. The photographer Josef Koudelka docu-
mented the invasion, smuggling his images out for
publication in the *Sunday Times,* under the pseudonym 'Prague Photographer' for fear of reprisals.
He was awarded the Robert Capa Gold Medal
anonymously in 1969 and kept his identity secret
until after his father died in 1984. He was granted
political asylum in Britain in 1970. The photographs
were not published in Czechoslovakia itself until
1990, but since the fall of the Iron Curtain Koudelka
has been able to return and now lives in Prague and
Paris.[4]

As a young man in Chile, Humberto Gatica was
involved in community arts projects with shanty
town dwellers, peasants and forestry workers. He
was detained following the Pinochet coup of 1973,
accused of taking part in a 'gathering in a public
place'. He was imprisoned for 10 months, at times
in an overcrowded cellar with 100 others, and
subjected to brutal interrogations until an international solidarity campaign secured his release.
He and his wife Gabriela were smuggled into
Argentina where they spent a year in a refugee
camp. They reached Swansea in 1975 and were
given university scholarships under a scheme to
help Chilean refugees. Through photography and
poetry he has explored the nature of his new country
and the history of Chile's 'disappeared'. In 2008 he
published a book tracing his exile's journey, sold in
aid of present-day asylum-seekers. His poem 'The
Emigrant' reflects experiences of refugees before
and since.[5]

Mona Hatoum has become one of the most
powerful and influential British artists of her generation, fusing the personal and political through
performance and video in the 1980s and sculpture
and installation since the 1990s. Often her work
combines elegance of form with challenging under-
currents of discomfort. She grew up in Lebanon
in a family that was already exiled from Palestine.
While on a short visit to London in 1975 the

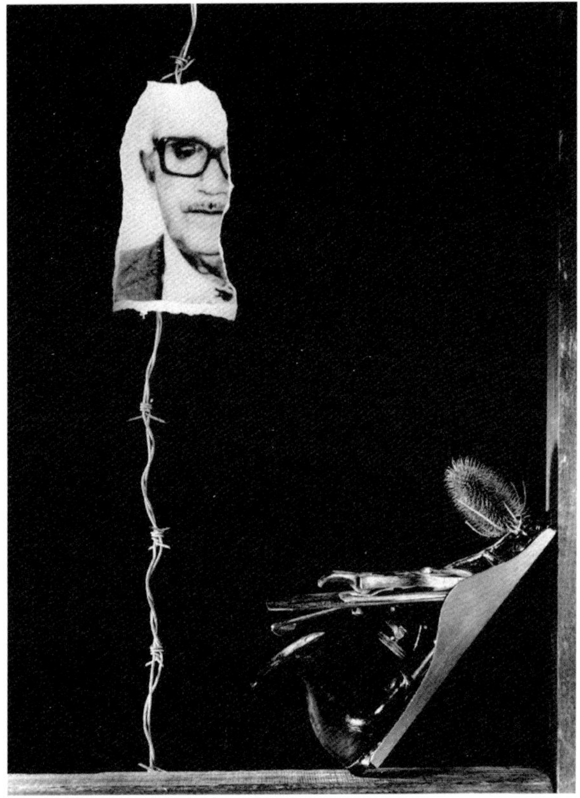 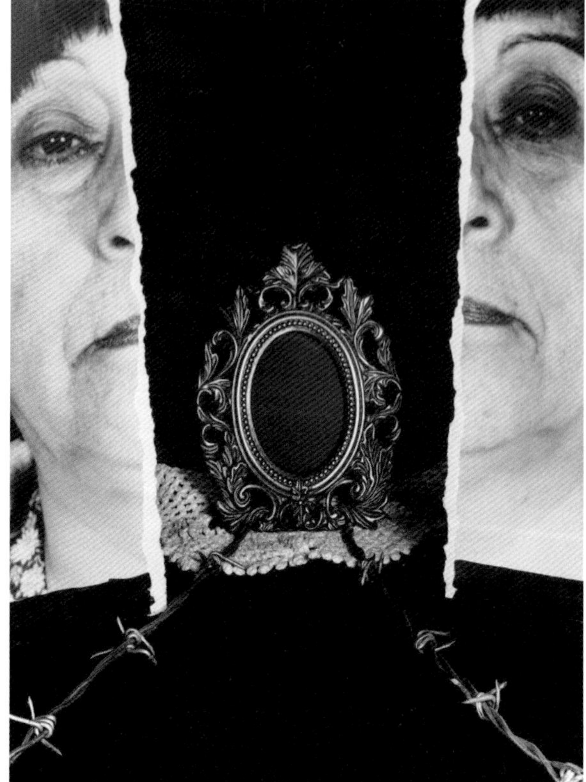

Humberto Gatica (b.1944) | *Vida (A Life)* and *Duelo (Grief)*
2008 and 2013 | silver gelatin prints | 28 x 25 cm
collection of/© the artist

These two photographs show arrangements of images and objects reflecting on the 'disappeared' who were imprisoned or murdered by the Pinochet regime in Chile. Gatica evokes layers of memory with solemnity and beauty.

The Emigrant
Neither
a castaway
nor a traveller
rather he is
a shattered man
knocking on
illusory doors
spending
his desperate
and obscene
language
secretly
erasing
his nightmares
and who awakes
every morning
surrounded
by labyrinths
and unbroken
dreams
Humberto Gatica (b.1944) | 1988

Lebanese Civil War broke out and prevented her from returning home. As a British passport holder she took 'refuge' but was never in the legal sense a 'refugee', echoing 1930s émigrés like Peter de Francia or Michael Werner who had no need to claim asylum. When she enrolled at Byam Shaw school of art, she says: 'I thought I might stay for a year and go back, but the war got worse.'[6] Some 60,000 people were killed over the next 15 years of conflict and thousands were displaced. Beirut was devastated. Rasheed Arean has written of her work that it 'centres around the experiences of dispossession, displacement, exile, alienation, and longing for return.'[7] *Measures of Distance*, a video work made during ongoing war in 1988, superimposes the Arabic script of letters written by her mother in Beirut over still photographs of her under the shower. It is accompanied by the artist reading an English translation. Hatoum sought to counter the Western stereotype of Arab women as 'a mass or herd without individual identity', hidden, passive and non-sexual.[8] For viewers,

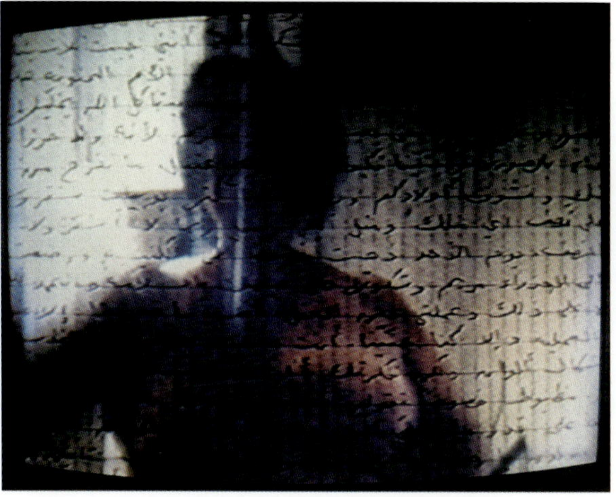
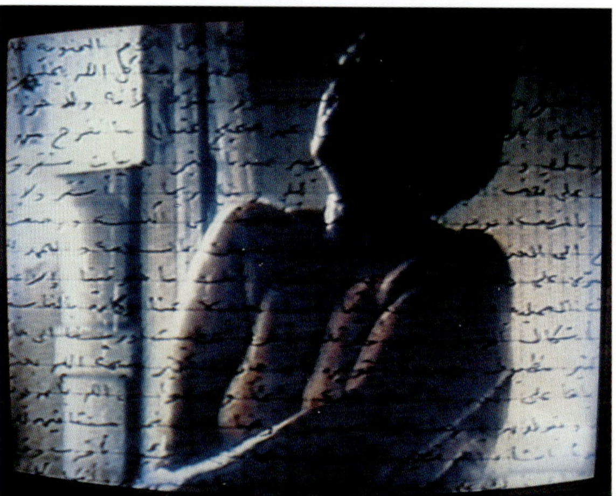

Mona Hatoum (b.1952) | *Measures of Distance*
1988 | colour video with sound | 15 minutes 35 seconds
A Western Front Video Production, Vancouver | collection of/© the artist

These stills taken from the 15-minute video combine letters to the artist from her mother in Beirut with photographs of her mother under the shower.

the personal, particular relationship expressed is all the more moving for the 2,500 miles that separated them.

In Iran, fundamentalist oppression of intellectuals and restrictions on women after the Islamic Revolution of 1979 caused many to seek freedom elsewhere. The young artist Zory Shahrokhi knew people who were imprisoned or executed. Having studied art in Tehran she left to continue her education in London. Both her culture and her experiences are important to her art:

> *My work is strongly influenced by Persian poetry, fabric and rug design. When still I was a teenager – a couple of years after 1979 revolution – I lost almost all the people dear to me. They were imprisoned, missing or executed due the government's crackdown on the opposition. The traces of those events are reflected in my work. [...] I investigate issues and perceptions around freedom related to displacement, exploitation, and gender oppression. Experiencing the dehumanisation of refugees and the ongoing struggle to be part of this society naturally is part of my work.*[9]

Amir a Nejad was tortured and imprisoned in Iran for his abstract painting, which the authorities deemed influenced by western art. He was condemned for owning a book about Picasso. With echoes of Josef Herman's experiences decades earlier in Poland he was arrested frequently and moved constantly to evade the police. His arms were broken to prevent him painting and he was locked in a darkened cell for months. His family paid bribes so that he could escape through a toilet window and got him out of the country. After gaining asylum he took a course in graphic design but he could not bring himself to paint again. Even his wife did not know he had been an artist until his daughter asked for help with her own drawings. When he returned to work after 12 years he realised his old style was tainted by his experiences and he instead painted photorealist portraits of people who had been through traumas.[10]

Perhaps the greatest number of refugee artists in the past 40 years have come from Iraq. The turmoil of the region from the regime of Saddam Hussein through two Gulf Wars to the atrocities of ISIS has brought several generations of artists to Britain. The painter and sculptor Dia Azzawi is the most celebrated contemporary Iraqi artist. He was born in 1939 and trained in art and archaeology in Baghdad. He first came to London in 1976 as an advisor to the Iraqi cultural centre but settled permanently after Saddam Hussein's rise to power. He pursues the cross-fertilisation of Arabic archaeology, visual traditions and calligraphy with modern art and is represented in major collections worldwide.[11] Walid Siti grew up in the Kurdistan city of Duhok and studied at the Institute of Fine Arts in Baghdad. When he went to Slovenia to continue his studies he sought political asylum in Britain in 1984. He makes drawings, installations and sculptures that show his emotional connection to Kurdistan and sense of exile from it through themes of militarized borders and waves of migration.[12] Jasim Ghafur came from Kurdistan in 2000. His art examines

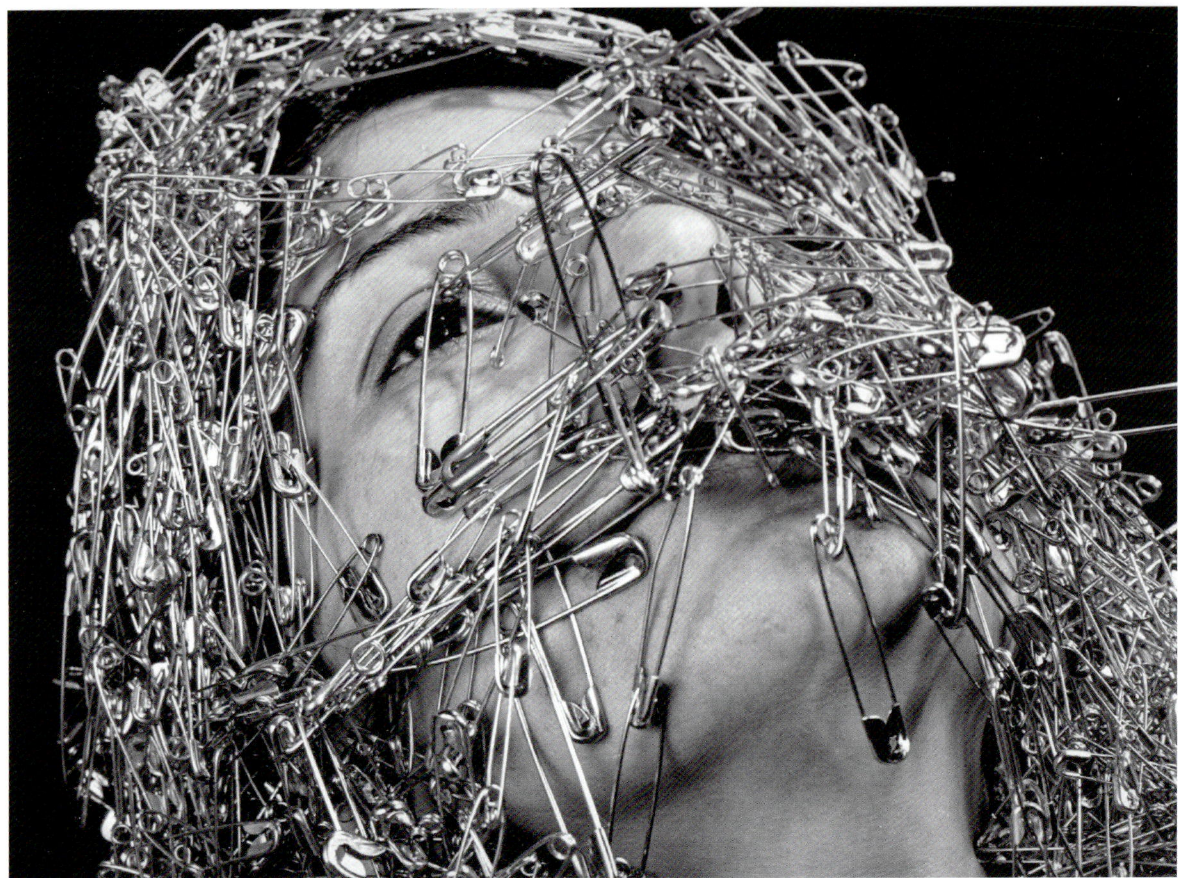

Zory Shahrokhi (b.1963) | *Masks; Veil #4*
2002 | photograph
collection of/© the artist

Shahrokhi used herself as a model in this photograph wearing a veil
of 4,000 safety pins, exploring both the confinement of the veil and
the act of resistance.

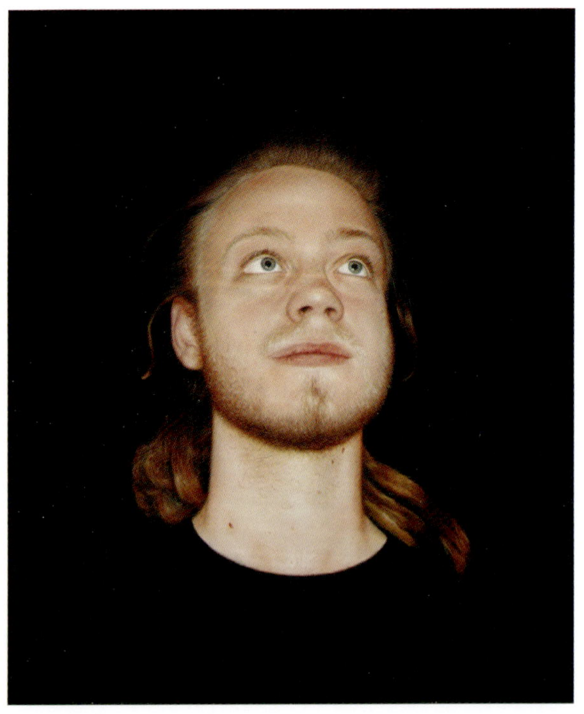

▶ **Amir a Nejad** (b.1971) | *Untitled*
*c.*2015 | oil on canvas
collection of/© the artist

After giving up painting for 12 years, Amir a Nejad began painting
former addicts and rough sleepers who had been through a hell of
their own.

▶▶ **Walid Siti** (b.1954) | *One Way Up*
2016 | plastic figurines and straw | 40 x 40 x 40 cm
collection of/© the artist

Tiny toy soldiers are drawn up into a towering, tsunami-like wave
built of straw in a metaphor for continuing conflict and failures
of reconstruction in the Middle East.

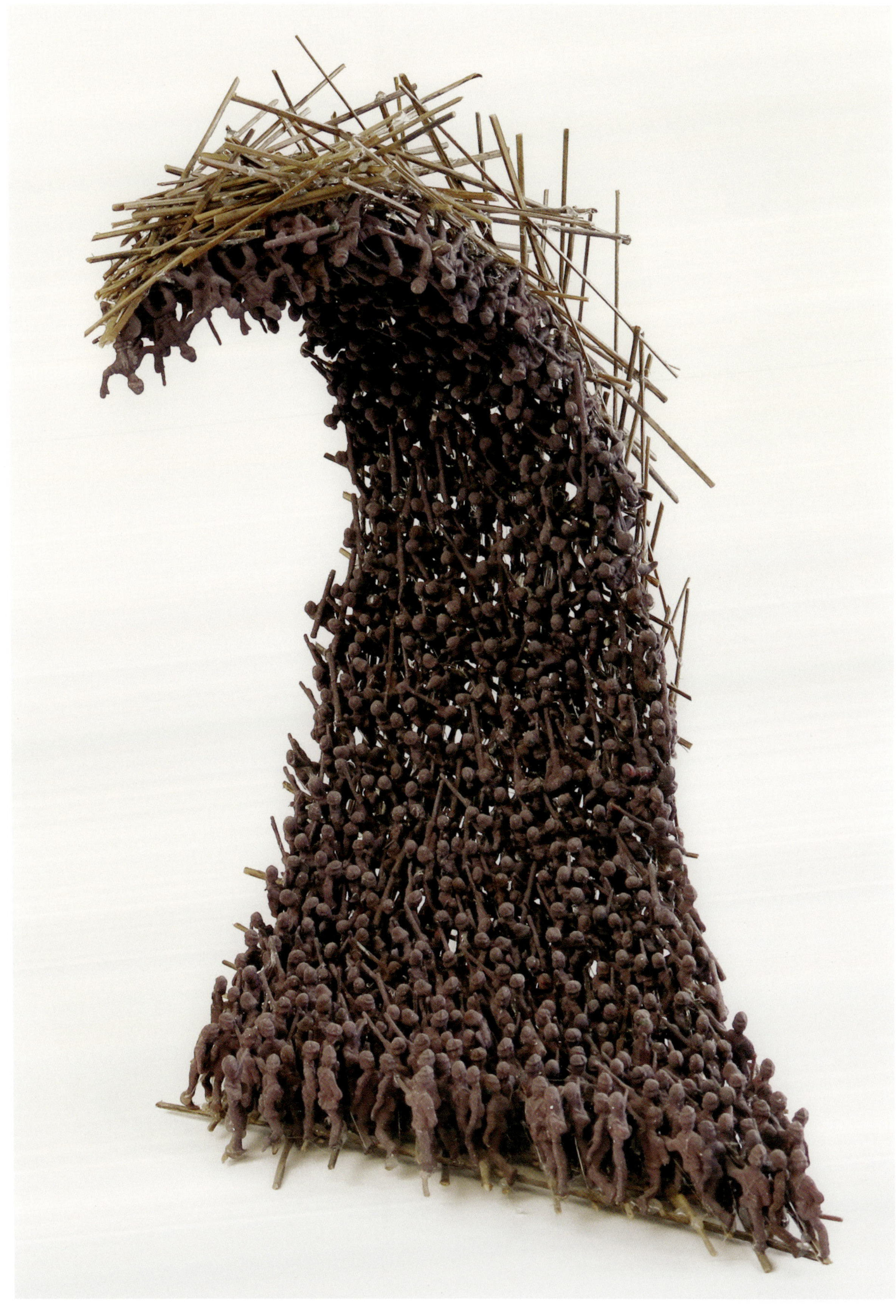

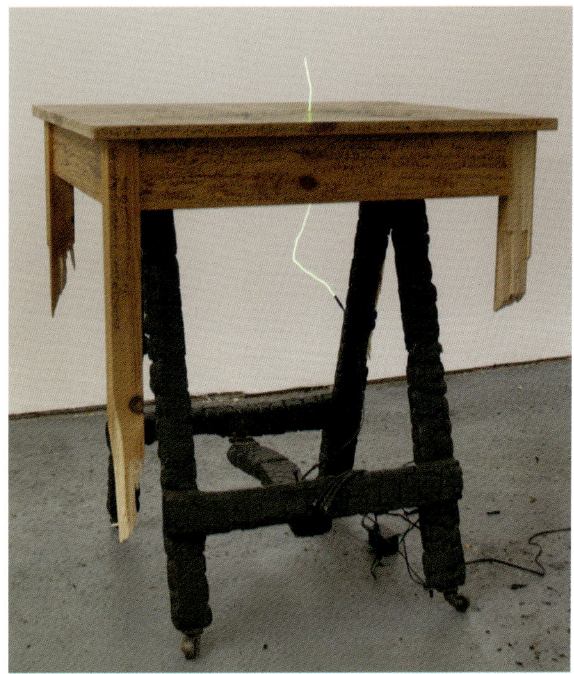

Hanaa Malallah (b.1958) | *Reading Table*
2014 | found table with burnt trestle and light filament
dimensions variable
collection of/© the artist

Malallah's work uses furniture, cloth, taxidermy and other found
objects, often combined with burning and with text.

violence against his people through harrowing
archival photographs, video and oral testimony
into which he inserts himself as witness. Into one
film he inscribed the words: 'I and all aspects of
my life were forced into exile. Life itself packed
its belongings and started its journey back to the
dark ages.'[13]

Several artists from Iraq settled in Britain after
the Second Gulf War as violence reached a new
peak. The Kurdish artist Behjat Omer Abdulla uses
drawing and video to explore contemporary history,
the refugee experience and its emotional impact.
He stayed in Britain to continue his studies before
settling in Sweden. Some refugees have rejected
their experiences as subject matter and turned to
life-affirming themes. Hasan Abdalla fled Kurdish
Syria during the Arab Spring and in Britain has
become refocussed and highly productive. When
Emad Al Taay had to leave Iraq at short notice
aged 33 he was working from his own studio in
Baghdad and had never been out of the country.
After resettling in Britain in 2009 he began to
paint Arab horses:

*I won't paint the blood or the killing; you can
see that every day in the newspapers. I was a
victim in Iraq, but I can't accept myself as a*

*victim forever. I can't change the world, but
I can help other people who are suffering to
leave that aside for half an hour while they
look at my paintings [...] there is peace
somewhere and we can find it.*[14]

Hanaa Malallah is one of the leading artists of Iraq.
She studied in Baghdad, from a diploma in graphic
art in 1979 to a doctorate in 2005, much of the time
with the revered modernist Shakir Hassan Al-Said.
Hostility towards her as a female artist and threats
against her life decided her to take a fellowship in
Paris in 2006 and settle in London the next year.
Through what she refers to as her 'ruins technique'
she reflects on her experience of decades of war:
'This does not mean that I am reproducing the
idea of war. Instead I am utilizing its intrinsically
destructive process to engender the visceral
experience'.[15]

In contrast to those Iraqi and Kurdish artists
whose work contemplates the devastation of their
country, Dobrivoje Beljkašić felt the need to look
back on the peaceful homeland he remembered
in Bosnia before the war of 1992. He had been
an artist, lecturer and curator in Sarajevo almost
all his life but when his studio was bombed most
of his work was destroyed. He moved with his
wife to Bristol in 1993 at the age of 70 and
painted for another two decades.

As a calligrapher and miniaturist, Samira
Kitman has brought traditional forms of visual
art from Afghanistan. She trained at the Turquoise

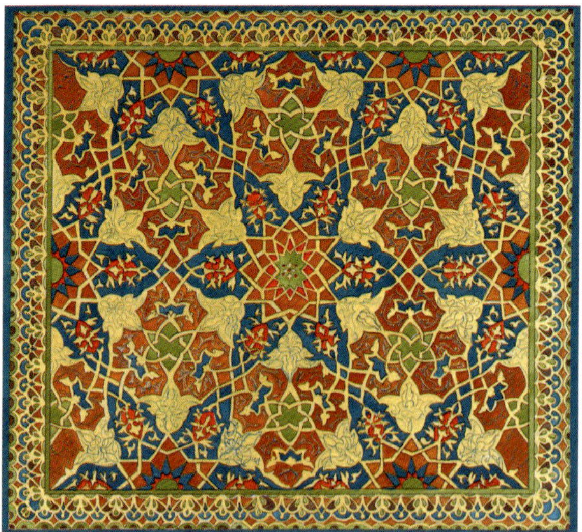

Samira Kitman (b.1984) | *Islamic Art Geometric Design*
2013 | tempera on paper | 35 x 35 cm
collection of/© the artist

This panel shows a symmetrical Islamic pattern with exceptional
detail. Kitman also produces 'shamsa' sunburst patterns,
calligraphy and representational paintings.

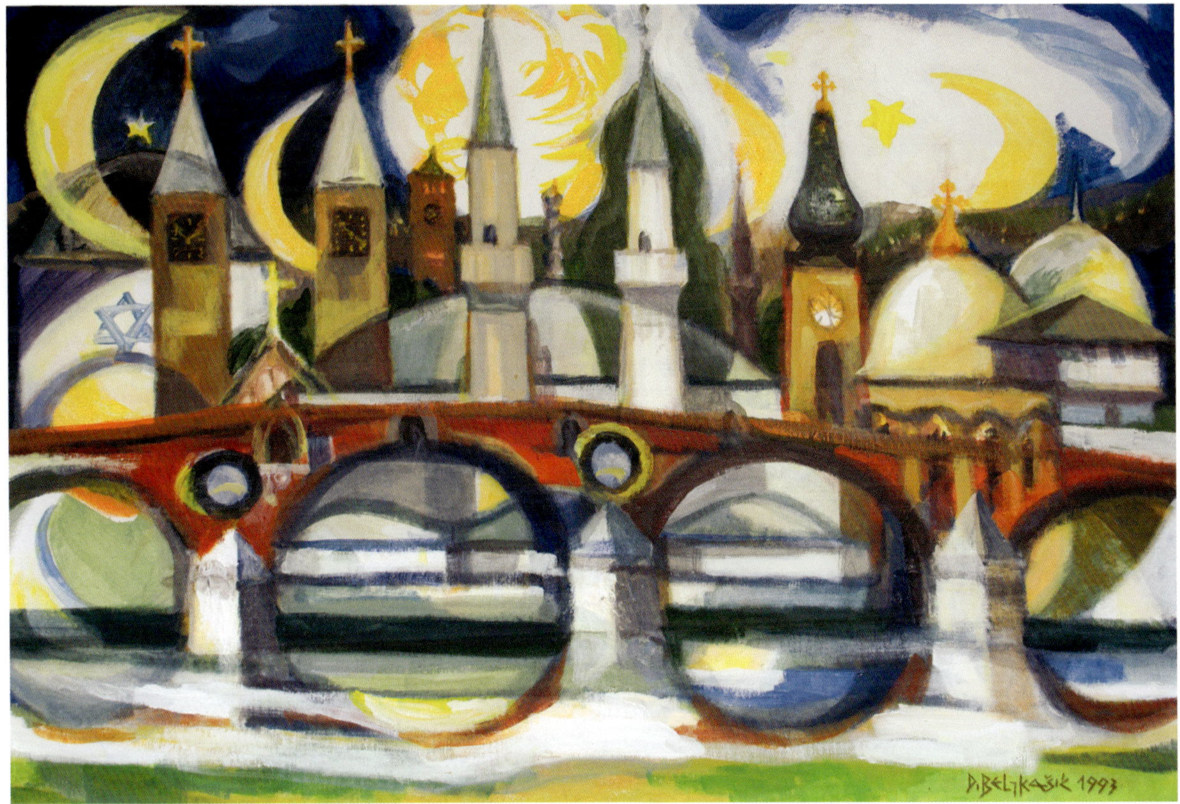

Dobrivoje Beljkašić (1923–2015) | *Memories of Sarajevo*
1993, acrylic on canvas, 75 x 53 cm
private collection | © Artist's Estate | photo: Lily Wildgoose

Beljkašić's paintings explored the countryside around his new home in
Bristol but he also looked back to his life in Bosnia before the divisive
war of 1992. This painting is his kaleidoscopic vision of Sarajevo
before it was torn apart: a bridge joining mosques, synagogues,
Catholic churches and Orthodox churches under a brilliant sky.

Mountain Institute (set up in 2006 to revive traditional crafts by Rory Stewart supported by the
Prince of Wales and the President of Afghanistan).
In her twenties she employed 15 women in Kabul
to fulfil commissions for major clients, set up
a charity that taught calligraphy and was voted
Afghan businesswoman of the year. Her high profile brought her to the attention of the Taliban and
she was subjected to a kidnap attempt and death-
threats. When she came to Britain she was initially
refused asylum but the Home Office reversed its
decision in 2017 when the extent of the risk to her
became apparent.[16] She now runs Kitman Arts from
her base in the UK.

The origins of the people who seek safety change
from year to year or even month to month. In 2018,
by far the greatest number given refugee status in
Britain came from Syria, followed by Iran, Eritrea,
Sudan, Afghanistan and Iraq. Syria demonstrates
how suddenly emergencies ignite. From 2011 to 2018
some 23,000 Syrians were granted asylum; yet before
2011 virtually no one from Syria had the need to
flee to Britain.[17] On opposite sides of the globe, new
crises have developed in Myanmar and Venezuela,
and others will emerge in future. War, persecution
or national collapse may come unheralded, while
the effects of climate change on crop failure and
rising sea-levels are anticipated everywhere.

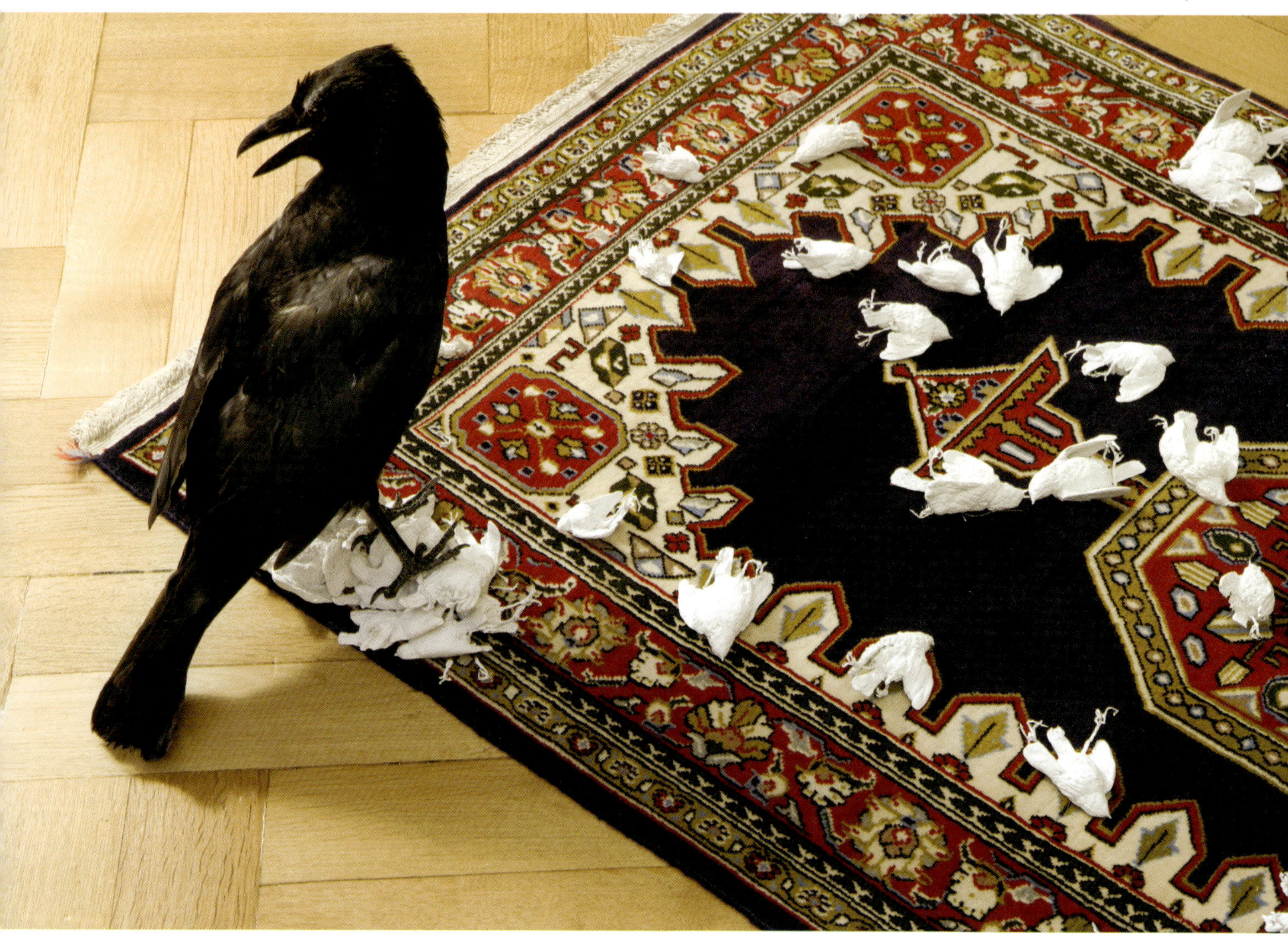

Zory Shahrokhi (b.1963) | *Where are We? (John Berger)*
2007 | rug, birds taxidermy, milliput and wires | dimensions variable
commissioned by the Foundling Museum and Arts Council East
collection of/© the artist | photo: Richard Davies

This installation view in the Foundling Museum, London, shows a
detail from a work in the series 'The Return of the Crows'. Under
a pair of full-size crows numerous bleached miniature birds lie
dead or dying.

Epilogue

EVERY ONE OF US IS A DESCENDENT OF MIGRANTS, and probably of people who were in some way refugees. Our prehistoric ancestors migrated through need as well as opportunity. We all know refugee narratives that stretch back centuries, from Mary and Joseph's 'Flight into Egypt' with the new-born Jesus to the seventeenth-century escape from religious persecution of the Pilgrim Fathers.

Britain's welcome of refugees has swung repeatedly from generous to suspicious, accepting to discriminatory. The nation has its xenophobic moments, just as other nations do, but it has a long tradition as a place of refuge. From time to time we need to be reminded that giving help brings benefits as well as fulfilling a moral imperative. John Willett wrote 35 years ago of how British culture's mongrel nature is regularly revitalized by new arrivals: 'might it not help us if more of today's Englishmen understood how rejuvenating for a rather elderly society such developments can be?'[1]

What have been the contributions of artist refugees in particular? Perhaps most distinctively, they have helped to tell Britain about itself, to see itself as others see it. German and Austrian photographers in the Depression went into industrial areas and urban slums and reflected them back to magazine readers in polite society; painters opened our eyes to British landscapes that were previously thought 'unpictorial'; artists from recent war zones have helped us pose questions about our foreign policies.

Migrant artists have contributed to the substance of British art. Our visual culture would be far poorer without Holbein's portraits of the Tudor court or Monet's atmospheric encounters with the Thames, without the landscape photographs of Bill Brandt or Schwitters' Dadaist Cumbrian barn. Some artists have developed in new ways as a result of their experiences. They have examined trauma, as Tissot did with his engravings of the siege of Paris or Meidner in his drawings of the concentration camps. They have looked back with distance on their former lives, like Josef Herman remembering his family in Warsaw, or examined their new present, as Camille Pissarro did in painting Norwood or de Saedeleer the mid-Wales hills. Occasionally, elements from British artistic traditions have cross-fertilised their work, whether Turner for Monet or Hogarth for Kokoschka.

Migrant artists have inspired and influenced British artists to make discoveries of their own. While influences can be over-stated, artists are changed when they encounter the new: stimulated to think afresh, motivated and excited, or attracted to ideas transferrable to their own practice. Naum Gabo's exotic presence and intellectual advocacy engaged major British artists, including Hepworth, Lanyon and Barns-Graham; Lotte Reiniger's induction of younger animators into her film projects boosted a creative animation sector that continues to this day.

Many refugees have become inspiring teachers and have energised generations of students with tangible connections to the wider world of art and experience. This was especially so among the teachers from German-speaking academies and universities from the 1930s onwards – Bloch, Henges, Koppel, Soukop and many more – whose professionalism paralleled the transformations wrought by refugees in art history, curating, publishing and dealership. As Daniel Snowman wrote: 'It is one of the great ironies of history that Hitler, by trying to stamp out a cosmopolitan culture that he abhorred, succeeded in the long run in bringing it to much of the wider world.'[2]

If these have been the potential contributions, why have some periods of migration or some individuals been more impactful than others? The length of their stay is critical. Some artist refugees have been short-term visitors – most refugees from the Franco-Prussian War were in Britain for only a year and those from the Great War only five or six, after which it was practical for them to return to their homes. Koudelka was able to return to post-communist Prague. For many others it was never possible to go back, especially for Jews after the Second World War whose families, neighbours and communities had been erased in Poland, Hungary, Austria, Germany, France and other countries. So complete was the divorce of many émigrés from Germany that their study is recognised as a freestanding discipline, *Exilforschung*.[3]

It is not too obvious to state that individuals could only contribute to British art if permitted to remain. John Heartfield might have achieved much more in Britain had he not been returned to East Germany. The tragedy of Otti Berger, who could not gain asylum and went home to die in the Holocaust, demonstrated that had Britain had a policy for adults in 1939 equivalent to the generosity of the *Kindertransport*, many times more lives might have been saved.

Personal factors were inevitably important. To change countries and tackle the challenges of a new language and new culture was infinitely harder for older people than for younger ones. Some artists had short lifespans as émigrés. Some were older when they came, such as Leonid Pasternak, who was in his late 70s, but some lives were cut short by trauma, such as the cartoonist Vicky, who killed himself aged 52. Settling in Britain has been difficult for many. Else Meidner could still say in 1979, four decades after she arrived: 'Here in London I walk about as in a dream and am surprised I'm here. Some plants thrive wherever you transplant them, but I could never put down new roots. My roots are in Berlin.'[4]

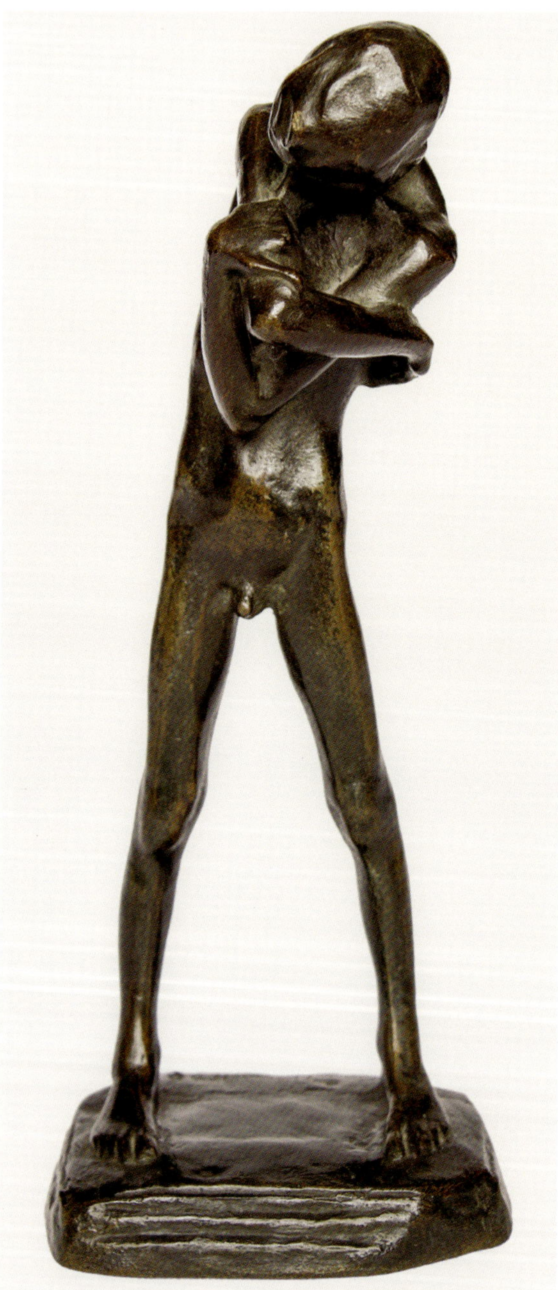

George Minne (1866–1941) | *Small Wounded Boy*
1898 | bronze | 25 x 10 x 7 cm
The Gregynog Trust

This vulnerable adolescent boy, arms clasped in pain, evokes the struggles of the refugee, made before Minne had become a refugee himself.

Yet perhaps the most important factors of all have been how artists were received by British contemporaries. The Impressionists might have had an impact much sooner on British art had they been more integrated beyond the community of temporary French refugees. The opportunity for Belgian symbolists like George Minne to work and influence British artists was lost largely by their isolation. The influence of Kurt Schwitters might not have been delayed so long had he not been alone in Cumbria. By contrast, the most profound effects have been when artists have had support and friendship. The importance in the 1930s of Fred Uhlman and fellow refugees in Hampstead with Herbert Read, the Nicholsons and others was fundamental in making connections for Gabo, Mondrian, Moholy-Nagy and many more. Communities also formed elsewhere that generated powerful influence – around Gabo in wartime St Ives, Herman and Adler in Glasgow, Koppel in Merthyr Tydfil.

Opportunity has been vital too. French artists might have gone hungry without Durand-Ruel to support them, and the galleries run by émigrés in London from the 1930s onwards were critical to the development of refugee artists' reputations as well as to the promotion of the modernism they influenced. Exhibitions of German art gradually acclimatised the British audience to what expressionism had to offer. Public commissions were vital to the impact of the muralist Hans Feibusch and the sculptor Siegfried Charoux. And in the post-war art colleges, key teaching roles for Potworowski, Frenkiel, de Maestre and others gave them opportunities to engage future generations.

Britain, for all its challenges, has brought hope and creativity for a multitude of artist refugees. When Josef Herman's wife Nini wrote about his arrival in a Welsh mining valley at the end of the Second World War she spoke for all our needs and all our possibilities:

Here was a homecoming in that sense of the word which is the domain of the soul. If, for the man, it satisfied his lifelong nostalgia for the community which had enriched his childhood years, that feeling of security where no one had to lock their door and each face was familiar in terms of human qualities; if for the child in the man a haven, like the arms of a mother, had seemingly been restored to him; for the maturing artist Ystradgynlais spelt home – home for the imagination furthered by an environment to fertilize it to fruition. A place in which to grow and rest.[5]

Surely, it is what every one of us deserves.

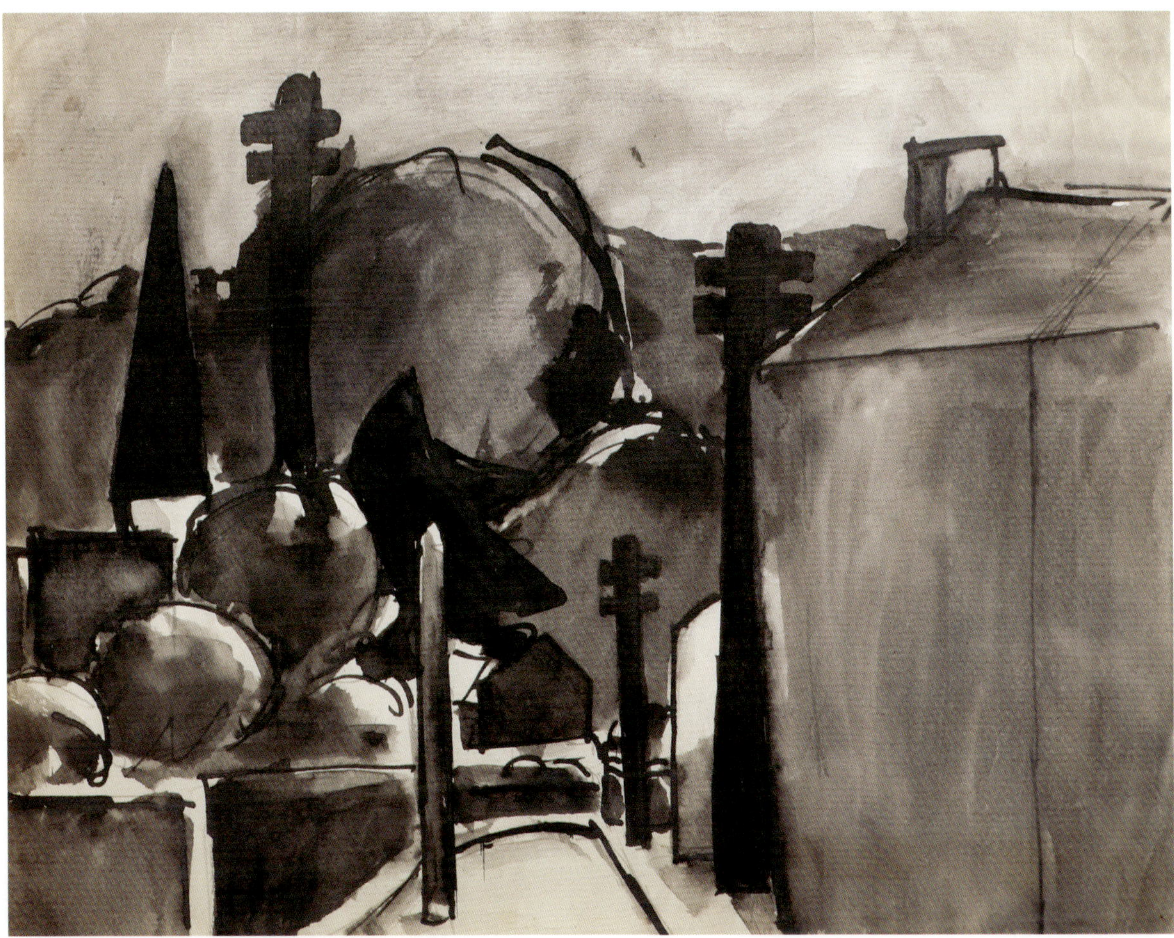

Josef Herman (1911–2000) | *Untitled night scene at Ystradgynlais*
*c.*1950 | ink on paper | 19 x 25 cm
private collection | © estate of Josef Herman/all rights reserved DACS 2019

Ystradgynlais was Josef Herman's place of spiritual as well as
corporeal refuge.

Notes

Preface
1. Daniel Snowman, 2002, p. 97, describes how Stephen Hearst, an Austrian émigré who later worked for the BBC, bought a newspaper in 1938 and found 'it was Len Hutton's Test Match score against Australia that filled the front page and he had to hunt to find, in small print, the fact that Hitler's troops were massing on the borders of Sudetenland.'

Introduction
1. John Berger, 1992, *Keeping a Rendezvous*, p. 12, quoted in Peter Gatrell and Liubov Zhvanko (eds), 2017, p. 1.
2. https://www.unhcr.org/uk/figures-at-a-glance.html; https://www.redcross.org.uk/about-us/what-we-do/how-we-support-refugees/find-out-about-refugees.
3. Robert Dinnis and Chris Stringer, 2013, pp. 137–47.
4. Tom Booth, 'What Happened to the Mesolithic?', *British Archaeology*, September/October, 2019, pp. 18–23.
5. Sarah MacDougall, 'Eva Frankfurther, artist (1930–1959)', https://evafrankfurther.benuricollection.org.uk/biography.php.
6. Bomberg, Gertler, Jacob Kramer, Bernard Meninsky and Isaac Rosenberg were helped to attend the Slade School of Art by the Jewish Education Aid Society. Tony Kushner, 2012, p. 55; Tony Kushner, 2015, pp. 28–9, 34.
7. Chien-Ying Chang obituary, *Telegraph*, 19 January 2004, https://www.telegraph.co.uk/news/obituaries/1452033/Chien-Ying-Chang.html
8. https://www.yadvashem.org/yv/en/exhibitions/nussbaum/about_nussbaum.asp?WT.mc_id=wiki
9. John Willet, 1984, p. 203.
10. Jutta Vinzent, 2006, p. 167.
11. Charlotte Salomon, 2017 and 2017a.
12. Foreword by Jeremy Hardy in Yasmin Alibhai Brown, 2002, p. 4.

Reformation and religious strife
1. Susan Foister, 2003, 'Holbein Family' in *Grove Art Online*; Karen Hearn (ed.), 1995, p. 35.
2. Karen Hearn (ed.), 1995, p. 63; Elise L. Smith, 'Hans Eworth', in *Oxford Dictionary of National Biography*, 2003.
3. Adam White, 2004. 'Colt, Maximilian' in *Grove Art Online*.
4. Tessa Violet Murdoch, 1982.
5. The Gentle Author, 'Marcellus Laroon's Cries of London', *Spitalfields Life*, 3 December 2014, http://spitalfieldslife.com/2014/12/03/marcellus-laroons-cries-of-london/
6. Lesley Stevenson, 2003. 'Monnoyer, Jean-Baptiste' in *Grove Art Online*.
7. David Cast, 2004. 'Chéron, Louis' in *Oxford Dictionary of National Biography*; D. Breme, 2003. 'Louis Chéron' in *Grove Art Online*.
8. Martin Myrone, 2001. *Henry Fuseli*, Tate: London; D.H. Weinglass, 2014. 'Fuseli, Henry' in *Oxford Dictionary of National Biography*; Georg Paula and David Blayney Brown, 2003. 'Füssli Family' in *Grove Art Online*.

When Paris came to London
1. https://www.musee-orsay.fr/en/events/exhibitions/archives/exhibitions-archives/page/6/article/gustave-dore-37172.html?S=&cHash=7d3d44ee04&print=1&no_cache=1&
2. Richard Shone, 'Pissarro in Norwood, Monet at the Savoy: What the Exiles Impressionists Saw in London', *The Guardian*, 20 October 2017.
3. Jon Whiteley, 2003. 'Gérôme, Jean-Léon', *Grove Art Online*.
4. Kathleen Adler, 2011, p. 27.
5. Frances Fowle, 2016, pp. 11–15.
6. John House, 1978, p. 636.
7. Simone Bartolena, 2011, p. 143.
8. Kathleen Adler, 1978, p. 43.

9. Kathleen Adler, 1978, pp. 48–9.
10. Kathleen Adler, 2011, pp.32–3.
11. Grace Sieberling, 1988, pp. 44, 55.
12. Christopher Lloyd, 1994, pp. 8–9.
13. Nicholas Reed, 1997, p. 2.
14. Grace Sieberling, 1988, p. 42; John House, 1978, p. 642; Kathleen Adler, 2011, pp. 34–5, 46; Richard Shone, 'Pissarro in Norwood, Monet at the Savoy: What the exiles Impressionists saw in London', *The Guardian*, 20 October 2017.
15. Kathleen Adler, 2011, pp. 32–3.
16. Kathleen Adler, 2011, p. 34.
17. Kathleen Adler, 2011, p. 37.
18. Christopher Wood, 1998, pp. 81–2.
19. Kathleen Adler, 2008, p. 47.
20. Kenneth McConkey, 1995, pp. 16–17, 18–19; Frances Spalding, 1986, p. 20.
21. Malcolm Warner, in Nancy Rose Marshall and Malcolm Warner, 1999, p.11.
22. Malcolm Warner, in Nancy Rose Marshall and Malcolm Warner, 1999, pp. 15–21; Christopher Wood, 1998, pp. 16, 81.
23. John M. Hunisak, 1996.
24. Anon, 2003. 'Drury, Alfred', *Grove Art Online*.
25. Fiona Pearson, 2003.

The war to end wars
1. Peter Gatrell and Liubov Zhvanko (eds), 2017, pp. 1–3.
2. Tony Kushner, 2012, p. 55; Tony Kushner, 2015, pp. 28–9.
3. Tony Kushner, 1999, p. 4; Michaël Amara, 2017, pp. 197–200.
4. Tony Kushner, 1999, p. 2.
5. Michaël Amara, 2017, pp. 200–3; Neil Evans, 2015, p. 29.
6. *Cambrian News and Merionethshire Standard*, 9 October 1914, quoted in Lorna M. Hughes, 2016, p. 214.
7. D. Cardyn-Oomen, 2003.
8. Oliver Fairclough et al, 2002, p. 182; Roger Avermaete, 2003, 'Permeke, Constant', *Grove Art Online*.
9. Quoted in Moira Vincentelli, 1981, p. 227.
10. Rowan, Eric and Stewart, Carolyn, 2002, pp. 91–123; Robert Hoozee, 'Minne, George', *Grove Art Online*.
11. Moira Vincentelli, 1981, p. 231.
12. Moira Vincentelli, 1981, Oliver Fairclough et al, 2002, p. 50.
13. Oliver Fairclough at al, 2002, p. 170.
14. Matthew Sturges, 2005, pp. 3, 30-33, 468–80.
15. *Sunday Times*, 17 January 1915.
16. https://nl.wikipedia.org/wiki/Joseph_Reubens
17. Christopher Lloyd, 1994, p. 46; Nicholas Reed, 1997, p. 38.
18. Simon Shorvon, 2011, p. 35.
19. Simon Shorvon, 2011, pp. 41–8.
20. Nicholas Reed, 1997, pp. 34, 42.
21. Matthew Sturges, 2005, pp. 391-2; David Peters Corbett, 2001, pp. 42–5.
22. Michaël Amara, 2017, pp. 200–3.
23. Michaël Amara, 2017, p. 204-5, 209.
24. *Report on the Work Undertaken by the British Government in the Reception and Care of the Belgian Refugees*, 1920, quoted in Michaël Amara, 2017, p. 210.
25. Michaël Amara, 2017, pp. 211–12.

The thirties
1. Jutta Vinzent, 2006, p. 23.
2. Marion Berghahn, 2007, p. 70.
3. Tom Ambrose, 2001, p. 66; Jonathan Petropoulos, 2014, pp. 166–8.
4. Margaret Garlake, 2005, pp. 170, 174.
5. Josef Herman, 2002, p. 52.
6. Imperial War Museum interview, quoted in Jessica Feather, 2004, pp. 12–13; David Buckman, 2002, 'Walter Nessler', *Independent*, 12 January 2002.
7. Quoted in Stephanie Barron, 1997, p. 14.
8. Jonathan Petropoulos, 2014, p. 169.
9. Quoted in translation in Jonathan Petropoulos, 2001, p. 274.
10. Jonathan Petropoulos, 2001, p. 271.
11. Monica Bohm-Duchen, 2013, pp. 119-121.
12. David Manson, 2010. *Willy Tirr (1915–1991): Figure in a Landscape*, Author House, Milton Keynes.
13. Janet Daws, 'Ernst Eisenmayer Obituary', *Guardian*, 25 April 2018.

14. Avram Kampf, 1990, p. 83.
15. https://www.yadvashem.org/yv/en/exhibitions/nussbaum/
about_nussbaum.asp?WT.mc_id=wiki
16. Barbara Warnock, 2018, pp. 31, 34–5; Daniel Snowman,
2002, p. 89.
17. https://www.bauhaus100.com/the-bauhaus/people/
masters-and-teachers/otti-berger/

The thirties émigrés
1. Nicola Baird, 2018; Anna Müller-Härlin, ' "It all happened in
this street, Downshire Hill": Fred Uhlman and the Free German
League of Culture' in Behr and Malet, 2005, pp. 241–65.
2. Norbert Lynton, 1998, pp. 102–3.
3. http://www.screenonline.org.uk/people/id/528134/
4. David Buckman, 'Walter Nessler', *Independent*, 12 January
2002.
5. https://www.britishmuseum.org/research/search_the_collection
_database/term_details.aspx?bioId=24914
6. Wolf Suschitzky, 1987, quotation p. 10.
7. Barbara Warnock and John March, 2019.
8. Frances Spalding, 1986, p. 107.
9. John Willet, 1984, pp. 202, 214.
10. *New Statesman and Nation*, 16 July 1938.
11. Shulamith Behr and Marian Malet, 2005, pp. 12–14.
12. Daniel Snowman, 2002, p. 280.
13. Norbert Lynton, 1998, p. 67.
14. Quoted in Rachel Dickson and Sarah MacDougall, 2015, p. 80.
15. Daniel Snowman, 2002, pp. 105–13; Suzanne Snizek, 2011,
pp. 11–15; Jessica Feather, 2004, pp. 4–6.
16. Margaret Garlake, 2005, p. 175; Klaus E. Hinrichsen, 1993,
p. 188.
17. Klaus E. Hinrichsen, 1993, pp. 191–5.
18. Sainsbury Centre, 2007, p. 55; Jessica Feather, 2004, p. 11.
19. *New Statesman and Nation*, 28 August 1940.
20. Rachel Dickson and Sarah MacDougall, 2015, p. 84.
21. Klaus E. Hinrichsen, 1993, p. 190; Christopher Masters,
'Paul Feiler Obituary', *The Guardian*, 22 July 2013.
22. Klaus E. Hinrichsen, 1993, p. 197.
23. Klaus E. Hinrichsen, 1993, p. 207.

The émigré achievement
1. Daniel Snowman, 2002, p. 113.
2. Klaus E. Hinrichsen, 1993, p. 188; Rachel Dickson and Sarah
MacDougall, 2015, p. 82.
3. Maeve Kennedy, 'Exhibitions', *Guardian*, 26 December 2017,
https://www.theguardian.com/artanddesign/2017/dec/26/
exhibition-wartime-artist-famous-mills-boon-covers-elizabeth-
friedlander
4. Joseph Flatter, 1980, oral history recording, Imperial War
Museum, ref 4765.
5. David Manson, *Will Tirr: Figure in a Landscape 1915–1991*,
Author House, Milton Keynes, 2010.
6. David Buckman, 1998, p. 1262.
7. Daniel Snowman, 2002, p. 318.
8. Rachel Dickson and Sarah MacDougall, 2015, p. 84
9. https://jussuf.abbo.uk/
10. Letter to Hilde and Walter Rosenbaum, 19/20 January 1943,
translated in Shulamith Behr, 'Exhibitions and Beyond: Ben Uri,
Politics and Émigré Identities in the Critical Years 1944–49', in
Rachel Dickson and Sarah MacDougall, 2015, p. 98.
11. Quoted from a personal communication in Avram Kampf,
1990, p. 87.
12. Keith Holz, 'Scenes from Exile in Western Europe', p. 51,
and 'Oskar Kokoschka in London', pp. 86–95, both in Stephanie
Barron, 1997.
13. Daniel Snowman, 2002, p. 227.
14. Barbara Copeland Buenger, 'John Heartfield in London',
in Stephanie Barron, 1997, pp. 74–9.
15. Daniel Snowman, 2002, pp. 333–42.
16. Margaret Garlake, 2005, p. 168.
17. Mark Brown, 'Naked ambition: £15,000 appeal to revive nude
sunbather statues', *Guardian*, 21 April 2017; Harriet Atkinson,
'Artists, Refugees and the Festival of Britain', in Monica
Bohm-Duchen, 2019, pp. 223–9.

18. *Jewish Chronicle*, 4 May 1951, p. 13, quoted in Rachel Dickson
and Sarah MacDougall (eds), 2015, p. 87.
19. Christopher Andreae, *Joan Eardley*, Lund Humphries, London,
2013, pp. 38–44.
20. 56 Group exhibition catalogue, 1963.
21. David Bell, *The Artist in Wales*, 1953.
22. Malcolm Yorke, *The Spirit of Place*, Constable, London, 1988,
p. 241.
23. Renate Koppel, interviewed in *Framing Wales*, BBC Wales,
2011.
24. *Times*, 21 May 1958, p. 3.
25. John Uzzell Edwards, personal communication to the author.
26. James Toub, 1994, 'Oskar Kokoschka as Teacher', *Journal of
Aesthetic Education*, vol. 28, no. 2, 1994, pp. 35–49.
27. Stephanie Barron, 1997, pp. 23–5.
28. http://www.baacorsham.co.uk/mparkin/p66.htm
29. Alina Polianskaya, 'George Adams', *Design Week*,
27 February 2019.
30. Stephen Gardiner, *Elisabeth Frink*, Harper Collins,
London, 1998, p. 29; Michael Parkin, 'Obituary: Willi Soukop',
Independent, 9 February 1995.
31. See Monica Bohm-Duchen, 2019.
32. Frances Spalding, 1986, p. 171.
33. Barbara Copeland Buenger, 'Kurt Schwitters in England',
in Stephanie Barron, 1997, pp. 80–5.
34. Tom Ambrose, 2001, pp. 71–3.
35. Daniel Snowman, 2002, p. 282.
36. Duncan Forbes, 2002, p. 7.
37. Margaret Garlake, 2005, *passim*.
38. Lynn Pearson, *Public Art 1945–95*, Historic England, London,
2016.
39. Philip Kemp, 'Lotte Reiniger', BFI,
http://www.screenonline.org.uk/people/id/528134/
40. David Herman, 2015, p. 114.
41. Fred Uhlman, *The Making of an Englishman*, Victor Gollancz,
London, 1960.

Continuing crises
1. Douglas Hall, 2008, *passim*.
2. 'Obituary: ChienYing Chang', *Telegraph*, 19 January 2004.
3. James Hamilton and Nathalie Levi, *György Gordon
(1924–2005): A Retrospective*, University of Leeds.
4. https://www.magnumphotos.com/newsroom/
josef-koudelka-invasion-prague-68/
5. Humberto Gatíca, 2008. *The Sand Garden/El Jardin de Arena*,
Hafan Books, Swansea.
6. Michael Archer et al, 2016, p. 8.
7. Quoted in Yasmin Alibhai Brown, 2002, p. 51.
8. Michael Archer et al, 2016, pp. 54–7.
9. http://www.tracesproject.org/zory-shahrokhi/
10. https://www.bbc.co.uk/news/uk-wales-south-west-
wales-34176860; personal communication to the author.
11. Saphora Smith, 2016. 'Befriended by a King', *Telegraph*,
17 October 2016, https://en.wikipedia.org/wiki/Dia_Azzawi;
Martin Gayford, *Apollo*, 22 October 2016.
12. http://walidsiti.com/
13. http://www.tracesproject.org/jasim-ghafur/
14. http://www.tracesproject.org/emad-altaay/;
https://www.desertheritagemagazine.com/NEW/articles/gallery/
44-emad-al-taay-gallery.pdf
15. http://hanaa-malallah.com/words/statement.html
16. Helen Pidd, 'Afghan Artist Wins Asylum Claim', *Guardian*,
26 March 2017.
17. Georgina Sturge, 2019. Asylum Statistics, House of Commons
Library, https://researchbriefings.files.parliament.uk/documents/
SN01403/SN01403.pdf

Epilogue
1. John Willet, 1984, p. 217.
2. Daniel Snowman, 2013, p. 12.
3. A review of exile studies in art is Sabine Eckmann, 1997.
4. https://www.juedischesmuseum.de/en/explore/fine-arts/detail/
else-meidner-painter/
5. Nini Herman, 1996, p. 85.

Select bibliography

Adler, Kathleen, 1978. *Camille Pissarro: A Biography*, Batsford, London

Adler, Kathleen, 2011. *A Time and a Place: Near Sydenham Hill by Camille Pissarro*, Kimbell Art Museum, Fort Worth

Alibhai Brown, Yasmin, 2002. *Celebrating Sanctuary: Conversations with Refugee Artists in the UK*, London Arts, London

Amara, Michaël, 2017. 'Belgian Refugees During the First World War (France, Britain, Netherlands)', in Peter Gatrell and Liubov Zhvanko (eds), pp. 197–214

Ambrose, Tom, 2001. *Hitler's Loss: What Britain and America Gained from Europe's Cultural Exiles*, Peter Owen Publishers, London

Archer, Michael, Brett, Guy, de Zegher, Catherine, and Spector, Nancy, 1997, revised edition 2016. *Mona Hatoum*, Phaidon, London

Baird, Nicola (ed), 2018. *The Making of an Englishman: Fred Uhlman, a Retrospective*, Burgh House & Hampstead Museum, London

Barron, Stephanie with Eckmann, Sabine, 1997. *Exiles + Émigrés: The flight of European artists from Hitler*, Los Angeles County Museum of Art, Los Angeles

Bartolena, Simone, 2011. *Monet*, Prestel, Munich

Behr, Shulamith and Malet, Marian (eds), 2005. *Arts in Exile in Britain 1933–1945: Politics and Cultural Identity*, Editions Rodopi, Amsterdam and New York

Berghahn, Marion, 2007. *Continental Britons: German-Jewish refugees from Nazi Germany*, Berghahn Books, Oxford, 1984, revised edition, 2007

Berghaus, Gunther (ed.), 1989. *Theatre and Film in Exile: German Artists in Britain 1933–1945*, Bloomsbury, London

Bohm-Duchen, Monica (ed.), 2009. *The Art and Life of Josef Herman*, Lund Humphries, London

Bohm-Duchen, Monica, 2013. *Art and the Second World War*, Lund Humphries, London

Bohm-Duchen, Monica, 2019. *Insiders-Outsiders: Refugees from Nazi Europe and their Contribution to British Visual Culture*, Lund Humphries, London

Bowlt, John E., 1981 'Art in Exile: the Russian Avant-Garde and the Emigration', *Art Journal*, vol. 41, no. 3, pp. 215–21

Buckman, David, 1998. *The Dictionary of Artists in Britain since 1945*, Art Dictionaries, Bristol

Camden Arts Centre 1986. *Art in Exile in Great Britain, 1933–45*, Camden Arts Centre, London

Cardyn-Oomen, D., 2003. 'Laethen-Saint-Martin', Grove Art Online

Cesarani, David and Kushner, Tony, 1993. *The Internment of Aliens in Twentieth-Century Britain*, Frank Cass, London

Corbett, David Peters, 2001. *Walter Sickert*, Tate Publishing, London

Dickson, Rachel and MacDougall, Sarah (eds), 2015. *Ben Uri, 100 Years in London: Art, Identity, Migration*, Ben Uri Gallery, London

Dickson, Rachel and MacDougall, Sarah, 2009. *Forced Journeys: Artists In Exile In Britain c.1933–45*, Ben Uri Gallery, London

Dickson, Rachel, 2018. *Out of the Bloodlands: A Century of Polish Artists in Britain – from Axentowich to Zulawski*. Ben Uri Art Gallery, London

Dinnis, Robert and Stringer, Chris, 2013. *Britain: One Million Years of the Human Story*, Natural History Museum, London

Dwork, Deborah and van Pelt, Robert Jan, 2009. *Flight from the Reich: Refugee Jews 1933–1946*, W.W. Norton, London

Eckmann, Sabine, 1994. 'Considering (and Reconsidering) Art in Exile' in Stephanie Barron, 1994, pp. 30–9

Evans, Neil, 2015. 'Immigrants and Minorities in Wales, 1840–1990, a Comparative Perspective', in Charlotte Williams, Neil Evans and Paul O'Leary, 2015, pp. 24–50

Fairclough, Oliver, Hoozee, Robert and Verdickt, Caterina (eds), 2004. *Art in Exile: Flanders, Wales and the First World War*, Museum of Fine Arts, Ghent

Feather, Jessica, 2004. *Art Behind Barbed Wire*, National Museums Liverpool, Liverpool

Forbes, Duncan, 2002. *An Exile's Eye: The Photography of Wolfgang Suschitzky*, Scottish National Portrait Gallery, Edinburgh

Forbes, Duncan, 2005. 'Politics, Photography and Exile in the Life of Edith Tudor-Hart', in Behr, Shulamith and Malet, Marian (eds), 2005, pp. 45–87

Fowle, Frances, 2016. *Daubigny and Impressionism*, National Galleries of Scotland, Edinburgh

Garlake, Margaret, 2005. 'A Minor Language? Three Émigré Sculptors and their Strategies of Assimilation', in Behr, Shulamith and Malet, Marian (eds), 2005, pp. 167–200

Gatrell, Peter and Zhvanko, Liubov (eds), 2017. *Europe on the Move: Refugees in the Era of the Great War*, Manchester University Press, Manchester

Grenville, Anthony and Reiter, Andrea (eds), 2009. *'I Didn't Want to Float; I Wanted to Belong to Something.': Refugee Organizations in Britain 1933–1945*. Yearbook of the Research Centre for German and Austrian Exile Studies

Grove Art Online, 2003. Oxford University Press, Oxford

Haftmann, Werner, 1986. *Banned and Persecuted: Dictatorship of Art under Hitler*, translated by Eileen Martin, DuMont, Cologne

Hall, Douglas, 2008. *Art in Exile: Polish Painters in Post-War Britain*, Sansom & Company, Bristol

Harrison, Charles, 1981. *English Art and Modernism, 1900–1939*, Allen Lane, London

Hearn, Karen (ed.), 1995. *Dynasties: Painting in Tudor and Jacobean England 1530–1630*, Tate, London

Herman, David, 2015. 'Postwar: Jews, Art and Refugees 1944–75'. In Rachel Dickson and Sarah MacDougall (eds), 2015, pp. 106–119

Herman, Josef, 2002. *Related Twilights: Notes from an Artist's Diary*, Tony Curtis (ed.), Seren, Bridgend

Herman, Nini, 1996. *Josef Herman: A Working Life*, Quartet, London

Hinrichsen, Klaus E., 1993. 'Visual Art Behind the Wire'. In Cesarani, David and Kushner, Tony, 1993, pp. 188-209

Hirschfeld, Gerhard (ed.), 1984. *Exile in Great Britain: Refugees from Hitler's Germany*, Berg/German Historical Institute, Leamington Spa

House, John, 1978. 'New Material on Monet and Pissarro in London in 1870–71', *The Burlington Magazine*, vol. 120, no. 907 (October 1978), pp. 636–639

Hughes, Lorna M., 2016. 'Finding Belgian Refugees in Cymru: Using Digital Resources for Uncovering the Hidden Histories of the First World War in Wales', *Immigrants & Minorities*, vol. 34, no. 2, pp. 210–31

Hunisak, John M., 1996. 'Aimé-Jules Dalou' in Grove Art Online, OUP, Oxford

Jeffrey, Ian, 1981. *Photography: A Concise History*, Thames & Hudson, London

Kampf, Avram, 1990. *Chagall to Kitaj: Jewish Experience in 20th Century Art*, Barbican Art Gallery, London

Kushner, Tony, 1999. 'Local Heroes: Belgian Refugees in Britain during the First World War', *Immigrants & Minorities*, vol. 18, no. 1, pp. 1–28

Kushner, Tony, 2012. *The Battle of Britishness: Migrant Journeys, 1685 to the Present*, Manchester University Press, Manchester

Kushner, Tony, 2015. 'Jewish Migration in Fin-de-Siècle Britain', in Rachel Dickson and Sarah MacDougall (eds), 2015, pp. 24–34

Lewison, Jeremy (ed.), 1982. *Circle: Constructive Art In Britain 1934–40*, Kettle's Yard Gallery, Cambridge

Lloyd, Christopher, 1994. *Pissarro*, Phaidon, London, 3rd edition

Marshall, Nancy Rose and Warner, Malcolm, 1999. *James Tissot: Victorian Life/Modern Love*, Yale University Press, New Haven

McConkey, Kenneth, 1995. *Impressionism in Britain*, Yale University Press, New Haven

Murdoch, Tessa Violet, 1982. 'Huguenot artists designers and craftsmen in Great Britain and Ireland: 1680–1760', unpublished thesis, Queen Mary, University of London

Nyberg, Anna, 2014. *Émigrés: The Transformation of Art Publishing in Britain*, Phaidon, London

Omasta, Michael, Mayr, Brigitte and Seeber, Ursula, 2006. *Wolf Suschitzky Photos*, Synema, Vienna

Pearson, Fiona, 2003. 'Sir William Goscombe John', Grove Art Online

Petropoulos, Jonathan, 2001. *The Faustian Bargain: The Art World in Nazi Germany*, Penguin, London

Petropoulos, Jonathan, 2015. *Artists under Hitler: Collaboration and Survival in Nazi Germany*, Yale, New Haven

Podro, Michael and Rossiter, Peter, 2007. *Martin Bloch: A Painter's Painter*, Sainsbury Centre for Visual Art, Norwich

Powell, Jennifer and Vinzent, Jutta, 2005. *Art and Migration: Art Works by Refugee Artists from Nazi Germany in Britain*, George Bell Institute, Birmingham

Powers, Alan, 2019. *Bauhaus Goes West: Modern Art and Design in Britain and America*, Thames & Hudson, London

Reed, Nicholas, 1997. *Pissarro in West London (Kew, Chiswick and Richmond)*, Lilburne Press, London, 4th edition

Rotas, Alex, 2012. 'From "Asylum-Seeker" to "British Artist": How Refugee Artists are Redefining British Art', *Immigrants and Minorities*, vol. 30, 2012, pp. 211–238

Rothenstein, John, 1962. *British Art Since 1900: An Anthology*, Phaidon, London

Rowan, Eric and Stewart, Carolyn, 2002. *An Elusive Tradition: Art and Society in Wales, 1870–1950*, University of Wales Press, Cardiff

Russell, James, 2018. *In Relation: Nine Couples who Transformed Modern British Art*, Sansom & Company, Bristol

Salomon, Charlotte, 2017. *Charlotte Salomon: Life? or Theatre?*, Overlook Duckworth, New York

Salomon, Charlotte, 2017a. *Charlotte Salomon: Life? or Theatre? A Selection of 450 Gouaches*, Taschen, Cologne

Schütz, C. and Simon, Hermann 2009. *Heinz Koppel: Ein Künstler Zwischen Berlin und Wales*, Verlag für Berlin-Brandenburg, Berlin

Scragg, Rebecca, 2005. 'Hanging Hitler: Joseph Flatter's Mein Kampf Illustrated Series, 1938–1942'. In Behr, Shulamith and Malet, Marian (eds), 2005, pp. 89–134

Seiberling, Grace, 1988. *Monet in London*, High Museum of Art, Atlanta

Shorvon, Simon, 2011. 'Lucien and Esther Pissarro – at home 1894–1914', in *Lucien Pissarro in England: The Eregny Press 1895–1914*, Ashmolean, Oxford, 2011

Snowman, Daniel, 2002. *The Hitler Émigrés: the Cultural Impact on Britain of Refugees from Nazism*, Chatto & Windus, London

Snowman, Daniel, 2013. *The Hitler Émigrés Revisited*, Research Centre for German and Austrian Exile Studies, University of London School of Advanced Study, London

Sorrell, Mary, 1953. 'Siegfried Charoux ARA', *The Studio*, July 1953, pp. 16–19

Spalding, Frances, 1986. *British Art Since 1900*, Thames and Hudson, London

Spector, Nancy and Brettby, Guy, 2016. *Mona Hatoum*, Phaidon, London

Sturges, Matthew, 2005. *Walter Sickert: A Life*, Harper Collins, London

Suschitzky, Wolf, 1987. *Edith Tudor Hart: The Eye of Conscience*, Dirk Nishen Publishing, London

Taylor, Brandon, 2004. *Collage: The Making of Modern Art*, Thames & Hudson, London

Tobin, Claudia, 2012. *Walter Nessler: Postwar Optimist*, J&C Marshall-Purves

Vincentelli, Moira, 1981. 'The Davies Family and Belgian Refugee Artists and Musicians in Wales', *National Library of Wales Journal*, vol. 22, no. 2, pp. 226–233

Vinzent, Jutta, 2006. *Identity and Image: Refugee Artists from Nazi Germany in Britain, 1933–1945*, Verlag und Datenbank für Geisteswissenschaften, Weimar

Wakelin, Peter, 2008. 'Cedric Morris and his influence in Wales', in Tony Curtis (ed.), *Following Petra: A Celebration of Seventy Years of the Contemporary Art Society for Wales*. CASW, Cardiff, pp. 93–104

Warnock, Barbara and March, John, 2019. *Berlin–London: The Lost Photographs of Gerty Simon*, Wiener Library, London

Warnock, Barbara, 2018. 'Refugees and emigres from Nazi Germany to Britain 1933–1938', in Wasensteiner, Lucy and Faass, Martin (eds), 2018, pp. 31–35

Wasensteiner, Lucy and Faass, Martin (eds), 2018. *London 1938: Defending Degenerate Art*, Liebermann Villa, Berlin and Wiener Library, London

Wasensteiner, Lucy, 2019. *The Twentieth Century German Art Exhibition: Answering Degenerate Art in 1930s London*, Routledge, New York

Willett, John, 1984. 'The Emigration and the Arts', in Gerhard Hirschfeld (ed.), 1984, pp. 195–217

Williams, Charlotte, Evans, Neil and O'Leary, Paul (eds), 2015. *A Tolerant Nation? Revisiting Ethnic Diversity in a Devolved Wales*, University of Wales Press, Cardiff

Wood, Christopher, 1998. *Tissot: The Life and Work of Jacques Joseph Tissot 1836–1902*, Phoenix Illustrated, London, paperback edition

Index

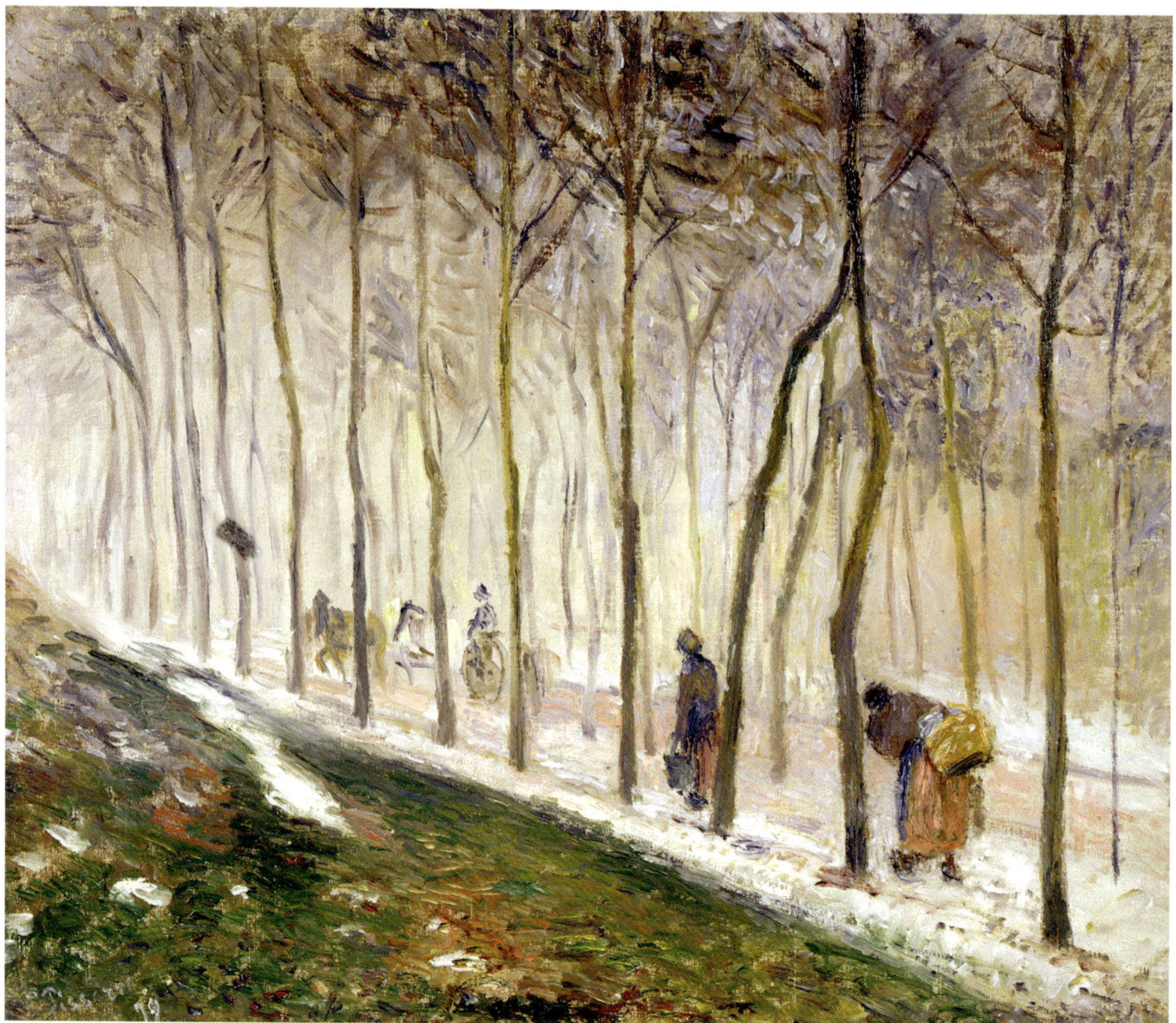

Camille Pissarro (1830–1903) | *La route, effet de neige*
1879 | oil on canvas | 45 x 55 cm
New Walk Museum & Art Gallery, Leicester, UK
reproduced courtesy of Leicester Arts and Museums Service
photo: © Leicester Arts & Museums/Bridgeman Images

Pissarro's painting of French peasants walking through the snow was made nine years after he and his family had been refugees in London from the Franco-Prussian War. He had returned home to find almost all his work before the age of 40 was destroyed.